Captives

PUBLISHED WITH A GRANT FROM

Figure Foundation

FREE AS THE FIRST AND THE LAST

BORDERLANDS AND TRANSCULTURAL STUDIES

Series Editors:

Pekka Hämäläinen
Paul Spickard

"[It is] equally accessible to advanced undergraduate students and researchers, with a wide range of studies and well-structured approach to captives as social beings that are organized in a coherent manner throughout. It should be the starting point for anyone seeking to understand the various facets of captive-taking and the lives of captives in small-scale societies."
—Liza Gijanto, *Historical Archaeology*

"*Captives* challenges archaeologists to consider captive-taking, an ancient and almost universal practice in human history, as a significant mode of cultural transmission and a source of culture change. . . . Here Cameron provides a framework that enables archaeologists to investigate the nature and scale of the roles that captives have played in small-scale societies."
—David H. Dye, *American Antiquity*

"A noteworthy cross-cultural study of captive-taking and its impacts on past societies and a convincing argument that archaeologist should pay considerably more attention to this ubiquitous class of people. . . . Although the author points out that this is only a first step in understanding the role of captives in prehistory, it nonetheless represents an impressive one. . . . [*Captives*] could have a significant impact on archaeological studies."
—Eric E. Bowne, *Journal of Anthropological Research*

"*Captives* is foremost an invitation to begin to see the past in a new way—to make visible individuals who have long been made invisible in archaeological interpretations but have nonetheless been there all along."
—Lydia Wilson Marshall, KIVA: *Journal of Southwestern Anthropology and History*

"[*Captives*] is useful for scholars in many fields interested in the topic, for classroom use, and the public. It is a significant contribution to the topic of captives and slaves, which remains urgent as we struggle

with our own national legacy of slavery, as well as human trafficking across the world and down the street."
—Kenneth M. Ames, *Oregon Historical Quarterly*

"Cameron accomplishes exactly what she set out to do: opening up a new space for investigation and laying out an agenda for further research. . . . She makes it clear that *Captives* is intended not to be the final word but, rather, the opening salvo. Archaeologists, anthropologists, historians, and ethnohistorians should heed [Cameron's] call."
—Matthew Kruer, *Ethnohistory*

"This moving book helps us understand: What was it like to be a slave? A slave-owner? How does slavery affect society? It demonstrates that archaeology—the social science of the past—can ask big questions about the human experience."
—Michelle Hegmon, professor in the School of Human Evolution and Social Change at Arizona State University and editor of *The Archaeology of the Human Experience*

"*Captives* challenges archaeologists to broaden their scope of inquiry to recognize the temporal depth, geographical breadth, and nearly universal presence of captives in small-scale societies of the past. Catherine Cameron's comparative approach to captives lays the groundwork, methodologically and theoretically, for understanding the lives of captives, their social locations, and their significance as agents of change in societies of all scales throughout human prehistory and, indeed, into the present."
—Brenda J. Bowser, associate professor of anthropology at California State University–Fullerton and coeditor of *Cultural Transmission and Material Culture: Breaking Down Boundaries*

| Catherine M. Cameron

Captives

| How Stolen People
| Changed the World

University of Nebraska Press | Lincoln

Library of Congress Cataloging-in-Publication Data
Names: Cameron, Catherine M., author.
Title: Captives: how stolen people changed the world / Catherine
M. Cameron.
Description: Lincoln: University of Nebraska Press, 2016. |
Series: Borderlands and transcultural studies | Includes
bibliographical references and index.
Identifiers: LCCN 2016022493 (print) | LCCN 2016040687 (ebook)
ISBN 9780803293991 (hardback)
ISBN 9781496222206 (paperback)
ISBN 9780803295766 (epub)
ISBN 9780803295773 (mobi)
ISBN 9780803295780 (pdf)
Subjects: LCSH: Social archaeology. | Captivity—Social aspects. |
Slavery—Social aspects. | Warfare, Prehistoric—Social aspects. |
Culture diffusion. | Social change. | BISAC: SOCIAL SCIENCE /
Anthropology / Cultural. | SOCIAL SCIENCE / Slavery.
Classification: LCC CC72.4 .C36 2016 (print) | LCC CC72.4 (ebook) |
DDC 303.4—dc23
LC record available at https://lccn.loc.gov/2016022493

Set in Sabon Next LT Pro by Rachel Gould.

To Tien Fuh Wu (1886–1973)
and other women who have survived slavery

Contents

List of Illustrations   xi

Acknowledgments   xiii

1. The Captive in Space, Time, and Mind   1

2. Captive Taking in Global Perspective   19

3. The Captive as Social Person   43

4. Captives and the Creation of Power   77

5. Captives, Social Boundaries, and Ethnogenesis   105

6. Captives and Cultural Transmission   133

7. Captives in Prehistory   163

Notes   175

References   177

Index   207

| Illustrations

1. *Setting an Enemy's Village on Fire*   5

2. *Conquering Warrior* effigy pipe   28

3. Guaraní women and children
   captured by slave hunters   60

4. Helena Valero and her family   72

5. *Chief Carried on the Back of
   a Slave* carved figure   84

6. *A Northwest Coast Village*   91

7. *A group of Cunivo [Conibo] Indians
   on the Rio Ucayali, Peruvian Montaña*   95

8. Native American prisoner halter   119

9. *Mujer conibo pintado ceramios*
   (Conibo woman painting pottery)   135

10. Portrait of Olive Oatman   151

| Acknowledgments

I trace the origins of this book to an email from Jim Skibo in spring 2005 inviting me to organize a Foundations of Archaeological Inquiry conference for the University of Utah Press (Jim was editor for the series). Encouragement from Jim and Jeff Grathwohl, then editor of the University of Utah Press, allowed me to develop an idea into a long-term study. The participants in the Utah conference and resulting book helped enormously in shaping my ideas about captives and I thank them all: Susan Alt, Ken Ames, Brenda Bowser, James Brooks, Warren DeBoer (who also pointed me toward some of the illustrations for the book), Judith Habicht-Mauche, Laura Junker, Noel Lenski, Debra Martin, Peter Peregrine, Peter Robertshaw, and Ann Stahl. My many conversations with Brenda Bowser were especially helpful. I wrote the first chapter for this book as a fellow with the University of Colorado's Center for the Humanities and Arts (2009–10). The fellowship involved meeting biweekly with a group of scholars from across campus who were studying migration (that year's topic) from a myriad of perspectives: historical, political, literary, and anthropological. Reading and talking about our work was tremendously stimulating and I thank: Pompa Banerjee, Ozge Celik, Céline Dauverd, Nan Goodman, Kira Hall, John Leffel, Anne Lester, Deepti Misri, and Marni Thomson.

I wrote much of the rest of the book as a residential scholar at the School for Advanced Research (SAR) in Santa Fe, during 2010–11. The year at SAR was a transformative experience for me. I worked with a close community of scholars who came from a variety of disciplines. We met often to enjoy food and explore each other's research. My thanks to Jamila Bargach, Gloria Bell, Lucas Bessire, the late Linda Cordell, Sarah Croucher, Doug Kiel, Teresa Montoya, and Melissa

Nelson, whose careful critiques made a significant impact on the book. James Brooks, then president of sar and a founding scholar of captive studies, was (and continues to be) enormously generous with his time and advice and I am most grateful. John Kantner, then vice president at sar, was also a great resource during that year.

My archaeological colleagues at the University of Colorado read and commented on several chapters of the book during our monthly "archaeology lunch" meetings. I thank Doug Bamforth, Gerardo Gutierrez, John Hoffecker, Art Joyce, Steve Lekson, Scott Ortman, and Payson Sheets. Payson also provided me with a wealth of articles on slaves and slavery from his wide reading. Very special thanks to Beth Dusinberre of the University of Colorado Department of Classics, who generously provided comments on a draft of the entire manuscript. At the University of Nebraska Press, Matt Bokovoy and Pekka Hämäläinen offered many helpful comments for developing the manuscript.

Also in Colorado's Department of Classics, Noel Lenski's work with slavery in the ancient world has been an inspiration. In fall 2013 Noel and I co-organized a conference with the theme "What Is a Slave Society" and then we jointly taught a class on global slavery. Both the conference and class took my knowledge of the slave experience worldwide to new levels. I thank Noel, the conference participants, and students in the class.

Many people have discussed captives with me, suggested references, passed on news clippings, and recommended new avenues for research. Although I won't attempt to name them all, they have my thanks, especially for listening and being interested. Mary Brooks, Joy Margheim, and Lindsay Johansson did a wonderful job editing the manuscript, which greatly improved it.

Finally, my interest in captives was stimulated in part by my childhood "aunt," Tien Fuh Wu, whose father sold her into domestic slavery when she was just five years old. This book is dedicated to Tien, to all of the girls and women through time who endured slavery, and to those who not only survived but contributed significantly to the cultures they joined and the world in which we now live.

Captives

Chapter One

The Captive in Space, Time, and Mind

An arrow fell behind us. The enemy had followed us and had waited until we entered the *shapuno* [a large, thatched enclosure]. Other arrows began to fall: tah, tai, tai. . . . Meanwhile the *tushaua* [leader] of the Shamatari [the enemy] had already entered. . . . Not even one man of those in the shapuno was standing up. The old Hekurawe was there, dead, with arrows in his body; the Aramamiseteri, too, was lying dead not far away. . . . Meanwhile the men began to bring the women prisoners together. They held them firmly by the arms. They were many and they were young. . . . Then they [the Shamatari] raised their shout: Au, au, au, with a cavernous voice and we began the journey. We marched and marched.

—HELENA VALERO'S ACCOUNT OF HER SECOND CAPTURE BY YANO-MAMÖ, QUOTED IN ETTORE BIOCCA, *Yanoáma: The Story of Helena Valero, a Girl Kidnapped by Amazonian Indians* (1965).

Tuesday 22 April 2014, Nigeria. Terror grips northern Nigeria after "Boko Haram" kidnappings: Last week's kidnapping of 230 schoolgirls in northern Nigeria, which is being blamed on the Islamist group Boko Haram, has plunged the region into chaos. Will the victims ever be seen again? Chibok boarding school in the remote state of Borno was attacked last week by the militant Islamic group, who burnt out the school before abducting its students. . . . The official number of missing girls has risen to an estimated 234.

—JONATHAN MILLER, FOREIGN AFFAIRS CORRESPONDENT, CHANNEL 4 NEWS, LONDON

In every corner of the world and through time people have stolen others, mostly women and children. Helena Valero's account of the attack of one Yanomamö group on another and the seizure of the defeated group's women has played out over and over again for millennia. Media reports a few weeks after the Boko Haram kidnapping followed a common pattern. A Boko Haram leader called the girls his slaves and said he would sell them or give them to his men in marriage (*Time Magazine*, May 26, 2014, 32). As I read these accounts, I recalled Helena and the hundreds of descriptions of captive taking I discovered in ethnohistorical, ethnographic, and historical studies during the decade in which I researched this book. A nighttime raid, men clubbed to death or shot, women and children hurried into a corner of the settlement by raiders, a long march that many did not survive, and at the end of the march, a new life.

People around the world hope for the recovery of the kidnapped Nigerian girls and as I write this, their eyes are on the spot in the bush where the girls are believed held. For the vast majority of women and children taken captive in the distant past, beyond the reach of historic records, no such hope existed. Not only were captives lost to their families, archaeologists have ignored the importance of their lives. This book brings this invisible class of people out of the shadows and explores the contributions they made to the societies of their captors.

As an archaeologist, I hope this book influences the scholarship of fellow archaeologists (as well as that of scholars in other disciplines), yet this volume is not an archaeological study. Nor is it a study of captives in a single society. It is a cross-cultural investigation of the common patterns and variability in warfare, captive taking, and the captive experience. It is a wide-ranging exploration of ethnohistoric, ethnographic, and historical sources, as well as the occasional archaeological study, that focuses on the lives of captives in small-scale ("nonstate") societies around the world. Because many captives became slaves, the slavery literature is an important component of the study. The broad comparative approach used here follows that of scholars of slavery, including sociologist Orlando Patterson (1982, 2008) and early twentieth-century scholar H. J. Nieboer (1900).

Small-scale societies rely primarily on kinship ties (real or fictive) as the basis for their social and political organization. They mostly fall into the category that archaeologists call "middle range"; in other words, they are not small bands or complex states. Service (1971) called such groups "tribes" (or "segmentary societies") and "chiefdoms." These terms carry outmoded evolutionary and conceptual biases and I employ them primarily when discussing parts of the world where their use is common. My focus on small-scale groups is partial, however. Captive taking operated on a large geographic scale that enmeshed societies of a variety of social levels and structured the complex relationships among them. Furthermore, captive taking did take place in band-level societies and at times I use examples from both band-level and state-level societies to support my points.

Captives typically entered captor settlements as members of a despised enemy group and their captors beat, abused, and mistreated them. They often remained marginal even after their captors married or adopted them. We might ask ourselves, What could these bedraggled, subordinate people contribute to the societies they joined? and Why are they worthy of archaeological interest? This book demonstrates that captives affected the societies they joined in a number of ways. Their presence created or increased social stratification in captor society. In small-scale societies where power derived from control over people, captives increased the power of their captors. Captives affected social boundaries in captor society by allowing captors to contrast themselves with their abject captives. Social boundaries were also strengthened when captives tried to conform to captor social practices in an effort to "fit in" and gain better treatment. My most important point, however, is that captives were a significant mode of cultural transmission and a source of culture change. They brought with them knowledge of new technologies, design styles, foodways, religious practices, and more that transformed captor culture.

I begin with a discussion of the pervasiveness and antiquity of raiding and warfare in small-scale societies, the source of most captives. I review the global scope of captive taking, as well as its selective focus on women and children. The next section defines captives and captors and discusses the scale of captive taking. The cross-cultural methods I use for the study are considered next, including a discussion of the concerns archaeologists have about the use of both analogy and the cross-cultural approach. Finally, I take a brief look at captive taking and slavery in the past and present. We have come a long way from the time when the majority of the world's people suffered in bondage, but the horror of the captive experience is still very real for far too many of today's women, children, and men.

Warfare, Kidnapping, and Captives

Most captive taking has resulted from warfare and raiding. Kidnapping was also common in many times and places, and the isolated herder, garden tender, or child left briefly alone was vulnerable. By proposing that captive taking was an ancient and almost universal practice and most often the result of warfare or raiding, I am, of course, implying that warfare and raiding were common, ancient practices (figure 1). Lawrence Keeley (1996) complained more than twenty years ago that archaeologists "pacified" the human past by ignoring the presence of warfare, especially in small-scale societies. R. Brian Ferguson and Neil Whitehead's *War in the Tribal Zone* ([1992] 1999) had launched a heated debate among anthropologists concerning the prevalence, frequency, and impact of war in small-scale societies. Ferguson, Whitehead, and many of the contributors to their edited volume argued that contact with Europeans created a "tribal zone" of warfare through the introduction of new trade goods, new diseases, and other factors, including an increasingly active slave trade (e.g., M. Brown and Fernandez [1992] 1999, 185–87). These scholars imply that before European contact, warfare in small-scale societies was uncommon and not particularly lethal. Countering this view of peaceful, precontact small-scale societies, archaeologists pointed to abundant material evidence of warfare in the past, including defensive structures, weapons of war, bodies showing

1. *Setting an Enemy's Village on Fire.* Created by Theodor De Bry, a Belgian
engraver who reportedly reproduced paintings made by artist Jacques
LeMoyne. LeMoyne accompanied French explorer Rene Laudonniére to
Florida in 1564, where they encountered the Timucua Indians.
Image courtesy of University of South Florida Tampa Library,
Special and Digital Collections.

evidence of violent death, and iconography related to warfare (Chacon
and Mendoza 2007a, 2007b; J. Haas and Creamer 1993; Keeley 1996;
LeBlanc and Register 2003; Lekson 2002; but see R. Ferguson 2013).

In the course of this debate, archaeologists working in a number of
parts of the world took up the study of violence and warfare and evaluated its impact on the societies they investigated (Arkush and Allen
2006; Chacoan and Dye 2007; Chacoan and Mendoza 2007a, 2007b;
LeBlanc 1999; LeBlanc and Register 2003; Martin, Harrod, and Pérez
2012; Maschner and Reedy-Maschner 1998). Surprisingly, few of these
authors mention one of its most common by-products: the taking of
captives. These studies, nevertheless, provide many insights concerning warfare in small-scale societies that are useful for understanding
the practice of captive taking (Arkush and Allen 2006; Keeley 1996,
32–33; Guilaine and Zammit 2005; LeBlanc 1999; LeBlanc and Register

2003; Lekson 2002). Tribal-level societies, for example, typically engaged in small-scale raids, while chiefs often maintained groups of high-ranking warriors who undertook much-larger-scale warfare.

The taking of captives, especially women, was not simply a by-product of warfare but often a major objective of raids or war (Golitko and Keeley 2007, 339; Keeley 1996, 86; LeBlanc 2002, 362; LeBlanc and Register 2003, 71; see also R. Ferguson and Whitehead 1999; also raiding for wives, Barnes 1999; Bowser 2008; DeBoer 2008; Jorgensen 1980; McLennan 1865). The ethnohistoric cases discussed in this volume make it clear that prestige and the acquisition of captives are powerful motivators of warfare in small-scale societies. In some cases the taking of captives was one of the most highly valued results of conflict. While R. Ferguson (2006) and others believe that warfare in small-scale societies was conducted only for material gain of land or resources and was undertaken primarily by groups suffering resource stress, other scholars disagree. They argue that the desire for prestige and status, revenge, and access to women were powerful motivations for warfare in small scale-societies and also essential to the success of these societies (Chagnon 1988; Maschner and Reedy-Maschner 1998; see also Bishop and Lytwyn 2007 for band-level societies).

There is no doubt that Western intrusion into small-scale societies increased the incidence of warfare, and especially slave raiding and captive taking. Western demand for labor in agricultural and extractive industries required a large labor force supplied in part by indigenous slaves who had been captured by other, more powerful indigenous groups (Gallay 2002; Thornton [1999] 2003). That any warfare was the consequence of Western contact, however, assumes that the "resulting transformations . . . occurred almost instantaneously" (Keeley 1996, 21). While warfare in every society was likely episodic and differed in intensity, it was a common social behavior long before contact in many, perhaps most, small-scale societies (Chacon and Mendoza 2007a, 2007b; LeBlanc and Register 2003). The earliest ethnohistoric accounts should provide useful data for exploring warfare in the past, but ethnohistory is especially important for the study of captive taking because the material evidence for captives in the archaeological record will be far less obvious than that of warfare. Defensive structures and weapons of war are relatively unambiguous, but individuals taken captive may be seamlessly incorporated into captor society, leaving little trace of their origin.

Captives who were the victims of kidnapping, often taken in isolated events involving one or a few people, are even more difficult to see. I do not join Patterson (1982, 115–22) in distinguishing between "genuine prisoners of war" and kidnap victims. He classifies raids made for the specific purpose of taking captives as kidnapping expeditions. I argue that such expeditions have a variety of social and political purposes and I restrict the term *kidnapping* to small-scale events in which a few captors target one or a few victims (see chapter 4). For some groups, kidnapping was a common method of obtaining captives; for example, the Comanches of the American Southwest frequently stole young Mexican shepherds to tend the vast herds of horses they had also stolen. In some band-level societies, such as the Tutchone of the Upper Yukon of Canada, low population density (less than one person per one hundred square kilometers [thirty-nine square miles]) precluded anything we might call warfare or even organized raiding. Yet even here more powerful families stole or appropriated the women and children of their distant neighbors and enslaved them (Legros 1985).

Geographic Scope and Scale of Captive taking

Captive taking was so prevalent worldwide that one is tempted to second DeBoer's (2008, 234) "rash" suggestion that the practice was almost primordial (see also Patterson 1982, vii; Taylor 2005). Ethnographic accounts and studies of slavery provide a sense of the geographic prevalence of captive taking. Nieboer's (1900) early cross-cultural study reports slavery on every continent except Europe (he was wrong about Europe) and throughout the Pacific. Slaveholders made up more than one-third of George Murdock's sample of 186 world cultures (Murdock and White 1969) and these groups ranged geographically from northeastern Siberia to New Zealand and from central Uganda in Africa to the Great Plains of North America (Patterson 1982, 350–52). Both Nieboer and Murdock considered only those societies that held slaves, but in many other groups captives were adopted or married into families. Cross-cultural studies of North America document raiding for women in a high proportion of Native American groups (Driver 1966; Jorgensen 1980; both cited in DeBoer 2008). Raiding for women and children is similarly well documented in a large number of small-scale South American societies (Bowser 2008; DeBoer 2011; Morey 1975; Santos-Granero 2009).

The Atlantic slave trade devastated and transformed the small-scale, "decentralized" societies of Africa, but evidence shows that raiding and captive taking were common practices among these groups from at least the first millennium (and likely long before) until well into the twentieth century (MacEachern 2001; R. Reid 2012, 19; Robertshaw and Duncan 2008; see also Lovejoy [1983] 2000; Meillassoux 1983, 1991; Thornton 1998). Warfare and captive taking also occurred throughout Europe prior to the modern era among state-level and small-scale societies, including among the so-called Germanic tribes and the small polities that formed after the fall of the Roman Empire (Bonnassie 1991; Lenski 2008; Patterson 1982, 150–57; Woolf 1997). Vikings raided throughout the North Atlantic and the Mediterranean, taking innumerable captives to labor in Scandinavian settlements or to sell to others (Helgason et al. 2000; Karras 1988). Similar maritime raiders were found across island Southeast Asia (Junker 2008; A. Reid 1983; Warren [1981] 1985, 2002).

War captives and slaves were common in ancient state-level societies (10–20 percent of Roman Italy [Lenski, forthcoming], one-third of the population of Greece from the fifth century BCE to the Roman period, 50–70 percent of Korea prior to the seventeenth century, and 15–20 percent of many Islamic states [Patterson 1982]), and ethnohistoric and ethnographic accounts suggest that small-scale societies also included significant numbers of captives. Slaves composed about 10–20 percent of the population of the Northwest Coast of North America, although the number of slaves in any one village varied considerably over time (Ames 2008, 141–42; Donald 1997, 185–90). Chagnon (1992, 106) reports that 12–15 percent of wives among the Yanomamö of Amazonia had been captured in raids. Among six slaveholding societies

in "tropical America" (which includes Amazonia, but not the Yanomamö) studied by Santos-Granero (2009), proportions of slaves ranged
from 5 to 19 percent of the population, not including servant and trib-
utary groups that made up more than 40 percent of some societies.
In Africa, slaves ranged from 1 percent to as high as 50 percent of the
population depending on the level of complexity of the group and
access to trade routes (Kopytoff and Miers 1977, 60–61). Slaves were
equally common in Europe. The Domesday Book census of 1086 CE
reported that England's population of slaves ranged from 5 to 25 percent (McDonald and Snooks 1986, 16–17); in Scandinavia the typical
twelfth-century farm had three slaves, suggesting a significant slave
population (Karras 1988, 78). Similar proportions are found among
the maritime chiefdoms of Southeast Asia, ranging from 10 to 30 percent (A. Reid and Brewster 1983, 161–62).

Captives, Slaves, Captors, and the Landscape of Captive taking

The term *captive*, as used here, refers to women, children, and men
who are unwillingly (and usually violently) seized, taken from their
homes, and introduced into a new society. Captive taking is a selective
process, and captives most often come from the lowest strata of society
as defined by gender, age, and social standing. Women and children
made up most captives in small-scale societies (Cameron 2008a, 2011;
Patterson 1982, 120–22). Adult males, who were a challenge to transport and manage, were most often killed in battle. Once separated
from natal kin, captives could be bartered, sold, or captured yet again
by another group. The captive role is temporary, and social positions
eventually opened to these people. Some captives became wives or
were adopted, and some became slaves; others occupied intermediate
positions between these two extremes as concubines, drudge wives,
household servants, or similarly marginal individuals (see chapter 3).

Slave and *captive* are overlapping categories used somewhat inter-
changeably in this volume. While not all captives became slaves, many
did. Some slaves were born into their status and had not been captured, but Donald (1997, 117) suggests that, at least on the Northwest
Coast, the rigors of life as a slave and lack of access to mates may have

limited reproduction. Patterson (1982, 132) disagrees but seems to be discussing state-level societies. Furthermore, among many small-scale groups, slavery lasted only a generation. The children of slaves were considered full members of the captor group and new slaves had to be recruited through raiding or warfare.

Scholars have spent a considerable amount of time defining slavery and arguing about the importance of slaves to the economy ("slave mode of production"; Finley 1980; Meillassoux 1991) as well as about what limits an individual must have on her access to independent action and the benefits of kinship in order to be termed a slave (Bonnassie 1991, 16–25; Copley [1839] 1960, 4–9; references in Davis 1966, 31–35; Engerman, Drescher, and Paquette 2001; Patterson 1982, 13; A. Reid and Brewster 1983). Because the individuals considered in this study occupy such a sliding scale of social roles, I will sidestep this debate. This study focuses on the effects of captives on captor societies; therefore, determining whether captives are considered "slaves" is less important than assessing the nature of the social roles captives played in captor society (Bowser 2008; Brooks 2002).

I use the terms *captor* and *captor society* often in this volume. Because captives are most often taken during raids or warfare, captors are commonly male warriors. But the face of the captor can change. Warriors may be required to hand over their captives to a chief or the individual who financed the raid. Warriors may give captives to female relatives or to others as a gift. Captives may be traded almost immediately to another group. In the discussion that follows, the captor is the person who initially takes the captive but also those individuals or groups ("captor society") that hold the captive during her lifetime and to whom she passes elements of her natal culture.

Captive taking took place at a large geographic scale and is only one of the processes, including marriage, migration, and refugee situations, that moved people around the landscape. "Predatory landscapes" (Bowser 2008; Stahl 2008) could enmesh societies of all social levels. Larger, more complex societies typically raided their smaller, less complex neighbors, but such relations could also be reversed, with the raided becoming the raiders (for Africa, see MacEachern 2001; Morrissey

1984; Robertshaw and Duncan 2008; for the American Southeast, see Bowne 2005, 2009; Gallay 2002, 40–69; Meyers 2009). The large geographic scale of slavery provides another reason for scholars to avoid conceptualizing historic or prehistoric groups as bounded social entities that persisted through time (Stahl 1999, 2008, 31; see chapter 5).

Raiding, warfare, and captive taking could dramatically affect cultural landscapes by changing settlement patterns, remaking ethnic affiliations, stimulating sociopolitical development, and reworking social relationships. Relations between predatory societies and the groups they raided were at times asymmetrical but not always negative; in some regions, they also involved mutual interdependence, like in marriage arrangements or trade (Albers 1993; Brooks 2002; Chernela 2011). Captive taking also functioned to maintain social boundaries, permit economic interactions, and establish kin relationships between groups that could be exploited in times of need. These topics are discussed in the chapters that follow.

Methods

This study is broadly comparative and like most archaeological work relies on analogy to reconstruct the past. Unlike the approach in most archaeological studies, however, I do not compare archaeological cases, nor am I making a direct analogy between material culture used in past and present societies. Instead, I explore the lives of captives in societies around the world in order to identify commonalities that we might use to understand people in similar circumstances in the past. I compiled cases of captive taking and descriptions of captive lives from a wide variety of secondary sources, described by region in chapter 2. Sources include those written by ethnohistorians, historians, anthropologists, and, occasionally, archaeologists. The surge of studies on captive taking and slavery among small-scale societies by anthropologists (Carocci and Pratt 2012; Donald 1997; Santos-Granero 2009) and historians (Brooks 2002; Campbell, Miers, and Miller 2007, 2008, 2009; Chatterjee and Eaton 2006; Colley 2002; Ekberg 2010; Foster 2003; Gallay 2002, 2009; Rushforth 2003, 2012; Snyder 2010) during the last decade is essential to my analysis. In addition, I rely on a range of other books, articles, and book chapters that focus on warfare, captive taking, slavery, coerced labor, and women as slaves. I occasionally use original sources, such as early explorers' accounts or captive narratives. Articles prepared for the edited volume *Invisible Citizens: Captives and Their Consequences* (Cameron 2008b) provide some of the foundational material for this book.

My goal is to develop an understanding of captive lives in small-scale societies prior to European contact. Only archaeological data *directly* addresses the past before written records, and such data on captives is currently limited; however, we can learn a great deal about captive taking and captive lives from ethnohistoric, ethnographic, and historic accounts, and these sources are the primary data upon which this study is built. I use data from historic periods to examine prehistoric times and apply the fundamental method of archaeological interpretation called "analogy."

There are well-known problems with the use of analogy, a form of inductive reasoning, but there is also agreement among archaeologists that analogy is an indispensable tool for understanding the past (David and Kramer 2001, 43–54; Gould and Watson 1982; Wylie 1985, 64). Much of this concern focuses on "source-side" considerations, in other words, the contemporary groups we select as analogues for the past (David and Kramer 2001, 48; Wobst 1978). Archaeologists are criticized for developing analogies that treat modern and historic non-Western societies (especially small-scale societies) as if they were timeless and unchanging ("people without history"; Wolf 1982) or for selectively studying only aspects of those societies deemed "traditional" (Stahl 1993; see also David and Kramer 2001, 43–54). European contact and colonization disrupted lives around the world, most profoundly in the sorts of small-scale societies considered here. Uncritically "upstreaming" contemporary conditions into the distant past, even for historically related cultures, either ignores change or makes our arguments for similarity teleological (or both; see Cobb 2005; Lekson 2011; Peregrine 2001, 2).

Comparison is fundamental to most archaeological work and archaeologists are increasingly willing to consider large-scale cross-cultural comparison, after several decades in which postmodern agendas and small-scale research dominated the field (Flannery and Marcus 2012; Michael Smith 2012; Trigger 2003). These new studies grapple with the fundamental question of how much of human behavior is determined by factors that operate cross-culturally and how much by factors unique to the history and development of particular cultures (Michael Smith and Peregrine 2012, 4; Trigger 2003, 3). They compare both archaeological data and ethnographic data that can be used to develop analogies to inform our knowledge of the past. The present analysis is of the latter sort and compares cultures around the world to show that captive taking was a widespread, perhaps almost universal practice and that commonalities are found in the treatment of captives and captives' influences on captor societies.

The two major criticisms of cross-cultural comparison are of concern for the present study. Critics accuse cross-cultural comparative studies of plucking traits from their cultural context for purposes of analysis and ignoring how those traits developed and functioned in the broader society (Trigger 2003, 21). Cross-cultural studies also tend to seek (and find) similarities instead of differences. Despite these concerns, a new generation of archaeologists has embraced these cross-cultural comparative studies, which have considerable power to help us identify and explore patterning in human behavior (Drennan et al. 2012). I see the present volume as a first step in the exploration of captive taking. Exposing the pervasiveness of this practice will allow archaeologists to investigate the presence of captives prehistorically around the world.

I do not use ethnographic or ethnohistoric data to interpret archaeological material in this study, but I do assume (based on analogy) that the vast number of historically documented accounts of captives in small-scale societies provide evidence of their existence in prehistoric societies and suggest similarities in their treatment. The examples of captive experiences used in this volume are selected from across time and space, yet each of the cultural groups discussed was the product of a distinctive history and a unique engagement with colonization. There is no doubt that European contact increased the prevalence of violence, giving us a potentially skewed view of the very practices we hope to understand. Competition for access to European trade goods and routes increased warfare, and Europeans often manipulated animosities among indigenous groups for their own benefit, creating more conflict. Among New World indigenous societies, a global market for slaves in some cases affected the value of captives to their captors. European diseases; social, economic, and environmental disruption; warfare; slavery; and ethnic erasure significantly reduced indigenous populations, destroying some societies completely (Cameron, Kelton, and Swedlund 2015). Remnant groups sometimes differed dramatically from their precontact ancestors.

When possible, to avoid some of the problems common to cross-cultural ethnohistoric comparison, I use sources that focus on the earliest explorers' accounts, especially those that aim to understand the time before contact (e.g., Donald 1997; Santos-Granero 2009). But the purpose of many studies of captive taking is to examine the *effects* of colonization. Of this group, those that try to link changes to precontact patterns are most useful (e.g., Brooks 2002; Gallay 2002; Santos-Granero 2009; Snyder 2009, 2010). Most of the accounts I use date to the postcontact period, yet they describe small-scale societies with lifestyles similar to those of the past. Studying captive-captor relationships in these societies provides insights that can be applied to the past.

While my interest is in small-scale societies, I occasionally use data on warfare, captive taking, and slavery in state-level societies. This is true especially in chapter 6, which explores the cultural practices captives contributed to captor society. In state-level societies, where documents are available, it is abundantly clear that captives introduced many important technologies or cultural practices into captor societies. Making the same sorts of links is difficult or even impossible for small-scale societies of the past. The best that archaeologists may ever be able to do is document the presence of captives at the same time that a new technology, design style, or architectural pattern is introduced. Patterns present in state-level societies can help us link these two lines of evidence.

This book develops a context for understanding how captives fit into captor society and their impacts on it. I argue that archaeologists can no longer afford to ignore the presence of subordinate people, including captives, in small-scale societies. But only by considering the lives of captives in ethnohistoric or ethnographic societies can we incorporate them into our accounts of the past. Captives may have clung to the lowest strata of the societies they joined, but this book contends that not only were they present in most prehistoric small-scale societies, their presence could be transformative.

The Captive's World

In the following chapters I use comparative research to characterize the impact of captives on the societies they joined. I begin in chapter 2, "Captive Taking in Global Perspective," by discussing the historic, ethnohistoric, ethnographic, and archaeological sources I use. Data on captive taking used in this volume is derived from eight broad regions of the world, and these regions are described. Four of these regions are in North America and data from these regions is used most intensively. Other accounts come from South America, Africa, Europe, and Southeast Asia.

The remainder of the book moves from microscale considerations of how captives are incorporated into captor society and captives' effect on its power structure to macroscale topics, including the role of captives in the formation and maintenance of social boundaries and the ideas and practices captives contribute to captor society. Chapter 3, "The Captive as Social Person," explores the social location captives were offered in captor society, which was an important determinant of the captives' level of impact on the societies they joined. Social locations for captives ranged from wife or adoptee to abject slave. A number of factors determined which of these social roles they took up. Perhaps most important was the captor's assessment of whether "others" could be civilized or properly trained in captor social practices. The captive's age, gender, sexuality, skills, and personal characteristics (intelligence, language ability, and so on) also affected access to more intimate social roles. Unlike the rigid racial divisions between slaves and masters in the American South, in most (but not all) small-scale societies, captive status evolved. With increasing age, marriage, the birth of children to their captors, or the ability to demonstrate interpersonal or technical skills, captives could improve their social standing.

The three chapters at the heart of the book explore the effects that captives could have on the societies they joined. Chapter 4, "Captives and the Creation of Power," suggests that captives may have been an important source of power prehistorically. Aspiring leaders need followers and control over the labor of others. Captives meet both of these needs without the reciprocal obligations involved in demanding the services of kin. Chapter 5, "Captives, Social Boundaries, and Ethnogenesis," investigates the effect of captives on the creation and maintenance of social boundaries. Surprisingly, even where captives make up a large proportion of a population, they do not necessarily blur the boundaries of the societies they enter but may strengthen them, either by assiduously following captor cultural practices or by serving as reminders of incorrect "ways of doing." Chapter 6, "Captives and Cultural Transmission," suggests a new mode of intercultural transmission, the captive. This chapter argues that, even though they were marginal, captives could introduce a variety of new cultural practices into the societies they joined. This chapter is especially important for archaeologists, who lack adequate models for how cultural practices moved between social groups (Cameron 2011). The final chapter, "Captives in Prehistory," reviews the book's major arguments and outlines archaeological avenues for finding captives in prehistory.

Slavery Past and Present

The news clip that opened this chapter shows that the horror of captive taking has not disappeared. Today we call it human trafficking and its victims are not typically taken during raids and warfare (although, as the Boko Haram raid shows, that still happens) but are kidnapped, sold by their parents or another relative, or tricked by deceptive offers of a lucrative job. Human trafficking is receiving increased attention from governments and the public. A 2012 report by the United Nations finds that since the 2003 implementation of the Trafficking in Persons Protocol, efforts to criminalize trafficking have increased worldwide (United Nations Office of Drugs and Crime 2012). One hundred and thirty-four countries now have laws criminalizing trafficking. Statistics in the report, however, remain grim. Globally, almost 21 million people (a more recent report by the Walk Free Foundation's 2014 Global Slavery Index puts the number at 35.8 million) are victims of trafficking for either sexual or labor exploitation. Fifty-five to 60 percent of trafficking victims are women; 27 percent are children. Two of every three child victims are girls. Even though many countries have laws against trafficking, conviction rates are low. Between 2007 and 2010, 16 percent of the countries covered in the report had no convictions.

As disheartening as the un report is and as devastating as trafficking remains for its victims, the world of slavery and human trafficking has changed dramatically in the past two hundred years. Adam Hochschild (2005, 2) observes that at the end of the eighteenth century over three-fourths of the population of the world was in some form of slavery or bondage. For an eighteenth-century person, whether slave or free, Asian, African, European, or American, this was simply the way the world was. Slavery supported ancient Greece and Rome, the Catholic Church during the Middle Ages, the great states of Asia, the striking cultural developments of ancient Islam, and the warlords of Africa. As this volume and others show, it was common in many small-scale societies, too (Brooks 2002; Cameron 2008b; 2011; Gallay 2002; Hämäläinen 2008; Rushforth 2012; Snyder 2010). It is no exaggeration to suggest, as historian Marc Bloch ([1947] 1975, 30–43, 161–70; cited in Bonnassie 1991, 1) has, that the most dramatic change the world has seen is the virtual elimination of slavery as an acceptable form of human relations.

Two hundred years is the blink of an eye in terms of human history, yet once slavery began to disappear, the memory of its pervasiveness was only selectively retained. While racial segregation the United States prevented African Americans from forgetting slavery, in other places memories of the nightmare of slavery were buried. At the end of the twentieth century, heritage tourism emerged in locations related to the Atlantic slave trade. But at the same time, memories of internal African slavery became part of what Carolyn Brown (2003, 219) calls "a haunting silence" (see Stahl 2008, 32–33). Similar "forgetting" occurs in many other places. In the San Luis Valley of Colorado, a wife whispers to an anthropologist about her Hispanic husband's ancestors, who had been indigenous slaves (Brooks 2002, 405). In the Ecuadorian Amazon, the recent descendants of captive women will discuss their origins only when no one else is around (Brenda Bowser, pers. comm.). On the Northwest Coast, the slave ancestry of neighbors is still the subject of gossip and derision (Donald 1997, 249).

Not only did people involved as slavers or the enslaved try to forget, so did historians and anthropologists. As Igor Kopytoff (1982, 207) observes, "Anthropology almost completely forgot slavery in the 1920 to 1960 period, when so much of the modern world view was being forged. The amnesia was, above all, theoretical." As references at the beginning of this chapter show, the amnesia is over and scholars and others are willing to consider captives and slaves and their effect on the world they inhabited. This book contributes to that conversation.

| Chapter Two

Captive Taking in Global Perspective

I have found the most detailed ethnohistoric, ethnographic, and historic accounts of warfare and captive taking in small-scale societies in eight regions of the world. European colonization impacted each region at a different point in time, but most accounts used here focus on the 350 years from 1500 to 1850 CE. A few are earlier (primarily late in the first millennium) and a very few extend into the twentieth century. Because the most recent and detailed work on captives in small-scale societies has been undertaken in the New World and because North America is my area of expertise, I concentrate on four broad culture areas of the North American continent: the Northeast, Southeast, Southwest, and Northwest Coast. In the following pages I present brief descriptions of each of these four regions, including the extent of territory encompassed and its general environmental characteristics, the nature of indigenous societies as they were known at contact, and the major sources used to understand the region. The effects of European contact on warfare and captive taking are discussed, as well as evidence for precontact captive taking.

The other regions I consider are large and diverse, yet each has small-scale societies in which warfare and captive taking have been described. In South America I focus primarily on Amazonia and, more broadly, on the region Santos-Granero (2009) calls "tropical America." The

continent of Africa is considered as a whole (following other scholars: Miers and Kopytoff 1977; R. Reid 2012; Robertshaw and Duncan
2008; Robertson and Klein 1983a; Stahl 2008); however, the majority
of the studies I use pertain to western Africa from the Sahel south to
present-day Angola, as well as the coastal areas of eastern Africa. Medieval Europe, especially Scandinavia, experienced widespread raiding and captive taking until about 1000 CE. A few studies allow me
to explore practices here. The final region is island Southeast Asia; a
few sources here consider captives in small-scale societies. For South
America, Africa, Europe, and Southeast Asia, I introduce the particular societies I consider, along with the sources I used in the analysis.

As with any other archaeological study that uses ethnographic or
ethnohistoric cases as an analogy for the past, I am concerned about
the transformations that European colonization caused in the small-
scale societies I examine. European economic systems demanded a
great deal of labor, and in many areas these demands increased captive
taking, enslavement, and the commercialization of slaves. The same
was likely true of non-European states. Slave labor built the Islamic
states of the tenth to fifteenth centuries and eastern Africa was plun-
dered for human booty. In small-scale societies, captives were valued
especially as prestige items, as sexual partners, or as a boost to community population, although captives certainly provided labor and
circulated as trade items or gifts. The presence of states adjacent to or
in contact with small-scale societies could shift the emphasis from taking captives for social aggrandizement to taking captives for trade, as
happened in areas colonized by Europeans, creating "predatory landscapes" (see chapter 1).

Certainly European intrusion had an enormous effect worldwide,
but it is important to recognize that even before the colonial era, many
small-scale societies were in contact with and reacting to larger political entities at variable distances. One exception may have been North
America. Except for a short period between about one thousand and
seven hundred years ago, North America was a land without states, although it may have been in contact with the great states of Mesoamerica. In South America there is evidence that the Andean states of the

west coast of the continent had contact with the smaller-scale societies in the Amazon jungles to the east. Furthermore, increasing information about the scale of prehistoric societies in Amazonia suggests
large-scale, perhaps state-level, polities in South America (Heckenberger 2002, 120). In Africa "states and stateless societies have existed side by side for nearly two millennia" (Curtin et al. 1995, 71). After
the fall of the Roman Empire, Europe went through various stages
in which large and small states were more or less influential (Davies
1996; Dornberg 1996). Trade with states on the mainland, including
China, connected the small-scale societies of island Southeast Asia. I
do not attempt to evaluate the effects of states on the small-scale societies I study, except to exercise caution in using postcontact sources. Still, we should consider that parallel, if smaller-scale, changes in
warfare, captive taking, and enslavement may have accompanied the
development of states in various parts of the world long before 1492.

North American Regions

The Northeast

The Northeast region includes societies located in and around the
Great Lakes. To the north the region ends where the boreal forest begins, and its southern boundary is marked by the watershed of the
Ohio River (Trigger 1978a, 1). It includes Iroquoian speakers to the east
and Algonquian and Sioux speakers to the west. On the east, primarily the English but also the Dutch settled the coastal region and inland
areas south of Lakes Ontario and Erie. The French settled the western portion of the region and called it the "upper country," or *pays
d'en haut* (Rushforth 2003, 2012; Peregrine 2008). The *pays d'en haut*
extended west to the Minnesota River and south to the confluence of
the Mississippi and Missouri Rivers (Rushforth 2012, 20; White 1991).

Historically known Northeastern people were hunters and fishermen, and most practiced horticulture. They lived in longhouses or
lodges clustered into settlements of varying size and permanence, with
the largest settlements holding fifteen hundred to two thousand people and the smallest an extended family (see articles in Trigger 1978b;

especially Fenton 1978, 306, for northern Iroquoian settlements; also Trigger 1976, 32, for the Hurons). Longhouses were occupied by kin groups and their affines. The patterns found at contact, especially maize horticulture, likely developed before 1000 CE, and after that point it is possible to link prehistoric and historically known cultures (Trigger 1978a, 2). The Northeast experienced frequent but nonintensive contact with European fishermen and explorers beginning at the end of the fifteenth century (Trigger 1978a, 2). The most extensive and devastating effects of colonization would not be felt until the first half of the seventeenth century and, unfortunately, this is the period of time in which most ethnohistoric and historic accounts of warfare and captive taking began to be produced. Most of the sources used in the present study date from about the 1630s to the 1750s.

Major sources used for Iroquoian groups include the work of archaeologist and ethnohistorian Bruce Trigger on the Hurons, especially his monumental *The Children of Aataentsic: A History of the Huron People to 1660* (1976) and the foundational study "Northern Iroquoian Slavery" by anthropologist William Starna and historian Ralph Watkins (1991), in which they argue that many of the Iroquois captives taken during seventeenth-century wars should be considered slaves. Historian Daniel Richter's (1983) "War and Culture: The Iroquois Experience" describes the intensive warfare of the late seventeenth century but addresses captives less directly, as does his more recent sweeping study of prerevolutionary America (Richter 2011). These scholars of the Iroquois use many historic documents but rely especially on *The Jesuit Relations*, the annual reports of French Jesuit missionaries first published in France in 1632 (Thwaites [1896–1901] 1959). The priests who produced these reports lived for years with various Northeastern groups, especially the Hurons and the Five Nations of the Iroquois League (Greer 2000). Their intimate knowledge of indigenous culture and their well-developed writing skills make *The Jesuit Relations* highly enlightening (Greer 2000, 1–2).

Captives in the *pays d'en haut* have been studied most recently and intensively by historian Brett Rushforth (2012) in his book *Bonds of Alliance: Indigenous and Atlantic Slaveries in New France* and in articles, including a study on captive taking and enslavement during the Fox wars (Rushforth 2006). Rushforth's (2012, 10) work focuses on the period between about 1660 and 1750, during which Indians and French colonists captured and enslaved thousands of indigenous people. His study emphasizes that indigenous societies in this region used captives for the creation of alliances among groups. French misunderstanding of this practice had profound effects on French and Indian relations (Rushforth 2003).

European contact during the sixteenth century was occasional, but still it was a time of significant change for Northeastern societies. Trigger (1978a, 2) argues that even prior to the penetration of Europeans into the interior of the Northeast, the fur trade and efforts to protect hunting territory and trade routes changed the sociopolitical landscape of the region and resulted in the formation of large tribal units and confederacies. A dramatic increase in warfare, which had become devastating by the mid-seventeenth century, is especially important for the present study. The fur trade, the introduction of guns, and especially European diseases that decimated Iroquois populations changed the nature of warfare among the Iroquois. The traditional Iroquois "mourning wars" that had once represented occasional revenge for the death of a group member became violent attacks that sought captives whose adoption would replace deceased Iroquois (Richter 1983). Iroquois attacks during the late seventeenth and early eighteenth centuries ranged widely throughout the Northeast and into the Southeast, destroying or displacing a significant proportion of the indigenous population of the Northeast and beyond. Similar violent warfare, especially the early eighteenth-century Fox Wars, disrupted the Algonquian and Siouan speakers of the *pays d'en haut*. These wars resulted from an effort by indigenous people to control trade routes and resist the incursions of Europeans and other indigenous groups into their territory (Rushforth 2012).

European descriptions of warfare, captive taking, and captive experiences cannot directly mirror the precontact period. Still, evidence shows similar activities were ongoing prior to contact and that some of the meanings surrounding these activities survived into the postcontact era. In an examination of the archaeology of southern Ontario and northern New York state, Trigger (1976, 144–45) presents evidence of increasing violence after 1300 CE, including palisaded villages, human remains with evidence of violent death, cannibalism (indicated by human remains that have been cut and cooked, as well as bones split for bone marrow), and few males ages sixteen to twenty-five in ossuaries. Young warriors, apparently lost during battle or taken as captives, were absent from family burial grounds. Following John Witthoft (1959, 52–56), Trigger suggests that the introduction of agriculture reduced emphasis on hunting, eliminating an important avenue for men to demonstrate courage and ability with weapons; warfare was a new avenue for the demonstration of male prowess and the acquisition of prestige. Arguing for continuity in the treatment of captives between pre- and postcontact periods, Trigger (1976, 145, 147) traces historic features of Iroquoian warfare such as the emergence of war chiefs and prisoner sacrifice well into the past, linking them with similar leadership positions and sacrificial cults known prehistorically in the Southeast and Mesoamerica.

Evidence for endemic warfare and captive taking during the period before contact is also found in the *pays d'en haut*, including palisaded villages, human remains with evidence of violent death, mutilated bodies that suggest ritual torture, and female-heavy sex ratios that indicate the presence of captive women (Rushforth 2012, 22). Language provides an additional line of evidence for the presence of captives in prehistoric societies. Starna and Watkins (1991, 48–49) describe links between Iroquois words for *slave* and *dog.* The verb root of these words means "to have as a slave or pet," and the expression for raising an animal is the same as that for mistreating or abusing a person. Analogous links between words for slaves and dogs or pets are found in Algonquian languages in the *pays d'en haut* (Rushforth 2012, 35–37), again suggesting temporal depth to the presence of slaves in these societies. Finally, evidence for the antiquity of warfare and captive taking is suggested by the fact that Native Americans often offered a gift of captives to the earliest European explorers in the Northeast as a sign of friendship (Ekberg 2010, 11; Rushforth 2003, 2012).

The Southeast

The southeastern portion of North America is conventionally considered a single culture area even though it contained a multitude of people with different languages and customs (Jackson and Fogelson 2004). The Southeast extends from the Ohio River on the north to the Gulf of Mexico on the south and westward from the Atlantic Ocean to the Trinity River in Texas (Hudson 1976; Wood, Waselkov, and Hatley 1989). This environmentally rich area was culturally distinct from at least 1000 CE, when maize agriculture was introduced (Gallay 2002, 23). With a mild climate and numerous large, slow-moving rivers, the Southeast was an area with abundant natural resources (Hudson 1976, 14–22), and a large indigenous population, estimated at around two hundred thousand at the time of European contact (Ubelaker 2006, 695).

Southeastern archaeologists call the centuries between 900 and 1700 CE the Mississippian period (Ethridge 2009, 3); this period included the most complex cultures developed in North America. Mississippian society was organized into chiefdoms that varied from simple to complex and in some cases included alliances of several groups ruled by a paramount chief. For a period of about 250 years (1050–1300 CE) the enormous settlement of Cahokia likely became complex enough to be called a state, but this was not characteristic of the region. Chiefdoms are unstable political entities with frequent conflict between groups, and archaeologists describe periodic collapse and reorganization of chiefdoms throughout the Southeast (Anderson 1994). More substantial disruptions also apparently occurred. Archaeologists have detected evidence of depopulation after 1400 CE in a wide area of the Southeast, which was unrelated to European contact (Cobb and Butler 2002).

Unoccupied areas often separated chiefly territories and served as buffer zones between hostile groups (e.g., Bourne 1904, 60–64). Chiefdoms consisted of towns and villages of varying size and generally had at least one ceremonial center with mounds or open space around which houses were built. Towns were typically built on high ground along rivers or streams, and some were surrounded by a palisade (Hudson 1976, 210–11). Southeastern societies were clearly hierarchically

organized. Sixteenth-century Spanish explorers described rulers surrounded by retainers and deferential commoners; some were carried
around on litters (Anderson 1994, 57; Bourne 1904; Hudson 1976, 203–
10). They dressed, ate, and lived considerably better than the commoners and also seem to have kept large numbers of slaves (Anderson 1994,
57; Bourne 1904; Gallay 2002, 29). Mounds found at ceremonial sites
were used by rulers as platforms on which they built temples or their
homes, and as burial places. Christina Snyder's (2010) *Slavery in Indian Country: The Changing Face of Captivity in Early America* is a valuable resource for the study of the captive experience in the Southeast.
Snyder is one of the few Southeastern scholars who focuses on the
captive experience and the roles captives played in the societies they
joined. Most of her ethnohistoric sources date to the seventeenth and
eighteenth centuries, after significant disruption by European colonists, but she links the pre- and postcontact practices of captive taking. These practices "adapted over time to meet changing needs and
circumstances" (Snyder 2010, 4). In *Vital Enemies: Slavery, Predation,
and the Amerindian Political Economy of Life*, Fernando Santos-Granero
(2009) describes the captive experience among the Calusas of southern Florida. Santos-Granero uses sixteenth-century historic documents
that provide a view of the Calusas prior to extensive European contact.
Slavery among the Cherokees has been well studied. Historian Theda
Perdue (1979), in *Slavery and the Evolution of Cherokee Society, 1540–1866*,
provides insights into the Cherokee conception of slaves and suggests
that the slave role also existed in precontact times.

As in the Northeast, the purpose and meaning of warfare and captive taking in the Southeast changed after contact, from revenge and
prestige building to supplying an international slave trade. The violence, intensity, and constancy of warfare increased as European colonists manipulated preexisting animosities and competition among
Indian groups and encouraged groups to attack each other (Gallay
2002; Ethridge 2009). The ease with which captives could be sold into
colonial markets provided an economic incentive for warfare and captive taking. Already reeling from the effects of European diseases on
their populations, Native American societies were further reduced by

war deaths, the taking and exporting of captives, and often by the destruction of indigenous subsistence practices (Cameron 2015). Several recent books focus on the indigenous slave trade and provide glimpses of the captive experience amid abundant evidence of the dismantling and reconstitution of Southeastern societies. *Mapping the Mississippian Shatter Zone: The Colonial Indian Slave Trade and Regional Instability in the American South*, a collection of papers edited by anthropologist Robbie Ethridge and historian Sheri Shuck-Hall (2009), focuses on the two hundred years after European contact, when Southeastern chiefdoms were largely destroyed. Historian Alan Gallay's (2002) *The Indian Slave Trade: The Rise of the English Empire in the American South, 1670–1717* describes the impact of the traffic in Indian slaves on both the indigenous societies and the early colonies of the Southeast; it was devastating for one, enriching for the other.

Palisaded settlements, weapons of war, and oral histories that glorify war and warfare provide considerable evidence of precontact warfare during the Mississippian period (Alt 2008; Dye 2004; Jeter 2012, 29; Milner 2007). Captive taking is more difficult to see. Useful lines of evidence for captives include isotopic analysis suggesting the presence of foreigners at some sites, human remains showing evidence of violent death (including retainer burials or "death companions"), and artwork depicting apparent war captives. The taking of captives was glorified in Southeastern oral traditions such as the Morning Star and Red Horn myths (Alt 2008). A figurine made at Cahokia, the largest Mississippian site (but recovered at Spiro Mounds in Oklahoma), depicts an individual interpreted as a warrior priest decapitating a bound and crouching captive (figure 2; Dye 2004, 199). At the Angel Site, a Mississippian site in Indiana, bone isotopes identified two distinct burial populations, and one of the groups seems to have been nonlocal (Schurr 1992, cited in Alt 2008, 211). The additional presence of stone pipes depicting kneeling and bound captives, as well as burials placed in unusual and seemingly subservient positions, suggests that some of the residents of this site were captives (Alt 2008).

2. *Conquering Warrior* effigy pipe. The object was found at
Spiro Mounds in Oklahoma but is thought to have originated
at the great center of Cahokia, just east of modern-day St.
Louis, Missouri. Photo courtesy John Bigelow Taylor.

The Southwest

The region contemporary Americans call the Southwest made up
the northern frontier of the great civilizations of Mesoamerica and
later of colonial New Spain. Today it includes the modern Mexican
states of Chihuahua, Sonora, and Sinaloa and in the United States
the states of Arizona and New Mexico and small portions of Utah,
Colorado, and Nevada. The Southwest is a varied but largely arid region. Its southern and western parts consist of north-south-trending
mountain ranges separating dry, low-lying basins. To the north is
the Colorado Plateau and beyond that high mountains. To the east

is the western edge of the Great Plains. Corn agriculture was introduced into this region about four thousand years ago, and by the beginning of the Common Era most indigenous groups relied on both agriculture and hunting and gathering (Cordell and McBrinn 2012, 19). Spaniards traversing the Southwest in the early sixteenth century encountered people living in multistoried pueblos to the north and dispersed communities of agriculturalists to the south. But they also encountered nomadic hunting and gathering groups who had arrived in the region at about the same time as the Spanish. The present study focuses on three of these nomadic groups for which warfare and captive taking have been studied: the Apaches, Navajos, and Comanches.

The Apaches and Navajos are Athapaskan speakers who migrated from Canada into the Southwest during the late fifteenth century, shortly before the Spanish arrived (Wilshusen 2010, 193; some scholars argue for an earlier arrival date). Initially nomadic or seminomadic, they subsisted on hunting and gathering but also practiced part-time horticulture. Raiding or trading with the settled Pueblo people was an important aspect of their subsistence. They lived in ephemeral dwellings that housed extended families. The separation of Apaches and Navajos as distinct cultural and linguistic groups likely took place during the seventeenth century (Wilshusen 2010, 195). The later-arriving Comanches, a Shoshonean group who originated in the Great Basin, established themselves in the southern plains by the late seventeenth century (Hämäläinen 2008, 18–21). Their territory included only the eastern edge of the Southwest, but raids and slave trading extended their influence throughout much of the region.

Captive taking, the indigenous slave trade, and a captive exchange economy developed rapidly in the Southwest after Spanish colonization and has been the subject of a number of studies that I found useful for the present work. David Brugge's ([1968] 2010) *Navajos in the Catholic Church Records of New Mexico, 1694–1875,* the result of research on Indian land claims in the 1950s and 1960s, examines baptismal and burial records containing information on the Navajo people. Brugge uses these data and other sources to quantify and describe the thousands of Navajos and other indigenous captives who became slaves or servants in Spanish society. He describes the experiences not only of captives in the Spanish society of northern New Mexico but also of those who became slaves of the Navajos. His later studies expand on this initial work (Brugge 1979, 1993a, 1993b). Ramón Gutiérrez's (1991) *When Jesus Came, the Corn Mothers Went Away* examines how marriage patterns shaped gender, sexuality, and systems of inequality in colonial-era New Mexico. Gutiérrez identifies the *genízaro* as detribalized Apaches, Navajos, and other indigenous people enslaved by the Spanish. The New Mexico elite defined the *genízaro*, who occupied the bottom of New Mexico's social hierarchy, as both intruders into Spanish society and outcasts from the society of their birth (Gutiérrez 1991, 155).

James Brooks's (2002) *Captives and Cousins: Slavery, Kinship, and Community in the Southwest Borderlands* emphasizes that Spanish and Southwestern nomadic cultures were based on similar concepts of male honor and shame that required the construction of avenues for intercultural transfer that involved raiding and captive taking. The Spanish brought with them memories of centuries of conflict and intermarriage with Moors that paralleled nomadic Southwestern society's male-dominated focus on raiding, trading, and the capture and control of women. Brooks demonstrates the important role of captive women as intercultural intermediaries linking multiple groups together.

Several recent studies focus on the Comanches. Pekka Hämäläinen's (2008) *The Comanche Empire*, one of the most detailed, traces the Comanches' transformation from a small band of hunter-gatherers, newcomers to the region, to the dominant force in the southern plains (see also Gwynne 2010). At the peak of their power, the Comanches controlled more territory than Euro-Americans and prevented Euro-American expansion into the Southwest until late in the nineteenth century. Warfare and raiding were central to the Comanches' expansion, and they eagerly joined the emerging slave-raiding and slave-trading networks that also involved the Spanish and other indigenous people. During the eighteenth and early nineteenth centuries, the Comanches raided Spanish and Pueblo villages and the camps of migratory indigenous peoples and took many children and young women captive. Hämäläinen provides a great deal of information on captive taking and the use of captives in Comanche society. Of even greater importance for the present study, Joaquín Rivaya-Martínez (2006, 2012) uses the testimonies of over eight hundred captives, taken between 1820 and 1875 and interviewed by the Mexican government after their rescue or escape, to explore how captives were incorporated into Comanche society.

Spanish colonization of the Southwest began at the end of the sixteenth century with the Spanish co-opting the Rio Grande and other New Mexico pueblos. Raiding and trading among the Spanish, their Pueblo allies, and a range of nomadic groups made violence and captive taking a constant feature of the subsequent two centuries (Cameron 2015). Pueblos, Spanish, Navajos, Comanches, Apaches, and others became enemies or allies as expediency dictated. Trade in indigenous slaves was the most lucrative business available for both European and indigenous entrepreneurs (Brugge 1993b, 97). The pueblos at the eastern edge of the Southwest (such as Pecos and Taos) shared a long history of interaction with Plains groups, and these patterns continued into the colonial era, albeit with new nomadic players. The exchange of slaves at fairs at Taos and Pecos continued as in prehistoric times (Brugge 1993b, 98). Many of the captives sold in these Spanish-controlled settlements disappeared into Spanish homes as "adopted" or "rescued" people and lived their lives as domestic slaves. Less fortunate captives were sold south to the mines at Parral in Chihuahua (Brugge 1993b, 98); the Comanches sold Apache women east to the French (Hämäläinen 2008, 43).

Linking precontact and postcontact patterns of warfare and captive taking in the Southwest is somewhat more difficult than in other regions because the indigenous people involved in these practices were newcomers; furthermore, the Spanish had neutralized Pueblo practices of warfare. Still, evidence of precontact warfare in the Southwest is considerable, especially in the three hundred years prior to Spanish contact. Evidence among the region's sedentary inhabitants includes large, aggregated, inward-facing villages, burned sites, indications of violent death, skewed sex ratios suggesting the absence of male warriors, and violent imagery on murals and rock art (LeBlanc 1998, 197–236; Schaafsma 2000). There is evidence that captives were taken. The first Spanish expedition to reach northern New Mexico in 1540 encountered Plains people held among the Pueblos (Brooks 2002, 47–48), which confirms that the colonial pattern of violent Plains-Pueblo encounters existed before the Spanish arrived. The same skewed sex ratios that suggest an absence of male warriors could also be read to indicate the presence of female captives (see Kohler and Turner 2006 for this pattern during earlier periods). Finally, bioanthropological studies identify populations of abused women in the northern Southwest who may have been captives (Harrod 2012; Martin 2008).

The Northwest Coast

The Northwest Coast culture area includes people who occupied the Pacific coast of North America, a narrow strip of land extending from southern Alaska to northern California and bordered on the east by coastal mountain ranges (Ames and Maschner 1999; Donald 1997). Rich in marine and riverine fish, mammals, waterfowl, and shellfish, as well as bulbs, roots, tubers, fruits, and berries (Donald 1997, 18–19), this was one of the most densely populated areas of North America when first encountered by Europeans (Ames and Maschner 1999, 43; Boyd 1990, 135; Lovisek 2007, 60; Ubelaker 2006, 695). It was also home to a diversity of linguistic groups, including the Tlingits, Haidas, and Salish (Ames and Maschner 1999). Northwest Coast societies are characterized as complex hunter-gatherers who subsisted on abundant but locally variable resources (Ames and Maschner 1999, 114). They collected, processed, and stored marine resources (fish, shellfish, sea mammals, and waterfowl), especially varieties of salmon, which were taken at specific locations along the rivers as they moved upstream to spawn. Because of the rich environment, Northwest Coast people were semisedentary, living much of the year in large plank houses in winter villages and then dispersing in other seasons to gather specific resources (Donald 1997, 24). The economy of the Northwest Coast was household based. Households were often large: thirty to over one hundred people who made up a single social group; especially large social groups might occupy several houses (Ames and Maschner 1999, 25). These kin-based social groups controlled access to resources and property. Villages were not integrated politically, yet social inequality on the Northwest Coast was highly developed (see chapter 4). Ranked and stratified groups included elite "titleholders" (and their less wealthy and prominent relatives), free commoners, and slaves (Ames and Maschner 1999, 27; Donald 1997; Kan 1989, 102).

Anthropologist Leland Donald's (1997) *Aboriginal Slavery on the Northwest Coast of North America* provides the most comprehensive and detailed study of practices of captive taking and enslavement for the region. Donald's work counters the perception that slaves played small and unimportant roles in Northwest Coast societies. Other scholars second his argument that slaves were numerous in Northwest Coast villages and that their labor and presence were vital to the maintenance of titleholder status. Two other useful sources are Yvonne Hajda's (2005) article on slavery in the Lower Columbia River region and Donald Mitchell's (1984) examination of the slave trade among indigenous Northwest Coast people. These three studies provide evidence of the impact of slaves on captor societies as well as a sense of the lives captives lived. Studies focusing on regions immediately adjacent to the Northwest Coast are also useful. Herbert Maschner and Katherine Reedy-Maschner (1998) show that warfare and captive taking extended beyond the Northwest Coast region to include the North Pacific rim. Dominique Legros's (1985) remarkable study of the Tutchones of the Upper Yukon confirms not only that slavery extended far into the interior but that it could exist even in the smallest of societies.

Among all the ethnohistoric material I gathered for this project, Donald (1997, 48–66) makes one of the best attempts to evaluate the potential biases in ethnographic and historical sources. He observes that visiting summer scholars who talked to very few people (often only one person) through a translator collected most ethnographic accounts of the Northwest Coast. Perhaps more problematic, ethnographers talked almost exclusively to titleholders, the owners of slaves. A very different perspective on the institution of slavery might have

been gained if slaves had been interviewed. With regard to historic accounts, Donald (1997, 60) observes that the Europeans who produced
these accounts arrived in the Northwest Coast with preconceived
views about Native American peoples that almost certainly colored
what they wrote. Writing in order to justify their activities in the region (whether trade, missionary work, or government intervention)
could also skew the view they presented, and the skewing increased
for accounts written long after the events recorded.

Despite the biases Donald notes, his work is of special importance
to the present study because of his goal of evaluating whether slavery
was present before European contact. European contact came late
to the Northwest Coast. There were occasional ships from Asia and
indirect overland trade, but significant interactions between Northwest Coast peoples and Europeans began only in the mid-1770s, when
Spanish, Russian, and British vessels and traders began to make regu-
lar voyages there (Ames and Maschner 1999, 10–11; Donald 1997, 201).
The decades immediately after contact brought great change to Northwest Coast societies, as they became involved in the global trade in
furs and other goods. Unlike in the eastern United States or the Southwest, Europeans in the Northwest Coast were rarely involved in buying and selling indigenous people, nor were they involved directly in
instigating indigenous wars. By the time Europeans became an important presence on the Northwest Coast, the British had abolished
slavery (1805) and there was a growing abolitionist movement in the
eastern United States (Donald 1997, 215). Europeans did, however, create a new market for furs and other goods that significantly affected
indigenous political and economic relationships. As in other parts of
North America, indigenous people competed for access to and control of indigenous and European trade. Captives taken in raids could
be traded with other groups for furs to sell to Europeans. The introduction of guns also led to wars of extermination and expansion instigated by groups who were first to receive these new weapons (Boyd
1990, 136). Raids and warfare could result in a high mortality rate; captives were generally poorly treated, shortening their lifespans and limiting their fertility.

There is substantial evidence for warfare and captive taking during the precontact era on the Northwest Coast. Trauma on human remains found in a burial population near Prince Rupert Harbor (head wounds, defensive forearm injuries, etc.) suggests an increased prevalence of warfare beginning as early as 3000 BCE (Cybulski 1990, 1994; Lovisek 2007, 61–62). Slaves in this burial population are suggested by the presence of bound and decapitated individuals (Ames and Maschner 1999, 190) and by sex ratios that show an overabundance of males, implying the existence of female slaves who were not given formal burials (Cybulski 1992). Other evidence also suggests the antiquity of captive taking. Captive taking was reported by the earliest European visitors to the region and words for slaves that seem to be ancient are found in several language groups (Donald 1997, 201–13). Archaeological indicators of intensity of household production, including house building, suggest that slave labor may have been required for the levels of effort observed (Ames 2008). Slaves were also frequent social actors in Northwest Coast oral traditions, demonstrating the antiquity of the slave status (Averkieva [1941] 1966, cited in Donald 1997, 45; Donald 1997, 177–81; see Ruby and Brown 1993, 42, for Chinook). After European contact, however, the scale and distance of raids may have increased (Donald 1997, 230–31). Donald also suggests that raids undertaken for the express purpose of taking slaves may be limited to the postcontact period.

Other Global Regions

South America

Like its northern neighbor, South America had a large and diverse indigenous population when first contacted by Europeans. For purposes of this study, I ignore the Andean civilizations of the west coast of South America and focus primarily on Amazonia and adjacent areas, where the impacts of European colonization occurred somewhat later. Following Santos-Granero (2009), I include the Caribbean, where European impact was immediate but where there are early accounts of indigenous warfare and captive taking, beginning with

Columbus's first voyage. The most important source for the present study is Santos-Granero's (2009) groundbreaking *Vital Enemies: Slavery, Predation, and the Amerindian Political Economy of Life*. Using the earliest available historical sources, Santos-Granero explores six indigenous slaveholding societies in the region he calls "tropical America." His work poses a direct challenge to scholars who have questioned the existence of slavery in this region during the precontact period (see also Carneiro 1991, which uses sixteenth-century accounts to describe the extensive slavery of the Cauca Valley of northern Colombia). Most intriguingly, Santos-Granero identifies an underlying worldview common to the people of tropical America that is consistent with warfare, raiding, and captive taking. In the following chapters I connect aspects of this worldview to captives in parts of North America.

In many South American societies captives were incorporated as wives rather than as slaves. Brenda Bowser's (2008) study of captive taking in Amazonia focuses on the variety of social locations captives were offered in different social groups, ranging from slave to wife; as understanding the nature of captive incorporation is an important goal of the present study, Bowser's article is especially useful. Janet Chernela (1992, 2003, 2011) emphasizes the role that captive women in Amazonia have played in linking groups across "tribal" or linguistic social boundaries. Using testimonies of Spanish women reclaimed from their indigenous captors in Argentina, Susan Socolow (1992) suggests that captive women may retain elements of their natal culture even after many years in another culture.

One of the most detailed and powerful captive narratives comes from Helena Valero, a Portuguese girl captured at age twelve in the 1930s by the Yanomamö, who occupied borderlands between Brazil and Venezuela (see chapter 3). After more than twenty years with the Yanomamö, two husbands, and three children, Helena escaped back to an unwelcoming white world. In interviews recorded by an Italian anthropologist years after she returned, Helena details her experiences as a captive. She was incorporated as a wife but occupied a liminal position as a perennial outsider.

Africa

African peoples have suffered capture and enslavement by Europeans since the time of ancient Greece and Rome. As Islam gained power in the late first and early second millennia CE, Arabs became major enslavers of African people, who were exported primarily from eastern Africa to labor on plantations and construction projects throughout the Arab world (Robertshaw and Duncan 2008, 57; Walvin 2006, 23–26). Africa, especially the western part, became a source of slaves for the New World beginning in the mid-fifteenth century, and the Atlantic slave trade created one of the largest diasporas in human history (but see Segal 2001). During the past forty years there has been an enormous outpouring of scholarly studies of slavery in Africa, much of it related to the Atlantic slave trade, and there has been an even larger volume of material published on African slaves on the other side of the Atlantic. My interest is in the contributions of captives to small-scale societies (African scholars call these societies "decentralized") rather than the role of slaves in global trade or industrial labor; therefore, I use only a small subset of this material. Peter Robertshaw and William Duncan's (2008) overview of African slavery in decentralized societies provides an important starting point for the present study. Like other scholars, however, they emphasize that states and decentralized societies have long been part of the social landscape in Africa (e.g., Curtin et al. 1995), making it especially important to recognize the dynamic context in which slavery in small-scale societies operated.

Unlike other regions considered here, it is generally not possible to use "earliest" explorers' accounts to understand captive lives in Africa prior to extensive outside contact. Early European slave traders dealt primarily with coastal groups who supplied them with slaves. Most accounts of slavery among groups in the interior date to the nineteenth or early twentieth centuries, after the Atlantic and Islamic slave trades had altered virtually every culture on the continent. The sources I use date either to this relatively recent period or to an unspecified "ethnographic present."

African literature is especially valuable because of its systematic attempts to examine the lives of women slaves in Africa. Men made up the majority of captives sent across the Atlantic as slaves (about 2:1 or 3:1; Thornton 1983, 39), but most of the captives who remained in Africa as slaves were women. Female slaves have been more intensively studied in Africa than in any other parts of the world. Recognizing the importance of women in African slavery, historians Claire Robertson and Martin Klein (1983a) published the edited volume *Women and Slavery in Africa*. Chapters of interest to the present study include those focusing on the labor of female slaves, arguments about their value in reproduction, and discussions of the different ways in which they were incorporated into the societies of their masters. More recently, *Women and Slavery*, vol. 1, *Africa, the Indian Ocean World, and the Medieval North Atlantic*, edited by historians Gwyn Campbell, Suzanne Miers, and Joseph Miller (2007; part of a two-volume series that includes *Women and Slavery*, vol. 2, *The Modern Atlantic* [2008]), explores the lives of women in household slavery, including domestic politics and the strategies of enslavement.

Almost forty years ago, Africanist scholars argued about the definition of slavery. Historian Suzanne Miers and anthropologist Igor Kopytoff's (1977) *Slavery in Africa: Historical and Anthropological Perspectives* includes articles by scholars from both disciplines that describe the range of institutions in Africa that have been called slavery or seen as similar to slavery. Most of the articles pertain to western sub-Saharan Africa, and they include several useful studies of slave lives in decentralized societies. The volume's introductory essay (Kopytoff and Miers 1977) has been criticized for suggesting a "slavery to kinship continuum" that seems to overlook the real limits to societal inclusion experienced by slaves in many parts of the world (Cooper 1979; Watson 1980, 5), but this scholarly disagreement does not detract from the value of the compendium for understanding the role of slaves in African societies.

Like other parts of the world, Africa has produced a considerable number of captive narratives, although most are from the late nineteenth and early twentieth centuries (but see Edwards 1967). They provide insight into the lives of slaves, their relationships with the families they served, and how they affected the societies they joined (Alpers 1983; McDougall 1998; Wright 1993). Some scholars have also used oral histories to investigate the role of slaves in African societies (Guyer and Eno Belinga 1995; Stahl 1991).

Africanist scholars assume that slavery has existed on the continent for at least the past two millennia, if not longer, but they recognize that evidence, especially archaeological data, is sparse (Curtin et al. 1995, 81; Kusimba 2004; Robertshaw and Duncan 2008, 57). Literary sources tell us that African slaves lived in ancient Greece and Rome and in Asia at least as early as the late first millennium CE (Alpers 2003; Segal 2001). The Garamantes of Libya captured and enslaved sub-Saharan Africans by the first millennium BCE (Carney and Rosomoff 2009, 29–30). There has been far less archaeological work on slavery in Africa than in the Americas and much of it focuses on West Africa's role in the Atlantic slave trade (DeCorse 2001; Ogundiran and Falola 2007). The Islamic slave trade in eastern Africa has been less frequently studied (Alexander 2001; Croucher 2015; Kusimba 2004). Alexander (2001) argues that archaeologists lack the ability to recognize the material culture signatures even of the large-scale chattel slaving that characterized the Islamic and Atlantic slave trades, much less that of ancient indigenous slavery; Kusimba (2004) is more optimistic that archaeologists will eventually contribute to an understanding of slavery in Africa.

Europe

The Roman Empire was built on conquest, and the capture and enslavement of the conquered was a routine part of Roman wars. At the height of the empire's power, slaves made up between 10 and 20 percent of Rome's population and staffed most Roman industries, large and small (Lenski, forthcoming; Scheidel 2012). At the same time groups glossed as "Germanic tribes" occupied northern Europe beyond the Roman border. Noel Lenski (2008) uses a variety of sources, including Roman accounts, but especially Germanic law codes, to examine the role of slaves in Germanic societies during the early centuries of the Common Era, including how people became enslaved, their incorporation into Germanic societies, and the nature of their labor. Ruth Karras (1988, 12–39) provides an overview of various types of servitude in Europe from the end of Roman rule through the fourteenth century. Other sources provide insights into the lives of European slaves after the collapse of the Roman Empire left medieval Europe fragmented and rife with raiding, warfare, and the taking of captives. Slaves (especially women) made up a considerable proportion of many European households (Woolf 1997, 68), and the Catholic Church operated its large estates using slave labor (Bonnassie 1991, 25–32).

Beginning in the eighth century, Viking raiders plied the North Atlantic and Mediterranean, taking large number of captives to use as slaves in Viking settlements or to sell. Slaves labored throughout Scandinavia, yet some of the most useful evidence of slave lives comes from Icelandic sagas and other oral traditions. For the present study, the most valuable source on the role of slaves in Scandinavian society is Ruth Karras's (1988) *Slavery and Society in Medieval Scandinavia*, which uses sagas and other historical sources. Karras's detailed reading of these sagas provides considerable evidence for the roles slaves played in Icelandic settlements. Kristen Seaver (2007) focuses specifically on the lives of female slaves in Norse societies, exploring the social and cultural isolation of women captives transported to settlements in Iceland and Greenland.

Because historic sources exist, archaeological data is less important for documenting slavery in medieval Europe. Genetic studies confirm the common understanding from oral and written accounts that Viking raids often targeted Ireland. The maternal DNA of contemporary Icelandic people still contains a significant Celtic admixture that points to female Irish captives taken to Iceland (Helgason et al. 2000).

Island Southeast Asia

Island Southeast Asia includes the extensive chains of islands (Indonesia, East Malaysia, Brunei, the Philippines, and Taiwan) lying within the tropical zone (Bellwood 1992). I use only a few sources from this region that help illustrate some of the common features of the captive experience here. Archaeologist Laura Junker (2008) explores the maritime chiefdoms of the Philippine Islands that operated on the eastern edge of the vast trading networks of the empires and kingdoms of the Indian Ocean and South China Sea during the interval between the twelfth and sixteenth centuries. She shows the vital importance of raiding and captive taking to the political economy and warrior ideology of the Philippine chiefdoms during this period. Most critically for the present study, she uses archaeological data to show that the captive women taken in large numbers to labor in chiefly societies brought aspects of their natal culture with them. Other studies of the region that expand on raiding, captive taking, enslavement, and the role of slaves in socioeconomic systems in this area include a volume edited by Anthony Reid (*Slavery, Bondage, and Dependency in Southeast Asia* [1983]; see also A. Reid 1992) and James Warren's ([1981] 1985) *The Sulu Zone: 1768–1898*, which focuses on piracy and its effects in the Sulu-Mindanao area (see also Warren 2002).

The global and diverse material used in this study satisfies the goals of this project, which are to highlight commonalities in patterns of captive taking and captive experiences in small-scale societies worldwide. The number of regions and variety of groups in which captive taking is found stresses the almost universal nature of the practice. Here I have described the major sources I have used—mostly secondary sources that are based on historic and ethnohistoric data. In the chapters that follow, I use many other articles and volumes to expand on various aspects of captives' experiences and influence on the societies they joined. As noted above, the broad use of analogy that I bring to the problem of finding captives in the past is not without problems. But I believe that it is the most appropriate approach at this initial stage of study. I hope to convince archaeologists that they must look for these so-far invisible people in prehistoric societies throughout the world. The next four chapters explore beyond the moment of capture and discuss what happens when the captive enters an alien society.

| Chapter Three

The Captive as Social Person

This chapter explores factors that affect the social persons captives become when they enter captor society. Captives undergo "social death," losing completely the social person they had been in the society of their birth (Patterson 1982; see also Bowser 2008; Peregrine 2008; Santos-Granero 2009). They are then "reborn" to the society of their captors, but the rights of social personhood extended to them vary from group to group and their status ranges from abject slave to full participating society member. Captives are most vulnerable at the beginning of their lives in captivity; with increasing age, marriage to or acquisition by powerful men, the birth of children to their captors, and opportunities to demonstrate skills or abilities in crafts or curing or as intercultural intermediaries, they can (though not all do) gain significantly in social standing. Yet even in societies in which captives are married, adopted, or otherwise appear to be fully integrated into captor society, their rights of social personhood may be limited, their alien origin never completely forgotten. Although I use the term *captive* throughout this book, from the point of view of captor society, this was a temporary state.[1] As soon as the captive was introduced into captor society a social place had to be created for this foreign individual.

The ways in which a new social location opens for the captive depend on a variety of factors relating both to captor society and to the captive herself. The first section of this chapter characterizes the captor and shows that in most cases captors were the wealthy and powerful individuals in the society. In turn, the most fundamental fact about captives is that, at the moment of capture, they existed outside the kinship network of their captors. The second section explores the ways in which captives become socially located as either kin or nonkin. The third section explores how captive identities are constructed within the captors' worlds and then used by captors for social, economic, or spiritual gain. Characteristics of captives that affect the ways they are integrated are considered next and include age, gender, sexuality, skills, and personal traits (intelligence, flexibility, language ability, etc.). The circumstances surrounding captive taking are considered with regard to how they affect captive social location. These include whether captives are taken great distances from their homes, whether captive takers and captive givers have an ongoing relationship, whether groups of captives live together in captor society, and the wealth and status of the family within which the captive resides. Finally, the captive narrative of the Portuguese girl Helena Valero illustrates the interplay of these factors.

Social Identity in Captor Society

This chapter explores how social identity is constructed for individuals who enter a new society as adults or near adulthood. Social identity is a basic but complex concept in social science and refers to a range of phenomena (Fowler 2010, 353; see Brubaker and Cooper 2000 for a critique). Identity consists of relationships of similarity and difference. It refers to a distinct set of characteristics that are shared, but because only some individuals share these characteristics, the construction of identity also necessarily stresses difference. These characteristics may include male/female, high/low status, ethnic ingroup/outgroup, kin/nonkin, and others (Fowler 2010, 353; Voss 2008a, 9–37). The processes of inclusion and exclusion through which social identity is assembled are key to understanding the social identity of captives. Because the social identities captives developed in their natal societies are erased and replaced, the construction of social identity for these individuals is different than for native-born children.

At the most fundamental level, the identities of captives and their captors are mutually constructed (see Robertson and Robinson 2008, 267, for slaves and owners; see also Patterson 1982 for "relations of domination"). While captors held the upper hand in opening a social location for captives, the presence of captives allowed captors to define themselves as superior beings in opposition to their captives (see chapter 5 for ways in which social and ethnic boundaries are constructed through situational opposition). As discussed below, captor social status could be created, maintained, or enhanced through relationships to captives—the lowliness of the captive reflected back as an increase in status for the captor. This mutual relationship may have been less potent in regard to women captives, as women are typically constructed as subordinate regardless of their status as captive or native-born. Yet captives often may have been supervised and directed in their daily tasks by female captors, which would have given these women the opportunity to demonstrate their superior status through daily performance of control over their captives (Foster 2003).

Who Were the Captors?

Captives were disproportionately owned by the wealthy and high-status individuals in society. This should be a familiar theme for anyone knowledgeable about slavery in the Americas, where a tiny white population owned a very large African and indigenous slave population. In the small-scale societies on which this book focuses, the wealthy generally financed and led raids and wars; their power allowed them to retain the high-value booty of war, including captives. Furthermore, warfare and captive taking were very often avenues to status and power for young men, with their captives the key elements of status enhancement. From the point of view of the captive, life in a high-status household at times offered more options for the expression of agency and influence (discussed below).

Accounts of captive taking around the world document the status and wealth of the majority of captors. Among the Kalinago of the

Caribbean, war leaders benefited most from captive taking, keeping one out of every two or three captives taken (Santos-Granero 2009, 54). Among the Otomaco of the South American Llano, the wealth and status of chiefs directly related to the numbers of captives held by the household (Morey 1975, 308). In the Cauca Valley, located in what is today Colombia, captive taking was an important avenue toward status for young men; the greater the number of captives taken, the higher status accorded the captor (Carneiro 1991, 177). In the North American Southeast, captive taking was linked to power and status, and chiefs owned many slaves, who served as their personal attendants and as the extra labor they needed to retain power (Snyder 2010, 80–85, 131). On the Northwest Coast, slaves were owned almost exclusively by "titleholders" who made up the nobility of these tribal societies (Donald 1997, 86–88). Slaves were important both in ceremonies that validated titleholder status and as daily symbols of their master's or mistress's status. In Africa, the Aboh of Nigeria accumulated slaves to demonstrate their affluence, and ownership of many slaves indicated a man's worth (Nwachukwu-Ogedengbe 1977, 141). Among the nineteenth-century Kongo of west Africa, slaves functioned as prestige goods used in political competition and "enhanced the importance of their owners" (MacGaffey 1977, 243). Robertson and Klein (1983b) note that women in Africa were often slave owners, especially of female slaves. Slave owning and control over the labor that slaves produced was an avenue that ambitious women used to enhance their power (see also Nwachukwu-Ogedengbe 1977, 141).

In most societies, captives created wealth for their captors (see chapters 4 and 6) and *represented* wealth and status. This could be a two-way street, however, as the wealth and power of captors at times opened opportunities for captives to advance their own status-seeking goals. The effect on captives of the social position of their captors is examined below.

Captivity and Kinship

Kinship was the basic organizing principal for the small-scale societies discussed in this book, and the captive was thrust into a society in which she had no kin. Captive taking, a carefully considered activity, advanced the social and economic goals of the captors; placing captives in the correct social location—either within or outside of the kinship system—was critical to this endeavor. Social locations ranged from complete exclusion through rigid systems of slavery to full inclusion through adoption or marriage (in a discussion of African and Asian slavery, Watson [1980] defines "closed" and "open" systems). Santos-Granero (2009, 174) distinguishes between "integration," as incorporation without full rights, and "assimilation," as incorporation with full rights, yet in small-scale societies these distinctions rarely were absolute. Slaves, through time and with initiative, might gain some rights in the society where they labored; conversely, captives incorporated through marriage or adoption might retain the stigma of an outsider. This section considers how captives were structured in relationship to captor kinship systems. In chapter 5 the role of captives as social nodes connecting the kinship systems of captive-taking and captive-giving societies is explored.

Some of the small-scale societies examined in this book excluded captives from their kinship systems, maintaining women, children, and men exclusively as slaves. This practice is most evident for some groups in Africa, in Europe during the early Middle Ages, and among the societies of the Northwest Coast. As chapter 1 explains, slaves are a subcategory of captives who have been much studied in state-level societies but less frequently in small-scale societies (but see Donald 1997; Santos-Granero 2009; Snyder 2010). In discussing the construction of the slave in Africa, Meillassoux (1991, 138–40) emphasizes that not only were slaves barred from the kinship system of the societies they joined, they actually functioned as "anti-kin," oppositional beings to full members of society. These disenfranchised individuals provided their captors with labor without the obligations that resulted from mobilizing labor within kinship networks (see chapter 4). In other words, the master-slave relationship functioned outside the struggles for power that engaged full kin. Furthermore, the slave wife had no family with whom her husband had to share her progeny.

Even within the category of slave, the captive experience in different societies varied. In small-scale societies, slaves were often part of the domestic scene (like household slaves in the more familiar systems of New World industrial slavery). They could be offered a sort of pseudokinship as "children" to their owners, yet as Kopytoff (1982, 215) remarks, this term conveyed authority and subordination, not closeness or nurturing. Depending on the construction of the "other" in captor society, slaves could also be vilified and suffer constant abuse. These are not necessarily opposite ends of a pole of slave treatment. Slaves experienced both paternalistic "care" and violent abuse in the same society (as well as in the same household). They engaged daily in a highly charged social dialectic with their captors. As discussed below, the personality of the captive and the ways captives engaged with their captors could affect their ultimate treatment.

Scholars of African slavery have spent considerable time discussing the factors behind differential incorporation of slaves. Some have suggested that the ways slave-owning societies incorporated captives, at least in Asia and Africa, relate to sources of wealth (Watson 1980, 11–12, following Goody 1971, 32). In Africa, where wealth was built through control over people, captives incorporated as wives or concubines increased the population and hence the prestige of the group (see also Nieboer 1910). Kopytoff and Miers (1977) argue that in Africa slaves are outsiders and slavery is an institution that allows slaves to be eventually incorporated into captor kinship systems. In other words, captives were processed through a slavery-to-kinship continuum in most African societies. Watson (1980, 2–9) points out that Kopytoff and Miers's continuum might work for many African societies, but not for Asian societies where kinship systems are "closed" to entry by captive slaves. Land was the primary source of wealth in Asia, and captives were rarely invited into kinship systems where they would have claims on kin land.

Kopytoff and Miers (1977, 22) also argue that the social location for captives in Africa is determined by the *nature* of captor kinship systems. The strict patrilineal kinship system of the Vai, a group located in what is now Sierra Leone, offered no place for an individual who lacked local lineage connections (Holsoe 1977). Slaves were considered unclean and often treated harshly (Holsoe 1977, 290–91). In contrast, the nearby and culturally similar Sherbro had a nonlineal and, as a result, more flexible kinship system (McCormack 1977, 22). Captives or purchased persons were adopted and served as a conduit to create alliances with the kin groups from which the captives originated.

In Europe and in Scandinavian colonies on Iceland and Greenland during the early Middle Ages, slaves were highly marginalized individuals excluded from the kinship systems of their masters (Bonnassie 1991; Karras 1988; Seaver 2007). Bonnassie (1991, 23) describes the European slave as a "de-socialized being," a nonhuman who by definition had no claim to membership in the human community. In Scandinavian legal systems, the amount of compensation—*wergeld*—paid to a victim's kin for killing their relative determined personal rights and status (Karras 1988, 100). Since slaves were not kin, no *wergeld* was paid for the killing of a slave, although the master would have to be compensated for the price of the slave. In other words, killing a slave was an offense against property, not against the honor of the victim's kin group. In a study of female slavery in Iceland and Greenland, Seaver (2007, 155) emphasizes the power of men over women, whether free or enslaved, but the most powerless and abject women were those who had no male kin to protect them—a position exemplified by the slave woman who had been captured and taken far from her home.

The Northwest Coast's intensive foragers also excluded captives from their kinship systems, and captives' slave status continued through generations. As in Asia, wealth and prestige was based on control of property, including resources such as salmon-fishing locations. This emphasis on control of property meant that captors never invited captives into their kinship system (Donald 1997, 101–2). Titleholders owned not only natural resources but also intellectual property (songs, dances, ritual paraphernalia, myths, and names), and their careers revolved around efforts to validate their ownership of and add to their supply of nonmaterial property (Donald 1997, 101). Captives had to be excluded from any claims to these scarce intellectual resources and were constructed as nonbeings beyond embrace of kinship networks.

For most small-scale societies, captive incorporation was much more flexible, with some captives becoming wives, others adoptees, and still others slaves, as consideration of captive taking in the North American Southeast, the Southwest Borderlands, the Northeast, and elsewhere illustrates. Control over women's labor and reproduction was the key to male power and success, and incorporation of female captives through marriage was evident in all but the most rigid slaveholding societies. When disease or warfare decimated groups (especially evident after colonial invasion in North America [Cameron, Kelton, and Swedlund 2015]), adoption of or marriage to captives maintained societies at functioning population levels.

Because women in most societies occupy subordinate positions, "wife" was a convenient social location into which captives (subordinate by definition) could be slotted. At times they became full wives with all of the benefits of that social position, but more often they did most of the difficult and unpleasant work of the household as marginalized secondary or "drudge" wives. Those who became full wives could prosper, but even these women might not be able to engage fully in the social life that native-born wives enjoyed, or they might be blamed or excluded when difficulties befell the group (for example, see the account of captive Helena Valero at the end of this chapter). Other women became concubines, barred from marriage and by definition ineligible for full benefits of societal membership. Again, this status varied, with some concubines functioning as disposable sexual partners and others as privileged and well-cared-for pseudospouses.

Finding an appropriate social location in captor society for male captives could be more difficult. Where one of the goals of captive taking was to increase population, men might be adopted (for example, in the American Northeast). In some cases, adopted men clearly became full or even prominent members of captor society, while in others they might remain marginalized and at risk of social sanctions (see chapter 5). As discussed below, the age at which males were captured significantly impacted the way they were integrated into captor society, with the youngest captives more fully integrated than older boys or men, depending on captor concepts of social personhood. Of course, women could be adopted, too, and in the same way at times become full members of captor society.

Examples illustrate the range of social locations available for captives in small-scale societies. In the Southeast, captives could be tortured to death, adopted, or "owned," with the latter group functioning as slaves (Snyder 2010). The sorting process began when warriors returned home with their captives. Decisions about the disposition of captives were largely the prerogative of high-ranking women who assessed each captive's health, strength, and bravery. "Those selected for fiery torture were painted black, given a rattling gourd, and forced to dance; lucky adoptees were embraced by their new relatives; slaves were retained by their captors or sold to others" (Snyder 2010, 93). Age and sex were a captive's most important characteristics, at least during the colonial era. Southeastern native people believed that men were dangerous and, as a result, they were often considered unfit for adoption. More easily incorporated children and women made up the bulk of captives taken (Snyder 2010, 94, 105–6).

Similarly, among the Comanches of the Southwest Borderlands, captives could be adopted, married, enslaved, or sold (Brooks 2002; Hämäläinen 2008; Rivaya-Martínez 2012). Comanches preferred preteen male captives who could function as horse tenders and women who could become wives. Women and children could be relatively easily incorporated into Comanche society. Yet some captives, even women and boys, could be denied entry into Comanche kinship systems and functioned as slaves throughout their captive lives. "Deprived of any inherent rights or social standing, and lacking Comanche kin, enslaved captives were absolutely powerless" (Rivaya-Martínez 2012, 51). Captive status could change with time as the captive aged and learned the Comanche language and social traditions. Captive personality and initiative, discussed below, also strongly determined the social location the captive eventually achieved in Comanche society.

Much has been written about captive-taking experiences in the Northeast, especially the lurid ceremonies of torture and death. Captives of the Iroquoian groups not killed generally underwent adoption

rituals that transformed them into kin (Lafitau [1724] 1977, 171–72, cited in Donald 1997, 262–63). There is good evidence that captives participated fully in Iroquois culture, but Starna and Watkins (1991) argue
that captives lived more marginal lives than many Iroquois scholars
acknowledge and that some occupied a slave-like status (see chapter
5). For example, Huron males might marry a female captive, but the
marriage was not officially sanctioned; in this "contract" marriage,
the woman functioned as a slave (Dannin 1982, 105, cited in Starna
and Watkins 1991, 51). Young female captives not yet taken as wives
were apparently in the most vulnerable and abject position (LeJune
in Thwaites [1896–1901] 1959, cited in Starna and Watkins 1991, 50).

    Among Amazonian groups in South America, Bowser (2008) ob-
serves that captives were incorporated into multiple social locations
that included slavery, marriage, and adoption. Even captives incorporated into kinship networks through marriage or adoption might still
be categorized as subordinate individuals (Bowser 2008, 273). Their
kin ties were apparently not as strong or binding as those of the native
born, and they occupied social locations like those of orphans who
had no kin to protect them. Among the Yanomamö, captive wives and
children were more likely to be tormented and abused; captive wives
of the Waorani usually survived for only a few months before they
died or were killed; and Achuar men were selectively violent against
orphan women, as they did not have to face the women's fathers or
brothers (Bowser 2008).

    When captives entered captor society in the small-scale groups
discussed here, they began a process of engagement with the kinship
system that continued until their release or death. Social locations
available for captives were not just inside or outside the kinship network but somewhere along a continuum of integration ranging from
full member to wretched outsider. Few captives, even those adopted
or incorporated through marriage, ever achieved full group membership; more often, captives were to some extent liminal members of society, embraced in good times and abused, sold, or slain in bad times.
Captors, of course, functioned as gatekeepers to kinship networks,
but as discussed below, the age, gender, and personal characteristics

of captives often determined the degree to which they could partake in the benefits of kin group membership.

Captors' Worldview and the Social Construction of Captives

The social location of captives was multilayered. Their relationship to captor kinship networks represented one level, but at another level, captors' worldview and their view of "others" were equally important in determining captives' social location. Social personhood for captives (as for all social actors) was always in the process of development, and the goal of this section is to highlight how the tension between captives and their captors continually formed and transformed the social locations that each occupied. The social person of the captive could change as she aged, expressed agency, developed skills, had children, or outlived her usefulness. Changing circumstances in captor society or the initiative of the captive could open opportunities for captives.

Captives are important elements in the striving of captors for power and full social personhood (see also chapter 4), and key to their use in these endeavors is their place in the captors' worldview. As the examples below show, worldview explains a group's place in the world and its relationship with other beings, whether humans, animals, material objects, or spirits. Captives come from the world of "others," and the captors' worldview defines how captives are used by their captors to achieve social, economic, and spiritual goals. Social personhood for both captors and their captives is created in the process. Even as subordinate individuals, captives were part of the web of relationships that encompassed every member of the society. Through daily activities and interactions with other persons, places, and things, captives changed not only their social place in the society but very likely society's basic conceptions of self and other.

Studies of personhood, not surprisingly, focus on society's most central concepts and actors, with marginal actors mentioned only in passing and for contrast. Here these marginal actors take center stage. A brief review of concepts of social personhood sets captive social construction in context. Cultural anthropologists (Busby 1997; Comaroff and Comaroff 2001; Strathern 1988) and more recently archaeologists

(Bowser 2008; Fowler 2004, 2010) recognize that concepts of "person-hood" and how it is socially constructed vary from group to group. The idea of persons as individuals or autonomous beings, common in Western societies, is emphatically unlike the ways personhood is constructed in many non-Western societies (Fowler 2004, 2010). The Comaroffs (2001, 267) dispute the idea that the autonomous person exists anywhere as "an unmediated sociological reality." Instead, personhood in many societies is seen as "relational"—constructed in the process of interacting with others, whether humans, animals, or things. Personhood is crosscut by many other aspects of identity, including gender, age, status (class, caste), kinship, ethnicity, and more.

Personhood is a process of becoming, a striving. Among the Tswana of southern Africa, "'the person' was a constant work-in-progress; indeed, a highly complex fabrication" (Comaroff and Comaroff 2001, 269). The Comaroffs describe how Tswana people, especially men, had to "build themselves up," constantly negotiating their rank and status in order to reach full social personhood. Part of this process involved creating alliances and acquiring "wealth in people," while another aspect of developing personhood involved protecting one's self from being attacked or "undone" by others. In contrast to the Western concept of the individual, the person is "dividual," a composite and multiauthored being composed of social relations with multiple others, in fact owing parts of himself or herself to others (Fowler 2004, 8).

In tropical America, Santos-Granero (2009) describes how the worldview of the slaveholding societies he studies creates both the ideology that justifies warfare and capture and the tension between captives and captors that constructs and transforms social personhood for each. Santos-Granero (2009, 199) labels the ideology of these groups "the political economy of life." The scarce resource at the heart of tropical Amerindian political economies is composed of the forces, substances, elements, and conditions necessary for life to continue (Santos-Granero 2009, 207). "The slave machine," an aspect of the political economy of life (Santos-Granero 2009, 199), allows the construction of the "other" as an inferior being who can be preyed upon like animals and justifiably attacked and enslaved.

As in Africa, personhood for Amerindian captor societies was a continual process of development. Here the process required the direct engagement with wild others from whom generative life forces, in the form of heads, teeth, scalps, blood, or souls, could be taken. These life forces were essential for the production of people, and self-identity necessitated the incorporation and taming of enemy substances (Santos-Granero 2009, 202). The ultimate goal of taking captives was to produce kin and to add to the generative life forces of the captor group. Santos-Granero (2009, 203) argues that the goal of taking captives for Amerindians was not to appropriate their identities but to take from these wild others the generative forces that represent life itself.

The worldview that impelled Amerindians into warfare and enslavement resulted in a distinctive social identity for their captives. Preyed upon much like animals were hunted, captives, from the captors' point of view, had to be domesticated, an initial step in the process of incorporation. They were conceived of as pets would be—quasi-animals to be domesticated and quasi-humans to be civilized (Santos-Granero 2009, 193–95). Santos-Granero (2009, 194) cautions that the pet analogy does not mean that captives were necessarily treated with caring and affection. Instead, these wild, less than human individuals were under the total control of their captors, subject to a variety of treatments, including death, trade, marriage, adoption, or enslavement. But most importantly, these "people in the making" had to be transformed into civilized human beings by their captors, who profited from the taming process by gaining additional "life force." This transformation from captive to kin was not complete, however. Captives were generally incorporated as affinal rather than consanguineal kin, and in some societies only the children or grandchildren of captives could be kin.

The worldview of Native Americans in the Southeast also emphasizes the wildness of the "other" and the necessity for taming them. The adoption of captives was based on the belief that the appearance and behavior of humans, animals, and plants was mutable and that beings (whether human or animal) who practiced established cultural norms could be trained to become kin (Snyder 2010, 102–3). But as

explained above, not all captives became kin. The term "owned people" translated for some groups as "domesticated animal" or "tamed"
(Snyder 2010, 128). It was the lack of kin ties that most distinguished
the owned people from the rest of the population. Slaves among the
Cherokees had a human form but could not live as humans because
they lacked kin ties (Perdue 1979, 16).

In the Southwest Borderlands, the worldview common to Native
Americans and their Spanish conquerors resulted in a somewhat different social construction for captives than that described for tropical
America and the Southeast (Brooks 2002). Yet as in these other places,
the Southwest Borderlands worldview and the captive taking it autho-
rized structured relations among groups there. Borderlands groups,
including the Pawnees, Comanches, Navajos, Pueblos, and others,
were involved in a system of "sacred violence and exchange" (Brooks
2002, 14). These dual concepts of honor and shame fueled raiding and
captive taking in native North America and brought gender and kinship to the forefront of indigenous exchange systems.

The Pawnee Morning Star ceremony, in which a young girl was captured and sacrificed, regenerated the complimentary male and female
powers that had first produced human life (Brooks 2002, 10–19). The
ceremony entwined violence, honor, and gender in ways that facilitated intersocietal exchange. "In their renewal of the very first act of human creation, Pawnee warriors engaged in an act of sacred violence
that confirmed the centrality of long distance interethnic exchange to
group genesis and survival" (Brooks 2002, 16). The Pawnees, like other Plains groups, used fictional kinship to establish relationships with
other groups for purposes of trade and diplomatic relations (individuals with whom one could not establish kin relations could be only
slaves or enemies; Weltfish 1965, 31, cited in Brooks 2002, 17). Captive
taking was a part of these mutually beneficial exchange relationships
(Brooks 2002). The accumulation of wealth created and enhanced
honor among the Pawnees—poverty was dishonorable. Pawnee males
gathered horses, wives, kin, and captive slaves, all of which represented wealth, status, and honor. This worldview impelled Pawnee males

to raid their enemies for captives, especially women and children, and "combined honor and shaming in a single action" (Brooks 2002, 16).

In Spain, seven hundred years of cultural interaction between indigenous Christians and invading Moors resulted in concepts similar to those in the Southwest Borderlands, where male honor/shame and status were closely tied to control of women and children (Brooks 2002). As the Moors in Spain retreated south, frontier areas were contested and violent, with captive taking the predictable result. Church and secular authorities on both sides encouraged intermarriage with converted captives. This construction of the self and other formed a conceptual framework for the incorporation of captives that came with the Spaniards when they entered the Southwest during the sixteenth century. "Native and Spanish men shared similar notions of honor, shame, and gender, with the control of women and children as a central proof of status" (Brooks 2002, 34).

Similarities in male concepts concerning honor, shame, and the control of women and children in both Native American and Spanish society formed one dimension of the economic and social interactions between them but also meant that similar social locations were opened for captives in both cultural groups (Brooks 2002). Like the African concept of "wealth in people," male honor was fed as captives swelled group size. Women's fecundity promised further increases and additional women and children for male control. Both indigenous and Spanish captors used kinship to incorporate captives, but with a difference. Captive women (whether Spanish or indigenous) might become wives of their Native American captors, but Native American captive women rarely became wives of Spanish men (Brugge 1993b, 95–99). Instead, the Spanish created fictional kin locations for these women and their children, who functioned as servants and concubines (Brugge 1993b, [1968] 2010). Children held by both indigenous groups and Spanish captors were usually easily assimilated, although those held by the Spanish could never achieve full personhood. In contrast, some young male captives kept in indigenous societies could become fully functioning members of the group (see also Rivaya-Martínez 2012). European demand for labor eventually enmeshed indigenous and Spanish societies in a continent-wide slave trade that transformed social relations across the Southwest Border-lands (Brooks 2002; Gutiérrez 1991).

The sale of children in an example from West Africa provides a use-ful illustration of how subordinate people are used by full members of their society in strivings for power and social personhood. Piot (1996) argues that concepts of personhood were one of the factors that result-ed in the sale of children by their kin among the Kabre of Togo during the seventeenth- to nineteenth-century slave trade that decimated and transformed West Africa. Persons among the Kabre were constructed through relationships with others, and these relationships were creat-ed through the prestation of material goods (land, animals, objects, etc.). According to Piot (1996, 45–46), the sale of a child, although a type of alienation, reaffirmed the prestational economy of the Kabre as well as the social position of the kin member who made the sale. Piot focuses on a time when centralized polities engaged in slave raid-ing and suggests that the Kabre may have been one of the groups that fled the unceasing violence of slave raids. Raids transferred Kabre peo-ple into the slave trade, but the Kabre also sold their own kin in mar-kets. These markets eventually took the place of raiding. Children were sold by their mother's brother, who, in asserting rights over the child, thereby immobilized rights claimed by the child's father. The cowrie shells received in return for the child were redistributed by the mother's brother back to the relatives who had been involved in pro-ducing the child (his sister, her husband, his own mother's brother, etc.). The mother's brother, through the sale, built a name for himself and strengthened the relationships on which his identity depended.

Captive and captor engaged in daily interactions mediated and de-fined by the captors' worldview, especially concepts of how "others" interacted with and operated within captor worlds. These interactions helped create a social location in captor society for captives. This so-cial location was never static, however, and captors used captives in their strivings to become full social persons. Captives might seem to be powerless, caught within a hostile and controlling environment, but as the next section shows, they were fully engaged in their own social positioning. The characteristics captives arrived with and the skills and initiative they displayed in captor society could affect their social position and likely affected the worldview of their captors.

The Captive

In the selective process of captive taking, captors chose their captives based on age, gender/sexuality, and sometimes skills. These characteristics also determined the social location captives would occupy in their new home. This section explores each of these characteristics and how they affected the process of incorporation for captives. Of course, age and gender/sexuality cannot be separated, as age affects the construction of gender/sexuality throughout the biographical development of each person. They are examined separately here in order to give each a more nuanced consideration. Our understanding of the ways social identity is constructed means that the characteristics a captive arrived with were only a starting point for her integration into captor society. Like for any social group member, daily social interactions, the aging process, and their own behavior and initiative constantly formed and re-formed captives' social identity. This process of social development is also explored.

Age

Because captives were most often taken during raids and warfare, captors selected their captives based in part on how well they might make the journey back to the captor's home (figure 3). The elderly, unlikely to survive the trip (and unlikely to be useful when they arrived), were generally not selected. Infants were similarly vulnerable and might be killed before the raiding party left for home (but see Keeley 1996, 65–66, for Cree raids on Inuit villages in which only infants were taken captive). Some societies focused especially on capturing children, who could be easily trained into captor cultural practices. The captors' worldview ultimately determined whether captives, regardless of age, ever achieved full rights of social personhood in the society of their captors. Describing slavery in Africa, Kopytoff and Miers (1977, 21–22) note that "there is often a preference for acquiring children, who can be

3. Guaraní women and children captured by slave hunters. Image by French artist Jean-Baptiste Debret, who lived in Brazil during the early decades of the nineteenth century. From *Voyage pittoresque et historique au Brésil* [A picturesque and historic voyage to Brazil], Imprimerie Nationale Éditions (Arles: Actes Sud, 2014).

molded into the society, or young women who can fit into the unusually well-developed niche of stranger-wife." As McCormack (1977, 190) reports for the Sherbro of coastal Sierra Leone, children intended for life as a slave are given early training for that subordinate role; they might receive the same training as free children, but for a longer period of time in order to learn perfect loyalty and obedience. But as late nineteenth- to early twentieth-century captive narratives from east and central Africa show, children might be required to accommodate themselves to a new captor cultures repeatedly before they find a permanent place (Wright 1993). Chisi-Ndjurisiye-Sichyajunga was captured during a raid at the age of perhaps seven or eight and given to the chief of the group that took her (Wright 1993, 81–90). After three years with that group, she was traded, escaped, and was taken in by another group, all before she matured. In this second group she married and had children before her husband tried to eject her during a time of famine; apparently she was never considered a full member of her husband's group.

The Comanches of the American plains valued male and female children but treated them differently based on their gender (here, of course, gender and age blur; Brooks 2002, 187–88; Hämäläinen 2008, 255–56; Rivaya-Martínez 2012). Female children were saved for marriage to male captors, the same treatment offered to young adult women. Age segregation was more pronounced for captive boys among the Comanches, who adopted the youngest and most culturally malleable but enslaved and often maltreated older boys. The Comanches continued to distinguish linguistically between native-born and adopted outsiders throughout their lives, meaning that captives might never attain full rights of personhood (Hämäläinen 2008, 257; Rivaya-Martínez 2012, 60–61). Captured boys could be assigned women's tasks and might learn only women's rather than men's conversational skills, a significant handicap to their acceptance within Comanche society (Rivaya-Martínez 2012, 61). Comanches at times incorporated adult males as replacements for members of their own group who had died, assimilating them into the deceased person's social space through a replacement ceremony. Other adult males remained slaves, although even they might achieve some social rights, including the right to marry, if they acquitted themselves well in battle (Hämäläinen 2008, 257).

Slave-owning tribes of the American tropics studied by Santos-Granero (2009) also treated male and female children differently. The Kalinago of the Caribbean raised captured boys as household servants and for eventual use in cannibalistic rituals. Girls, as well as young women, were destined for use as concubines and household servants (Santos-Granero 2009, 53–54). Girls had their hair cut and boys might be emasculated. Adult men were typically executed soon after they entered captor villages (Santos-Granero 2009, 130). The Conibo of the Amazon region took young women as concubines and young girls as prospective spouses for captors' sons (Santos-Granero 2009, 131). Concubines never attained full personhood in captor society but served as drudge wives to native-born wives. The Conibo seem to have particularly targeted children in captive taking. These children became servants for the older members of the captor household, and most Conibo men had several such captives (Santos-Granero 2009, 132). Even when captive boys became adults, they were charged with the most laborious and time-consuming tasks.

Girl captives could gain status as they matured, married, or were taken as a sexual partner by their captors and eventually had children. At the far end of the age spectrum, the status of older women often declined as they lost sexual appeal. In East Africa during the late nineteenth century, slave prices document the decline in value of female (and also male) slaves as they aged. Women over the age of thirty-five sold for a little more than one-quarter of the price paid for reproductive-aged women (Deutsch 2007, 137, table 5.1). Older women, often under threat of sale to distant provinces, generally sought protection from their children who were considered "free"—they could not be sold (Deutsch 2007, 140).

Gender/Sexuality

Gender was a fundamental criterion for the selection of captives and for their integration into captor society. As the examples in the previous section indicate, children were considered (or were treated as) gendered persons in captor society in terms of their social location and the occupations planned for them. Gender is widely understood as the cultural construction of biological sexual difference. Busby (2000, 16) sees gender as produced through language, representation, and material practice; she gives ontological status to the body, but biological status is not fixed.

Voss and Schmidt (2000, 2) urge archaeologists to distinguish gender from sexuality in order to aid research, although they also note that "it would be inappropriate to study gender without considering sexuality, and vice versa" (Voss and Schmidt 2000, 21). They define sexuality as "including sexual activities, eroticism, sexual identities, sexual meanings, and sexual politics" (Voss and Schmidt 2000, 2) and encourage us to think beyond the narrow confines of Western sexual categories that grant normative status to reproductive heterosexuality while treating as abnormal (or ignoring) nonreproductive and nonheterosexual sexual expression. This section explores the ways that gender and sexuality affect the values placed on captives in captor society and therefore captives' social position. It emphasizes that captors often "degendered" the labor of their captives and that captive labor was often supervised by captor women. Both circumstances influenced the social locations captives occupied in captor society.

For most of the groups discussed in this book, captors were typically adult (often young) males whose most highly prized captives were reproductive-age women. The value of these young women can be broadly cast into three intertwined categories: their use as a sexual partner, their reproductive abilities, and their labor. Young women became concubines in many societies, where their value as a sexual partner may have been foremost. Reproduction may have been most important when "wealth in people" or population replacement was a primary objective of captive taking. Captive labor, especially for labor that was gendered female (regardless of the biological sex of the person undertaking the labor), seems to have been important in most societies.

Every society that took captives almost certainly used captive women as sexual partners, but this was probably not their primary value in most societies. Even where captive women became concubines, this role and the value of their sexuality likely decreased with the passage of years. Among slaveholding groups in tropical America, the use of female captives as concubines did not preclude their use as domestic servants (e.g., among the Kalinago; Santos-Granero 2009, 53–54). Similarly, in the colonial Southwest, indigenous female captives were incorporated as domestic servants into Spanish households but also served as secret concubines for their masters (Brooks 2002; Brugge 1993b, 97).

Sexuality, but especially reproduction, was a primary value of female captives among groups (generally state-level) where powerful males kept harems that produced, both biologically and culturally, heirs. Harems were ancient institutions in Africa and Asia, but they were not exclusively associated with Islam and existed in many other societies, too (Klein 2007, 64). In Islamic harems, slave-concubines generally came from non-Islamic areas; Islamic men were permitted four wives but could have an unlimited number of concubines. As they aged, sexuality for harem women changed. In the Ottoman Empire, a concubine who bore the sultan a son no longer had sexual relations with him but became a teacher and politically active advocate for her son (Klein 2007). In Kano (Nigeria), slave women who worked in the palace could at times become concubines but were more often married off to male slaves after a period of service (Klein 2007, 64). Women in large harems had nominally been acquired because of their sexuality and reproductive potential, yet many never bore children and some never even had sexual relations with their masters (Klein 2007, 75). Older women who remained in the harem were freer to interact with the outside world because they were no longer involved in reproduction.

Harems were not typical of small-scale societies, of course. More generally, African scholars have debated the contrasting values of female slaves relative to their gender-based labor or reproductive abilities (Robertson and Klein 1983b, 8). Among the horticultural societies of Africa, crop production relied on the labor of women, whether native-born wives or introduced captives. Meillassoux (1983, 49; 1991, 113) argues that native-born women were valued for their reproductive abilities but slave women were valued chiefly for their labor. In most African societies, women, regardless of their slave or nonslave status, worked at many more kinds of tasks, especially agricultural, and for longer hours than men (Meillassoux 1983, 55). Slave women suffered low fertility, and purchase or capture rather than reproduction replenished slave populations (Meillassoux 1983, 51–55).

Taking up the question of the value of female slaves to Western Sudan, Klein (1983) analyzes late nineteenth- and early twentieth-century demographic and pricing data for slaves and concludes that female slaves were valued first for their labor and ability to produce a surplus. That women more easily assimilated into Sudanese societies, were less likely to try to escape, and helped integrate male slaves constituted secondary values. But the role of female slaves in reproduction was not insignificant, especially for concubines, and the offspring of other female slaves represented a bonus for their master (Klein 1983, 89;

but see Miller 2007, 12, for the argument that slave women in Africa were most highly valued for their reproductive abilities).

Their labor contributions made female captives valuable in many parts of the world, but the subordinate status of most captives meant that gender roles could be blurred or ignored when captives labored (see Ames 2001, 4; Foster 2003; Hudson 1976, 256; Meillassoux 1991, 100–101; Robertson and Klein 1983b, 10). This regendering of labor had important effects on captive social positioning (see also chapter 4). Because of the low status of women's labor in most small-scale societies, assigning women's tasks to male captives was often used to infantilize and emasculate them. Snyder (2010, 110) reports that in the Southeast the onerous task of fetching wood and water, typically the work of women and children, was assigned indiscriminately to male or female captives. In Africa male slaves were assigned female tasks and female slaves were de-gendered—assigned both men and women's work (Coquery-Vidrovitch 2007, 57). For example, female slaves in African Islamic societies traded and procured supplies, while free women were secluded at home (see also Deutsch 2007, 133). Donald's study of Northwest Coast slavery perhaps expresses best how the daily labor slaves were forced to do reinforced their social position with regard to other members of the society. "Slaves were undifferentiated labor power. It is not inappropriate to demand that a male slave do 'women's work,' because a male slave is not a 'man' in the fullest cultural sense" (Donald 1997, 135).

Of course, captors were gendered, too. While the industrialized slavery of the American South might lead us to envision overseers as male, labor relationships in nonstate societies differed. Since captives were typically set to tasks normally accomplished by women and children, they most likely worked alongside and were directed by female captors. For example, a study of female slavery based on Swahili literary sources found that although slaves were owned by men, it was the men's wives who made use of slave women's labor (Bromber 2007, 115). In other parts of Africa, as Robertson and Klein (1983b, 13–16) make clear, women not only directed many female slaves but also owned them. Adult captive women among the Conibo in tropical America worked under the direction of the female household head (Santos-Granero 2009, 131). Among the Tukano, their Makú female captives "had to perform most of the agricultural activities so that 'their mistresses could lie at ease in their hammocks.' Often the female captives were even in charge of breast-feeding their mistresses' children" (Santos-Granero 2009, 132, citing Reichel-Dolmatoff 1971, 19).

Women captors most often supervised the labor of English and indigenous captives held in New France by indigenous tribes and by the French during the seventeenth and eighteenth centuries; both the tasks and the supervision humiliated male captives and reinforced their social location as subordinate, de-gendered beings (Foster 2003). "For an enslaved Huron captive . . . simply being set to tasks he had traditionally consigned to his wife or daughters accomplished the intended humiliation readily enough. But for enslaved Anglo-Americans . . . the real degradation . . . was that they were directed in these activities by women" (Foster 2003, 10). Women's normally low status in most societies meant that female captives were likely accustomed to low-status tasks as well as to supervision by other women. The same would not have been true for men.

Captives' Skills, Characteristics, and Agency

While the characteristics of age, gender, and sexuality most often conditioned the selection of captives and their social location in captor society, some captives were also selected or retained because of special skills or dispositions they brought with them. Technological knowledge or skill in craft production seems to have been especially valued. Personal characteristics, such as intelligence, aggressiveness or passivity, flexibility, and trustworthiness, among others, might also allow the captive an increased degree of agency in captor society. Captives might develop skills in captivity that could also affect social positioning, including knowledge of multiple languages and cultures that allowed them to situate themselves as cultural intermediaries. In many important ways social identity was based on the degree to which captives were able to express agency (Robertson and Robinson 2008, 267–73).

Assessing factors that affected the treatment of slaves, Patterson

(1982, 179) argues that skilled captives might have received better treatment by their captors than unskilled captives. Ancient Greek, Roman, and Islamic societies relied heavily on their enslaved craftsmen for urban industries, and skilled slaves occupied prominent positions that gave them a degree of agency and autonomy. Slaves imported into the Lower Mississippi Valley during the eighteenth century arrived from Africa with skills as woodworkers, weavers, and blacksmiths, making them highly valued merchandise in the local slave trade (Usner 1992, 55–56). The skilled slaves created competition for the region's nonslave craftsmen, many of whom solved the problem by buying skilled slaves for their own craft businesses. In New France during the late seventeenth and early eighteenth centuries, a number of the New England captives taken during the French and Indian Wars were weavers (Foster 2003). The weavers may or may not have been directly targeted for capture in raids, but regardless, captors seem to have immediately recognized their value. A French female entrepreneur who developed the first textile industry in Canada purchased a number of them.

Small-scale societies valued skilled individuals as well. The Tlingits of the Northwest Coast placed a high value on slaves able to carve totem poles (Patterson 1982, 197). Another Northwest Coast group, the Mowachahts, captured a white man named John Jewitt in the first years of the nineteenth century. His life was spared because he was a blacksmith and could make iron harpoons for the chief who held him (Ames 2001, 4; Stewart 1987). In a study of female slaves among the Mangbetu of northeastern Zaire, Africa, "opportunities emerged in slavery which allowed slaves to move from their original complete dependence on their captors toward greater responsibility and status. Many of the opportunities were determined by factors specific to each slave's situation: ethnic group; intelligence and speaking ability; fertility; skill at farming or handicrafts; owner's age, status, and personality; and so forth. Generally the more valuable the slave was or could become to the owner, the more likely he or she was to be integrated quickly into the new society" (Keim 1983, 148–49). The same was true of Spanish captives held by the Navajos, among whom long-held Spanish captives could became prominent men (Brugge [1968] 2010, 128).

The captive's attitude and initiative often significantly affected her experience as well as her place in captor society. In Africa, among the Vai of Sierra Leone, Holsoe (1977, 290) reports that slaves who worked hard and were well-behaved could increase their status, even approaching the status of the freeborn in the household in which they were held. The slave who distinguished himself in war was especially valued. Still, the treatment of the slave depended on the character and social position of the master. In the Northwest Coast, "within the family group, a pleasant and industrious slave was well off" (Marian Smith 1940, 52, cited in Donald 1997, 85).

The captive must not only have a good attitude; if she were to improve her status, she had to succeed in endeavors that furthered captor goals. Among the Comanches, captives could move from enslaved outsiders to fully integrated members of the society, with the individual performance of the captive key to the level of incorporation she achieved (Rivaya-Martínez 2012). Female captives could become wives but still occupied the lowest status in polygynous families, where they were subservient to Comanche wives (Rivaya-Martínez 2012, 57). Yet motherhood could raise a captive woman's status in the family and in the group (Rivaya-Martínez 2012, 53, 57). Male captives, especially those who had not been adopted, significantly improved their status by distinguishing themselves in warfare; with sufficient success they gained the same rights as native Comanches (Rivaya-Martínez 2012, 58–59). Raiding allowed a male captive to obtain wealth, and with wealth he could acquire wives and become an accepted (if not actually full) member of the group.

Captives brought with them knowledge of other languages and other cultures, which often made them invaluable to their captors. They formed important links between groups of captive takers and captive givers that facilitated vital exchanges (see also chapter 5). Certainly not all captives maximized such roles, but some did, which significantly enhanced their status in captor society (and in the society of their birth, if they returned). In the Southwest Borderlands, many female captives operated as "cultural intermediaries" between Spanish and indigenous cultures. Brooks (2002) explores the lives of several women—captives or former captives—who, because of their knowledge of multiple languages and cultures, carved out positions as go-betweens among the groups in which they had lived, a position that enhanced their level of influence (see also Barr 2007; Brugge [1968] 2010, 127–28). For example, in 1680 a band of Navajo raiders attacked a Spanish ranch in northern New Mexico and captured a seven-year-old girl, Juana la Coyota, of mixed Indian-Spanish descent. She was likely the product of a Spanish master's sexual abuse of her mother, an Indian from Zia Pueblo (Brooks 2002, 99–103). As a result of Juana's mixed origins, her captivity (she was redeemed and returned to Spanish society after a number of years with the Navajos), and her mixed children, she was able operate successfully between the Zia, Spanish, and Navajo worlds, a position that gave her wealth and influence.

The Circumstances of Captive taking and Captive Social Position

The circumstances surrounding her capture partly determined a captive's social location; they set the tone for how she would be received and treated in captor society. Many captives were taken during warfare, and captives entered captor society accompanied by a wave of violent and negative feelings toward the captive's social group, especially if captor-society warriors had been lost in battle. Where the captors' worldview saw others as amenable to "taming" and believed captives could be trained to become kin (for example, in the Southeast), negative feelings might subside. Where captives became slaves or occupied more liminal positions, their association with a hated enemy might be remembered long after the act of capture and constrain their social position and opportunities for social advancement.

When captives served as social nodes for interactions between captive takers and captive givers (see above and chapter 5), their role as intermediaries offered opportunities to enhance their social position. But some captives were taken or traded far from their homes. In Africa slaves were moved far away from home so they could not escape (Baier and Lovejoy 1977, 399; Klein 1983, 77; Kopytoff and Miers 1977, 53). Gallay (2002) reports that the Iroquois of the Northeast made long-distance raids into the Southeast; southeastern captives might also be given or traded to a distant tribe. On the Northwest Coast slaves were often taken from neighbors and near neighbors, but an extensive slave trade network meant that captives could pass from hand to hand and end up far from home. Sometimes Northwest Coast warriors made long-distance maritime raids along the coast (up to 1,000 km, or 620 mi.) in which captives were taken (Donald 1997, 103–16; Mitchell 1984). Long-distance riverine slave raids were common in tropical America, and sometimes raiders traveled more than 600 km (372 mi.) to attack their victims (Santos-Granero 2009, 46, 49–51, 56). Captives taken such great distances were isolated, which diminished their ability to enhance their social position using natal linguistic or cultural skills.

Because persons who occupied positions of wealth and high status typically held captives, captives could at times use the status of their captors to their advantage. For example, female slaves in Africa might achieve an influential position as a wife or retainer of a king (Robertson and Klein 1983b, 16–17). Marriage to slaves was advantageous to African rulers because, as noted above, slave women were without kin ties and unlikely to have their loyalties divided between their husband and their natal family. In a study of Spanish women captured by Indians in Argentina in the seventeenth to nineteenth centuries, Socolow (1992) suggests that these women actually gained social status in moving from a position as the wife of a Spanish peasant to one as the wife of an Indian chief.

Socolow's study highlights another factor that captives at times used to their advantage. She discusses a Spanish woman in South America who was captured by Indians as a child and had been taught the Spanish language by other captive women, an obvious effort to maintain natal identity despite their captivity (Socolow 1992, 88–89). Socolow's example reveals that large numbers of captives from the same or similar cultural traditions held captive together might be able to maintain some natal traditions and practices. They might use these practices to enhance their social position in captor society, as has been found among slaves of African origin in the American South (i.e., Fennell 2007; L. Ferguson 1992; see also Chernela 2003).

A Captive's Story: Helena Valero, Napagnuma of the Yanomamö

In 1932 Helena Valero was a twelve-year-old Portuguese girl traveling with her family up the Rio Dimiti near the border between Brazil and Venezuela when she was captured by a group of Yanomamö (figure 4; Biocca [1965] 1996). Her riveting first-person account of more than two decades living as an Indian woman in the Amazon jungle illustrates the complex social interactions into which captives are plunged, as well as many of the patterns that the cross-cultural discussion in this chapter highlights. Helena's enormous intelligence and courage helped her survive her initial captivity. That she was a source of interest, affection, jealousy, and rage is almost certainly typical of the experiences of captives in many parts of the world. Because she was "other," because of her age, sexuality, and gender, she was valuable and hence eventually taken as a wife by a powerful male. But her ultimate flight from the jungle with her children and her heartbreaking attempts to return to Hispanic society demonstrate her precarious position as "wife" in Yanomamö society. In times of tension, her "otherness" was not only remembered but foregrounded and placed her life and those of her half-Hispanic children in frequent danger.

Helena was initially taken by a group of Yanomamö called the Kohoroshiwetari, but soon after her capture the Kohoroshiwetari were attacked by another group, the Karawetari, who killed the Kohoroshiwetari babies and children and took the women captive. Helena later heard that the battle between the two groups had been waged over her—the Karawetari wanted control of this white girl. They called her Napagnuma ("white woman" or "foreign woman"), and by this name she was apparently widely known among Yanomamö groups. Her sojourn with the Karawetari was not long. During yet another attack, she was taken by the Shamatari, and in this group she was the object of both interest and fear. Some Shamatari wanted to kill her but eventually she was given to the chief's father-in-law so his wife could care for her. This family and other Shamatari women were kind to her for a time, but the Karawetari women who had been captured with her were jealous of the good treatment she

4. Helena Valero with three of her children, her second husband, Akawe, and her father. From Ettore Biocca, *Yanoáma: The Story of Helena Valero, a Girl Kidnapped by Amazonian Indians* (New York: E. P. Dutton, 1970), 377.

received. One day she collected and cooked a toad that turned out to be poison. A child she was caring for ate it and died. The immediate calls to kill her were countered with pleas to save her life. The woman with whom she was staying told her to run into the jungle. Still a prepubescent child, she lived alone for seven months, surviving on what she could gather in the jungle or scavenge from abandoned gardens.

Found by another group, the Namoeteri, she had now become "of consequence" (mature) and was desired by many of the men of the group. Fifty of them came for her one day, and in the fight over her, she was almost killed. Eventually the chief's mother and daughters saved her. After she recovered, another woman lied to the chief about things that Napagnuma allegedly said about him. He came immediately to kill her, but she vaulted the enclosure palisade and escaped into the jungle. Hidden in the jungle near the *shapuno* from which she had fled, she was the subject of an intense search by the Namoeteri. Eventually the chief, Fusiwe, captured her as she came to a stream late at night for water. He still wanted to kill her, but his mother, father, and another man convinced him to spare her. Instead he took her as his fifth wife; two of his other wives were captives from other Yanomamö groups.

Fusiwe was a significant chief who controlled not only his own group but also three other groups when they were together. His oldest wife loved Napagnuma and treated her kindly, but the other wives were often cruel. Because she was white, they thought she should be able to make European-style machetes, clothing, and cooking pots and they beat her when she said she could not. The oldest wife often put Napagnuma in charge of the other wives and eventually they followed her commands. Her influence as "other," along with her personal strength, combined to make her influential. She once saved a young girl of mixed parentage from rape by shouting and facing off the attackers. Yet when her first baby was born, the women of her group wanted to kill it because it was white and hairless—different from their babies. "Put him on the ground, put a tree-trunk over his neck and tread on the trunk," they said (Biocca [1965] 1996, 162). But Napagnuma's husband intervened to save the baby. Illogically, Napagnuma was blamed for the hostility of another band toward the Namoeteri, who said their enemies would "avenge themselves for the women we have stolen from them; we did it on account of this woman here, Napagnuma" (Biocca [1965] 1996, 176).

Napagnuma's husband was killed in a protracted feud among related bands of Yanomamö and she and her two children were taken in by yet another related group. Some there argued to kill her and she fled with her children. After days in the forest she ended up with a group of her dead husband's enemies. Following calls by many to kill her and her children, the chief insisted they be spared, but men accosted her, wanting to take her for a wife (Biocca [1965] 1996, 274–75). One day an old woman who lived near a big river came to visit; she said that whites were traveling along the river in boats. Napagnuma decided to go with her to try to return home, and she and her children snuck away. But even here, there were people who wanted to kill her children because they were boys of an enemy group.

Again they fled, and Napagnuma used vines to cross a raging river with her two boys clinging to her. They took refuge with yet another band. Here she was taken as a wife by Akawe, a man "who had many women, one here, one there; to have more, he was prepared to kill" (Biocca [1965] 1996, 293). With him, Napagnuma gave birth to her third and fourth sons. But Akawe blamed her for his imagined misfortunes and tried to kill her. She was now old and he wanted younger women. Her first two children were sent off to live with other groups.

Because she was now by the big river, Napagnuma determined to escape back to the white world. She stole her two older children away from the groups that held them and fled with all four children and her abusive husband, who was being hunted for his misdeeds. She came upon an Anglo who knew her father, and the family was conducted down the Rio Orinoco and back into the world of the white man.

Back with her family, Helena was once again an outcast. Her Portuguese brothers were ashamed of her Indian appearance and her mixed-blood children. Her husband, Akawe, returned to the jungle. She asked for help from the government, but it only wanted her sensational story and offered no assistance. She was told to get a job, if she could. He sons were deemed "backward" and denied entry into the schools. She and her children often lacked food. Eventually she was able to get some education for her children and she returned to live in a half world—with other Indians, but near a mission. In her despair she said, "I thought everything would be different among the white men" (Biocca [1965] 1996, 329).

Helena Valero's story embodies many aspects of the experience of captives in small-scale societies everywhere. She is admired, reviled, loved, and used. She is captured over and over again or flees certain death to another group. Some people are kind to her and treat her as one of their own. Her intelligence and initiative and her association with the chief of her group make her, at times, a highly influential member of society. Yet in times of turbulence, she can instantly be pushed outside social group boundaries. The death of her first husband leaves her and her children vulnerable. Her children at various times are considered outsiders and threatened with death. During her time with the Yanomamö, Helena is called variously wife, sister-in-law, mother, and daughter-in-law, but she is always called Napagnuma, "the foreigner," a name that never left her. Her liminal and contextual social location is part of the captive experience. Helena's tragic attempt to reenter the white world is also consistent with the experience of many captives—the taint of the "other" followed her and her children.

Captives, at the moment of capture, became ultimately vulnerable and powerless and, most significantly, surrounded by people to whom they claimed no kinship. As the hours and days of their captivity advanced, their captors created a social position for them, a position carefully calculated to make maximum use of these exposed people. The new social position was somewhere along a continuum of belonging. They might be located outside the kinship system in a slave status or marginally within the kinship system as affinal kin (wives) or adopted as consanguineal kin, replacing captor dead and building captor population. Even when they seemed to occupy one or the other extreme along this continuum, their position was rarely fixed and could change through time and with changing circumstances. In most situations, captives were used to enhance the already high status of their captors. The captors' worldview and goals for the development of their own social personhood dictated the social person the captive would become.

Captives were selected for capture because of their age, gender/sexuality, and sometimes their skills or knowledge. They almost immediately entered into a complex relationship with their captors in which the captors held the upper hand. Captives were not entirely without power, however. They maneuvered to improve their lot, but always in tandem with the needs and goals of their captors. Captives who became mothers, were skilled craftspersons, acquitted themselves well in war, or served as cultural intermediaries negotiated a better position for themselves in captor society. But this generally occurred only when their actions furthered the social, economic, and spiritual goals of their captors. The relationship between captors and their captives, played out over the duration of their captivity, resulted in a constantly shifting social position for the captive and a continual striving of the captor to maximize use of the captive.

| Chapter Four

Captives and the Creation of Power

> Scholars have increasingly become aware that slavery cannot be studied as
> an isolated phenomenon, detached from its broader social and political
> context.... Ignoring the larger context would run the risk of transforming
> native forms of slavery into epiphenomena—curious and exotic customs
> without any grounding on the configurations of power and meaning
> that generate them.
> —FERNANDO SANTOS-GRANERO, *Vital Enemies* (2009)

The development of complex societies and the ways in which people
gain power over others constitute one of the major questions for archaeologists attempting to understand the history of human culture change.
Most theories involve control of resources: critical means of production
(land, raw materials), food itself, or high-value goods. Control over resources that others need or desire results in power over others; the more
people an aggrandizing individual (that is, ambitious people; Hayden
1996) controls, the greater his power. Leaders who successfully develop
or manage crucial resources attract followers. Or when leaders use coer-
cive methods to appropriate crucial resources, the people who depend
on those resources naturally follow. No archaeologist would fail to acknowledge that power accrues to those who gain the largest number of
followers, and some even suggest that warfare was a causal factor in the

development of complex societies, yet only a few archaeologists have suggested (usually in passing) that captives played a key role in creating or increasing power bases for leaders (see Carneiro 1991; Robertshaw 1999). This chapter does not argue that captives were a primary factor in the development of complex societies. Instead it begins an exploration of the ways captives were involved in power acquisition in small-scale societies.

There are two major but entwined avenues for the creation of power that involve captive taking. The first are situations where power is directly related to the number of followers a leader can amass. Captives immediately become followers and simply by their presence increase the social power and status of their captors. In the second, power results from control over labor and the production of surplus or valuable goods. Captive taking creates laborers, and captives become tools for increasing production, which brings leaders wealth and power. Scholars studying small-scale societies disagree about whether captives are economically profitable or whether they are simply luxury goods used primarily as status symbols for their owners. Donald (1997, 131) points out that captives can function as both a source of prestige *and* a source of economically valuable labor and that there is no contradiction in these two roles (but see Watson 1980, 13–14, for the argument that Chinese domestic slaves were status symbols only).

The chapter begins by exploring the social and economic avenues toward power that captives create. These avenues range from newly arrived captives forming low-status groups and instantly raising the status of others in captor society, to captives being highly productive laborers and regularly producing a surplus for their captors. Three case studies that illustrate the use of captives to gain or express power in small-scale societies follow this discussion. They emphasize that the arrival of captives opens avenues outside the imposed limits of kinship that captors may exploit in their strivings for power. The case studies also underscore the highly interrelated ways that captives produce power for their captors.

The Acquisition of Power in Small-Scale Societies

This section examines the nature of power in small-scale societies, beginning with a discussion of social stratification among such groups and the role of warfare in the creation of power. One of the most important messages for archaeologists is that there can be significant social stratification even in the "simplest" societies. Then two major sources of power in which captives had the potential to play important roles—social and economic—are discussed. Individuals who are already wealthy and powerful often gain the most from war and captive taking. These activities also allowed status-seeking young men to build a retinue of followers and a foundation for future status gains.

Social Stratification in Small-Scale Societies

Leaders in small-scale societies generally consist of family or lineage heads. In tribal societies, power is usually situational (e.g., a leader emerges during times of war) or diffuse (a religious leader is influential but lacks the economic base necessary for the effective use of power). Tribal societies have a variety of crosscutting social institutions, beyond basic kin ties, that integrate members of the society. Different elements of the society may join together or separate depending on external challenges. In these societies, individuals gain status and power through individual acts and often through hosting feasts or other displays of wealth. In chiefdoms, lineages are graded on a scale of prestige in relation to a senior lineage that is headed by a chief (Earle 1997, 5–6; Yoffee 1993, 61–62). In other words, social organization remains kinship based but is more hierarchically organized than in a tribal society. The role of chief is hereditary, and prestige and rank are determined by how closely one is related to the chief. A chief can demand food and other goods from his followers, but he must also reward family, followers, and warriors for their loyalty. In these social formations, more people means more power, and the larger social unit an aggrandizing individual can put together, the greater status that individual can amass. Because rewarding followers is essential to maintaining their loyalty, power and status are also based on a leader's ability to control foodstuffs and other goods. While most archaeologists assume small, band-level societies are largely egalitarian with social differences based primarily on age and gender, ethnohistoric accounts establish that even these societies exhibit significant social stratification, including slaveholding.

Warfare is common in both tribes and chiefdoms, and in many chiefdom-level societies it is considered endemic (Arkush and Allen 2006; Guilaine and Zammit 2005; Keeley 1996, 32–33; LeBlanc 1999; LeBlanc and Register 2003; Lekson 2002). Tribal-level societies typically engage in small-scale raids, while chiefs often maintain groups of high-ranking warriors and undertake larger-scale warfare. Both tribes and chiefdoms take captives during war and raids against other groups, and in many cases the taking of captives, especially women, is a major objective (Golitko and Keeley 2007, 339; Keeley 1996, 86; LeBlanc 2002, 362; LeBlanc and Register 2003, 71, 208; see also R. Ferguson and Whitehead [1992] 1999, 23–24; also, on raiding for wives, see Barnes 1999; Bowser 2008; DeBoer 2008; Jorgensen 1980; McLennan 1865). Warfare and captive taking are important elements of male status striving in small-scale societies. Local legends, myths, and epic accounts of "warrior elites" often celebrated captive taking and the high rank accrued to successful raiders (e.g., Junker 2008, 119). Such cultural beliefs not only fueled raiding and warfare but validated the taking and keeping of captives; as a result, captives became well-recognized and accepted social actors in the captor societies that held them.

Maschner and Reedy-Maschner (1998), in an article that examines warfare among complex hunter-gatherers on the north Pacific Rim, are explicit about the role of status-seeking young males in captive taking among the village-based societies of this region. They use archaeological data to show that violence and warfare evident in the ethnographic record extend several thousand years into prehistory. Arguing against scholars who see warfare and raiding as the result of conflict over land or food or as the result of colonial intrusion, Maschner and Reedy-Maschner (1998) emphasize that warfare was a way for young males to gain status. In fact, they argue that in societies where there has been a decrease in subsistence hunting (a traditional source of male status), men turn instead to violence and warfare as avenues for achieving social status (this idea was proposed by Trigger [1969, 52] with regard to a decrease in hunting among the Hurons of the northeastern United States). The primary motives for warfare expressed in ethnohistorical accounts from the north Pacific Rim were exacting revenge and acquiring slaves and women (Maschner and Reedy-Maschner 1998, 42).

Even in band-level societies where hunting remained a major subsistence strategy and warfare was limited, stealing or appropriating women and children increased the status and power of certain families. The Tutchone Athapaskans of the Upper Yukon River basin of Canada lived in a harsh environment and depended on hunting and fishing for the majority of their food (Legros 1985). When first described in the mid-nineteenth century, they had a population density of less than one person per one hundred square kilometers (thirty-eight square miles) and lived mostly in groups of one to three nuclear families, but a few groups included as many as ten families (Legros 1985, 46). In spite of a low population density, the Tutchones exhibited significant social stratification. Larger groups controlled the best fishing, hunting, and resource extraction areas, as well as trade with external groups. These families consolidated power through strategic intermarriages that prevented alliance with poor families. Poor families often faced starvation in the marginal areas remaining to them. Furthermore, powerful men could increase the size of their group and their productive power by stealing or simply appropriating the women and children of the poor, incorporating them as slaves in the semipermanent settlements over which they presided (Legros 1985, 59–61). Slaves could also be purchased or created when the poor sold themselves to the rich in order to survive. The status of slaves among the Tutchones was clear; they could be beaten or killed at the whim of their owner. Legros (1985, 62) reports that other band-level societies in the same region and elsewhere exhibited similar levels of social stratification.

Captives and Social Power

Captives opened avenues for the creation of social power in several ways. By their mere presence, captives created a stratified social system. In some societies they helped create not only an elite class but a

leisure class that did little or no work. Captives functioned as attendants and retainers and were living symbols of the high status of their
owners. The entry of captives into captor society, as well as the reproductive abilities of women captives, allowed leaders or status-seeking
men to increase the size of their family or number of followers without incurring obligations of bride price or debts to other kin groups.
In situations where increased population results in power for leaders
and status seekers, captives are a key source of power.

In small-scale societies, captives entered captor society at the lowest
rung of the social ladder and their presence created a system of stratification. As Patterson (1982, 33) notes in his influential study of slavery,
in small-scale societies where there were few differences in social status, slaves might be the only form of wealth that created permanent
status distinctions. In a study of the ways captives were incorporated
into the indigenous societies of Amazonia, Bowser (2008) emphasizes
the marginal social location captives typically occupied, even when
they were admitted into the social system through marriage. For example, among the Tupinamba of the Brazilian coast, a captured woman could be taken as a secondary wife, subordinate to the first wife.
Captured wives among the Yanomamö of Venezuela and Brazil were
more likely to be abused by their husbands, like Yanomamö wom-
en who were without kin (Bowser 2008, 272). Among the Arawakans
of the Peruvian Amazon, captive children, especially girls, were frequently accused of witchcraft and executed (Bowser 2008, 276). In Africa, captive men, women, and children, regardless of how they are
integrated into the society, may be the first to be sloughed off through
sale, trade, or expulsion during times of economic downturn or famine (Isaacman and Isaacman 1977, 117; Klein 1977, 343; Kopytoff and
Miers 1977, 12).

Captives not only highlight captor power through their low status and poor treatment, they become visible symbols of their master's
status in other ways. Captives might relieve him or her of the most
onerous domestic and subsistence tasks (gathering firewood, fetching water, preparing food). In societies with an elite class (even small-
scale societies), the elite may do little real work. In both small-scale

and state-level societies, labor is often scorned by the elite. As Patterson (1982, 34, following Finley 1964; see also Karras 1988, 16; Patterson 1977) notes, it is not labor itself that is despised, but labor for others that is conceived as demeaning. "Among the tribes with a slave standing, work had become dishonorable" (Patterson 1982, 84–85). The often stark disparity in quotidian routines between masters and their captives constantly stressed their relative status. Captives might serve as attendants, retainers, or warriors; they carried the master's goods and sometimes his or her person (figure 5). They were an outward display of the wealth and power of their captors, a constant visual reminder of the power of the master over others. Captives frequently served as sacrificial victims, demonstrating the owner's wealth through his ability to destroy his most valuable goods (Donald 1997, 34; Miers and Kopytoff 1977; A. Reid and Brewster 1983, 24–25). In other words, by their presence, the tasks they accomplished, and sometimes the manner of their death, captives not only created power for their captors but also symbolized it.

Captives increased the number of followers a leader or status-seeking male controlled, thereby increasing his status. The reproductive capabilities of female captives promised further increase in the size of a status-seeking man's family or lineage. As Patterson (1982, 33) points out with regard to slaves in small-scale groups, "there was not a mass consumption society with ever increasing demand for commodities, but a society with mass demand for persons as retainers in the escalating demand for power. Power over slaves, then, was both the direct exercise and enjoyment of power and an investment in the means of reproducing and accumulating power over others." In other words, increasing the number of their kinsmen and dependents was the primary method aggrandizing men in small-scale societies used to increase political and social power. Thornton ([1999] 2003, 16) points out that legal systems in Africa did not recognize land as private property; rights over people were what mattered, and this "gave special impetus to slavery as an institution for private, revenue-producing wealth. Indeed, ownership of slaves in Africa was virtually equivalent to owning land in western Europe or China" (see also Isaacman and

5. *Chief Carried on the Back of a Slave* carved figure. Attributed to the
Kwakwaka'wakw people. The distinctive headdress of the upper figure
indicates a person of status, while the crudely carved face of the lower figure
suggests his subordinate role. Courtesy UBC Museum of Anthropology,
Vancouver, Canada. Photograph by Derek Tan. MOA ID# A17154.

Isaacman 1977, 117). Watson (1980, 11–12, following Goody 1971, 32), in an attempt to understand how captives or slaves were integrated into the societies that held them, highlights the importance of demography. In Africa's sparsely inhabited landscape, land was plentiful and people were the scarce resource. Here captives acquired during warfare and raiding, women especially, could be incorporated into society as wives or concubines, increasing the size and prestige of the group.

Captive women can be taken without incurring any obligations to another kin group, as captives are by definition without kin (Cooper 1979, 117; Robertshaw and Duncan 2008, 71; Robertson and Klein 1983b, 6). These women and their offspring increase the size of their captor's social group, but without kinship restrictions and entanglements. The taking of captives could be potentially revolutionary because the individual who controls captives—whether men, women, or children—develops a power base independent of other kinship groups, giving him a decided edge (Cooper 1979, 107).

Captives as Economic Power

The most familiar system of slavery today is the American plantation system in which slaves, captured in Africa or born into slave status, composed a highly segregated and stigmatized class whose extracted labor produced goods that supported an elite class. In spite of the fact that captives in some small-scale societies could be defined as slaves, most became an intimate part of the captor's domestic scene. As wives or secondary wives, adoptees, concubines, personal servants, or supplemental labor, captives often slept in the same houses as their masters and undertook the same sorts of tasks as other members of the society. Captives do not generally seem to have been a drain on household resources (e.g., see arguments in Donald [1997] regarding the Northwest Coast). Instead strong evidence shows that captive labor allowed captors to accumulate and control surplus food and other goods essential to hosting status-enhancing public ceremonies and to attracting and keeping followers. Food and other goods could be used (along with the captives themselves) in power-generating systems of trade and exchange.

This is true even at the smallest social scale. The Tutchones of the Upper Yukon, described previously, traded a variety of commodities (fur robes, embroidered coats, etc.) with the coastal Tlingits, neighboring Athapaskan groups, and other Tutchone subgroups (Legros 1985, 46). Powerful family heads monopolized all trade interactions with other groups. Tutchone slaves were forced into the most difficult and demeaning tasks (fetching water, gathering firewood, preparing meat and hides), which created free time for their owners to produce commodities for trade. Slaves also produced commodities for their masters, further increasing their wealth and status.

Unlike among the Tutchones, subsistence in most of the small-scale societies considered here was based on horticulture, although some were complex hunter-gatherers whose rich environment offered surplus food. In horticultural societies, women provide much of the agricultural and other productive labor, and captive women could add significantly to the labor force (Patterson 1982, 179). This was especially true in Africa, where labor-intensive hoe agriculture depended primarily on female labor (see chapters in Robertson and Klein 1983a, especially Meillassoux 1983, 49–50, 1991; Robertson and Klein 1983b, 9–10). In a study of the development of states in fifteenth-century Uganda, Robertshaw (1999) argues that the labor of captive women may have been an important element in an increased agricultural production that permitted co-opting of power by prominent chiefs.

Similarly, among complex hunter-gatherers women also provide much of the labor involved in food procurement and processing. Among the tribes of the Northwest Coast, women's labor was essential for processing and drying salmon, a food that could be gathered only at limited times of the year but was needed at other times (Donald 1997, 25). As described below, the forcing of captive women and captive men into women's labor roles allowed the production of surplus in these societies (Donald 1997). Captives, especially women, therefore, added significantly to the labor force in horticultural and complex hunter-gatherer societies, allowing the production of a surplus in areas where it otherwise might not have been possible.

Captive labor was important in the creation of surplus, but how did aggrandizing males convert surplus to power? The labor of captive women is implicated here, too. In small-scale societies, power is often created and displayed through what Hayden (1996, 127) calls "competitive feasting." He sees the competitive feast as an important avenue for developing hierarchical and centralized political control. Competitive feasts involve competition for both economic gain and control over labor. They occur only in societies where the creation of a surplus is possible (Hayden 1996, 129). Aggrandizing individuals make contractual arrangements with other community members or with other groups in order to gain the surplus they need to stage a competitive feast. Aggrandizers achieve social and economic gain not only by amassing goods but also because the people who participate in the feast are now indebted to them.

Captives can accelerate the process of amassing surplus for competitive feasts and open new avenues for the acquisition of power (Hayden [1996] does not mention captives). Women who were skilled at horticultural tasks as well as in the production of foodstuffs and alcoholic beverages usually featured at competitive feasts. As demonstrated in the case studies below, aggrandizers used captive women as a labor source that was independent of ties of kinship and the gift giving and repayment usually involved in creating a surplus. Cooper's (1979, 107) assessment, cited previously, is pertinent here: captives provide aggrandizers with an independent power base unavailable through normal means. For example, as discussed below, DeBoer (1986) found that among the Conibo of Amazonian Peru, captive wives not only supplied the additional labor needed to increase the output of manioc and maize but also undertook the laborious process of turning these products into beer, which was used at status-enhancing feasts that attracted followers to aggrandizing males. Clearly, taking captives was an important strategy for acquiring power.

An additional, and often complimentary, avenue toward the accumulation of wealth and power is control of the production of craft goods and other portable objects used in trade or gift exchange. The types of materials vary, of course, but commonly include containers, textiles, furs, tools, decorative objects, ritual objects, prestige goods,

88

CAPTIVES AND THE CREATION OF POWER

raw materials for ornament production, and the like (see, e.g., articles in Costin and Wright 1998; Hruby and Flad 2007; Shimada 2007; Stark, Bowser, and Horne 2008). At the simplest level, among the band-level Tutchones slaves accomplished much of the drudge labor (gathering water and wood and processing fish, meat, and hides), leaving their wealthy owners time for producing status-enhancing prestige items or goods for trade (Legros 1985, 61). In more complex societies captives could be a labor force for larger-scale craft production. Tribal-level societies typically do not have full-time craft specialists, but certain individuals or even villages may specialize, part-time, in the production of a particular object that requires knowledge of a somewhat complex technology, such as pottery or metal objects (see Cordell 2006; Spielmann 1998). Craft producers can distribute the product to nearby villages or more distant locations in return for needed agricultural or other subsistence goods. In somewhat more complex societies the chief may support craft specialists who produce a particular product. The chief then distributes these goods to gain the support of his followers or trades them in return for other wealth (however, Lass [1998] shows considerable variation in the amount of control Hawaiian chiefs exerted over specialists who produced different crafts).

Captives are a ready labor force that can be set to craft production and controlled by an aggrandizing individual. Captors sometimes even targeted skilled craftspeople during raids and warfare specifically because of their abilities (see chapter 6; see also Cameron 2011; Patterson 1982, 179). Women's work was important here, too. Women were often potters, textile makers, processors of hides, and producers of other easily transported goods. For example, captives among the protohistoric North American Plains tribes were apparently involved in the labor-intensive production of bison robes and hides. Habicht-Mauche (2008) suggests that Plains men used captive taking as one way of increasing their access to women's labor. Multiple wives working together significantly increased the number of hides produced each year. Men who amassed hides to exchange with other groups gained significant wealth and status.

Captives not only made portable wealth, they also *embodied* it.

Trading or selling captives over wide areas after their capture ensured
in part that they were far enough from their home that escape or rescue was impossible (Baier and Lovejoy 1977, 399; DeBoer 1986; Junker 2008; Klein 1983, 77; Kopytoff and Miers 1977, 53; Mitchell 1984, 42;
Santos-Granero 2009), but it also occurred because they were highly
valuable and constituted a source of wealth for aggrandizing individuals. Patterson (1982, 148) argues that captives may have constituted
the earliest article of external and long-distance trade. As discussed
below, Ames (2008) documents slave trade routes among the indigenous peoples of the Northwest Coast that apparently operated prehistorically (see also Mitchell 1984). Northwest Coast trade extended to
inland regions, where, Legros (1985, 60) reports, Tlingit trading parties occasionally entered the territory of the Tutchones to sell slaves
in exchange for furs. Among the chiefdoms of the Cauca Valley of
Colombia, the earliest European accounts describe an extensive trade
in captives as well as the presence of slave markets (Carneiro 1991). In
the American Southwest in the postcontact period, Brooks (2002) describes widespread raiding and trade of captives that enmeshed a variety of indigenous and European groups (see also Brooks 1998).

Extensive trade in captives has been well documented historically
for many parts of the Old World, including ancient Greece and Rome,
the Islamic slave trade in Africa that commenced before 1000 CE, the
extensive Viking-era slave trade (eighth through eleventh centuries),
and eventually the Atlantic slave trade (Patterson 1982, 148–64; Walvin 2006). In fact, Patterson (1982, viii) argues that Islam would not
have existed and spread without slaves, as they gave the elite an ability to gain power (see also S. Haas 1942). Captives in these societies
functioned as more than simply social persons. Around the world,
they are repeatedly described as media of exchange (Brugge 1993b, 97;
Taylor 2001, 35; Warren [1981] 1985, 186, 201). Patterson (1982, 167–71) recounts the many places in the world where slaves were used as mon-
ey. For example, in early medieval Ireland, the *cumal*, or female slave,
was the highest unit of value. She was a standard unit of value for fines,
she was used as a measure of the value of land, and *cumal* were also
used as a method of payment. Similarly, among the Kalinago of the

Caribbean, the frequent exchange of captives also resulted in a fixed rate of exchange: one captive was worth one *calloúcouli*, a metal ornament (Santos-Granero 2009, 151). The high value of women, especially those with skills, to ancient Greeks is also evident in Homer's *Iliad*. At the funeral for Achilles's friend Patroklos, first prize in the chariot race was a woman "skilled in all useful arts," while fourth prize was "two talents of gold" (Homer 1898, XXIII).

Captive Taking and Power in Three Small-Scale Societies

Three societies that practiced captive taking illustrate how captives could be a source of power for aggrandizing individuals. These examples highlight both the variety of ways captives are used in power acquisition and the fact that these different avenues toward power are often parallel.

The Northwest Coast

The environmentally rich and demographically dense Northwest Coast was home to complex hunter-gatherers who exhibited significant social stratification (see chapter 2 for a full description of this region). Northwest Coast communities had at least three social classes: titleholders, commoners, and slaves (Donald 1997, 25). The titleholder class included "chiefs," who held many hereditary titles, rights, and privileges, and other titleholders, who owned a few titles (Ames and Maschner 1999, 27). Titleholders had no real power or authority outside their own kin group, although they might have considerable prestige in the community. No multicommunity political units existed. As Ames and Maschner (1999, 178) report, "Chiefs could be quite authoritarian, and act with great dignity and pomp, but they had little or no power to make people do their bidding. Chiefs had to wheedle, cajole, or persuade their people to do what they wished." Both men and women held hereditary titles. Women were only rarely household heads, but high-status women could still exhibit enormous prestige, influence, and authority (Ames and Maschner 1999, 179).

Raiding and warfare were common among Northwest Coast societies both historically and prehistorically (figure 6). "Powerful and

6. *A Northwest Coast Village.* Men are returning from a raid, with bound captives and trophy heads. By François Girard, courtesy Canadian Museum of History, I-A-42, S95-23505.

high-ranking war leaders led their lineages and clans on raids that might involve hundreds of warriors in dozens of 18m [60-ft.] war canoes" (Ames and Maschner 1999, 195; see also Ruby and Brown 1993, 57, 187, 244, 261, 263 for accounts of raids). Warfare has been documented prehistorically as early as the Early Pacific period (4400–1800 BCE), although its intensity varied over time (Ames and Maschner 1999; see also chapter 2). The major cause of warfare was revenge for real or perceived slights, but the capture of slaves was especially important (Ames and Maschner 1999, 197; Donald 1997, 105; Mitchell 1984, 39). During battle, men were most often killed because they were dangerous and they could provide valuable trophy heads (Donald 1997, 112; see also Lovisek 2007, 53). A raider who killed an adult male might also appropriate the songs, dances, or rituals the dead man had controlled in life. Women and children were preferred as slaves and preferentially taken during warfare. Individuals who had previously been enslaved were often captured over and over again because their position in captor society was so vulnerable (Donald 1997, 112).

Raids for captives provided an immediate avenue toward the creation of wealth. Not only an economically important labor source, captives also functioned as a source of wealth in status-enhancing ceremonies and as trade items (Mitchell 1984). Slaves were held almost exclusively by titleholders, and a titleholder's status was measured in large part by the number of slaves he held (Donald 1997, 87). Titleholders inherited their rank but had to validate it with potlatches and other activities; giving away or destroying slaves was part of title validation. "Descent from a high ranking family was necessary to assert or maintain high status, but the possession of wealth was crucial. Though numbers of wives . . . and sons . . . as well as dentalia [shells] and other property . . . were said to be important for chiefly status, the possession of slaves was mentioned most often" (Hajda 2005, 570). Titleholder kin groups rather than individuals generally owned slaves. Still, the most prominent men controlled the use of the slaves and might assign them to their wives or daughters as personal servants.

Commoners and slaves on the Northwest Coast may have worked at the same tasks, but activities apparently differed for elite titleholders (Donald 1997, 124). Most of the daily drudgery in titleholder households fell to slaves, including domestic work (carrying water, gathering firewood, preparing fish and game), while the head of a household group undertook mostly managerial and ceremonial labor and shunned everyday tasks (Donald 1997). Among some Northwest Coast groups, female slaves served as constant attendants to the daughters of important titleholders (Donald 1997, 127). Oberg (1973, 87, cited in Donald 1997, 124) states, with regard to highborn Tlingits, "Common labor is quite impossible if he wishes to maintain his prestige. *Anyeti* [titleholder] women are not taught the common art of weaving . . . in fact girls who have never worked are considered special prizes to be won in marriage" (for the Chinooks, see Ross [1849] 1969, 92, cited in Donald 1997, 132; Ruby and Brown 1993, 39–74). In Northwest Coast societies, both titleholder men and women had many slave attendants who answered their every need, including accompanying their masters on war expeditions and even fulfilling commands to commit murder (Donald 1997, 127–28; Ruby and Brown 1993, 62–63).

Some scholars assert that the contributions of slaves to Northwest Coast economies were negligible and in fact that slaves were a noneconomic drain on their owners' resources (see Drucker 1965, 52; Rohner and Rohner 1970, 79, cited in Donald 1997, 39). But others argue that raiding for slaves was an important method of creating wealth (Mitchell 1984, 46). Donald (1997, 135) shows that captives were a key source of labor in the procurement and especially the processing of salmon, one of the most important resources for Northwest Coast tribes. Ames (2008), using archaeological data, supports Donald's conclusions, showing that slave labor was likely necessary for the levels of processing and storage evident at prehistoric Northwest Coast sites, and he agrees with Donald that slaves were essential for producing the wealth necessary for elites to maintain their status.

As in many societies, slaves on the Northwest Coast provided labor for titleholders without the reciprocal obligations that came with requests to kin for their labor. As scholars note (Ames and Maschner 1999, 178; Donald 1997, 137–38), kin were obligated but not required to perform labor for titleholders in their community, whereas slaves *had* to comply with such requests, under threat of death. Because demands made by titleholders on slaves were fulfilled without incurring any reciprocal obligations, slave labor was free labor. The surplus produce that slave labor created allowed titleholders to increase their power by holding feasts and ceremonies. Gift giving at these ceremonies validated titleholder claims to their title and position, and when titleholder guests received gifts, they publicly acknowledged their host's claims (Donald 1997, 31). Donald (1997, 297) describes four ways slaves contributed to the ability of titleholders to host feasts: slaves helped amass the food and other goods necessary for the feast; slaves became gifts to other titleholders invited to the feast; slaves could be traded for furs and other goods to be given away at the feast; and slaves might be killed to demonstrate the wealth and power of the titleholder host.

Slaves were important items of trade. Among the Chinooks, captives were the highest priced trade item, second only to the highly valued "coppers" that circulated along the Northwest Coast (Mitchell 1984, 40, citing Ray 1938, 51; see also Donald 1997, 150–51, which gives the value of slaves in terms of coppers for many Northwest Coast groups). Using historic records, Donald (1997, 139–56) reconstructed major northern and southern slave-trading routes in the Northwest Coast that could move slaves hundreds of miles. Ames (2008, 144–46) shows the close correspondence between the prehistoric movement of obsidian and Donald's southern slave trade route, implying that these slave trade routes may have operated long before European contact.

A series of events in the late 1830s, well documented in the journals of the Hudson's Bay Company, illustrates the key role captives played in the creation and display of wealth (Mitchell 1984, 41; Donald 1997, 114). A group of warriors from the area of the Skeena River traveled south to Vancouver Island, captured twenty women, and traded them to other groups for furs. The furs were then taken to Fort Simpson and exchanged for European goods. These goods were the wealth used by a titleholder in the raiders' group to host a large feast that validated his status. Other sorts of transactions also used slaves as wealth items. For example, they were part of the exchange of goods between families at the marriage of titleholders. When someone was killed, slaves could be given to the deceased's family as compensation (Donald 1997, 156–64).

The Conibo of the Ucayali Basin

The Conibo are one of the Panoan-speaking groups that live along the Ucayali River in eastern Peru (figure 7; Steward and Métraux 1948, 567–69). The Ucayali flows northward along the eastern base of the Peruvian Andes through lowland tropical forest and eventually joins the Amazon River. This relatively flat landscape, much of it covered by water, is characterized by rich, fertile soil and diverse riverine and riparian fauna (DeBoer 1990, 83; Santos-Granero 2009, 23–24). When first contacted by the Spanish in the sixteenth century, the Conibo were one of a number of large, complexly organized, and competing polities living along the river, while away from the river were many smaller, less sedentary, and less complex groups (DeBoer 1990, 83–84). These horticulturalists, who grew maize and sweet manioc, also relied on fishing, wild plant collecting, and hunting (Steward and Métraux

7. *A group of Cunivo [Conibo] Indians on the Rio Ucayali, Peruvian Montaña.*
Some of the women in the front may be captives. Photograph by either
Charles Kroehle or George Huebner, late 1880s. Courtesy National
Anthropological Archives, Smithsonian Institution, photo lot 129.

1948, 567–69). A sixteenth-century European explorer reported that
the Conibo lived in large villages consisting of two hundred to four
hundred houses with populations perhaps larger than two thousand
people (Santos-Granero 2009, 23; see DeBoer 1981, figure 1, for later population estimates). Villages might include two or three local
groups, each ruled by its own headman, that banded together for de-
fense (Santos-Granero 2009, 22–23, 25). Myers (1974) reviews the reports of early explorers to confirm the presence of large villages along
the Ucayali. His interpretation of these data suggests that the Conibo
and other major riverine tribes could be considered to have a chiefdom level of political organization.

The Conibo engaged in frequent warfare against their neighbors,
often traveling hundreds of miles in flotillas of large canoes to attack
other villages (the following discussion is taken from Santos-Granero
2009, 55–63, unless otherwise noted). "No-man's-lands" along the Ucayali River were observed by early Spanish explorers, suggesting long-
standing warfare in the region (DeBoer 1981; Myers 1974, 141). The

Conibo also conducted raids against the smaller groups who lived on tributaries of the Ucayali, and these raids were the most productive in terms of captives and booty. Raiders embarked on their trip with almost empty canoes in anticipation of returning fully loaded with clothing, blankets, salt, valuable ornaments, other goods, and many captives. The goals of Conibo raiding were to destroy the settlements of their enemies and take captive as many women and children as possible. Raiders generally killed adult men so they would not pursue the raiders; killing the men was also intended to make captive women and children forget their past lives—they had no home to escape to. Some scholars suggest that the focus of captive taking was on women who could be incorporated as wives, but Santos-Granero's (2009, 61) careful analysis of early documents shows that the capture of children was equally important, if not more so.

The Conibo practiced head elongation and female circumcision and took captives mostly from groups that did not follow these practices. As a result, regardless of how long captives lived with the Conibo, their physical characteristics marked them as "wild" and "uncivilized" (Santos-Granero 2009, 178). In Conibo villages, captives underwent rituals intended to both incorporate them into Conibo society and distinguish them from "true" Conibo (Santos-Granero 2009, 111–12). Their hair was cut in distinctive ways, and they were referred to by the same words used for pets or domesticated animals (Santos-Granero 2009, 179).

Female child captives were often raised to be spouses for the sons of their captors. At puberty, they might be circumcised (considered civilizing), an act that rendered them suitable as wives. Adult women too old for the circumcision ritual were considered "uncivilized" and could only become concubines. Women who became concubines functioned as household servants rather than as wives (Santos-Granero 2009, 131). These servant women did far more of the most arduous household work than Conibo wives, including planting; harvesting; carrying loads; weaving clothing, bags, and mosquito nets; and making maize beer. Captive children cared for the elderly, and most Conibo men owned one or more of these children (Santos-Granero 2009,

132). As they grew, captive boys took on more laborious tasks, carrying firewood, clearing gardens, paddling or carrying canoes, and loading and unloading cargo. They also made canoes, an enormously time-consuming process but a key element in the raiding and captive taking practices of Conibo society (Santos Granero 2009, 132).

Captives did the most difficult and time-consuming work for their household. Their Conibo masters were not completely relieved of daily domestic or subsistence tasks but worked alongside their captives. The labor of their captives increased household wealth and prestige, however. Captive females' labor could increase the status of their male masters while at the same time reducing the amount of work required of Conibo wives (Santos-Granero 2009, 132). Because male captives took on time-consuming jobs such as clearing gardens and building canoes, male masters had more time to devote to raiding and trading, activities that brought status and wealth.

Conibo men's status depended on their success in war, and the most successful men were able to have multiple wives (Santos-Granero 2009, 55–63). Raiding and taking captives allowed younger Conibo men to obtain wives when the older, more powerful men had co-opted women within the group (see also DeBoer 1986). While most men had no more than two wives, war leaders had three or more (Santos-Granero 2009, 62). The ideal of the successful Conibo man centered on his courage and success in warfare; after death, successful warriors were thought to enter an afterworld where they engaged in tournaments and were served by beautiful women (Santos-Granero 2009, 63).

Status production for males among the Conibo was in many ways similar to that in the Northwest Coast. Using historic documents from the seventeenth to the nineteenth centuries, DeBoer (1986) argues that female labor was fundamental to the development of Conibo men's power and social status and was a primary reason they raided for women to become their wives or concubines. Women were responsible not only for most of the agricultural production but also for the time-consuming production of beer made from manioc. Beer was a key element of the competitive feasts that were the primary avenue for men to achieve social status. Therefore, the more women a man had, the greater his chances of being able to host a large feast. Archaeological evidence presented by DeBoer (1986) suggests that the practice of competitive feasting extends well into prehistory. It is more difficult to demonstrate prehistoric captive taking, but DeBoer (1986) believes the same patterns seen historically were also common in the past.

As in the Northwest Coast, Conibo masters traded or sold their captives, usually shortly after capture but sometimes after the captive women had served as concubines or captive children had been raised for a time in a Conibo home (Santos-Granero 2009, 154). Seventeenth-century explorers reported that after a successful Conibo raid, they would trade captives with groups on the lower Ucayali for iron tools (Steward and Métraux 1948, 562). Sometimes trade in captives went the other way, with Conibo exchanging iron tools for captive children held by interior tribes away from the main waterway (Santos-Granero 2009, 154). If captives had a "wealth" value as well as a "labor" value historically among the Conibo, it is likely that precontact trade in captives provided another source of wealth and power for Conibo men.

Maritime Chiefdoms of Coastal Philippines and Adjacent Parts of Southeast Asia

Even prior to the first historic records (prior to the current era) island Southeast Asia consisted of groups representing a variety of socioeconomic levels: band-level hunter-gatherers, tribal agriculturalists, and socially ranked chiefdoms (Bellwood 1992, 55). For most of the last two millennia it was a region of low population with groups living in disconnected territories. The region has a strong maritime orientation, and slave raiding and trading is one aspect of this adaptation that has been well documented by historians of the early modern period (after 1500 CE) using abundant historical documents and ethnohistoric accounts (A. Reid 1983, 27–33; Warren [1981] 1985). These practices also extended into the precontact period (Junker 2008). In explaining the causes of low population during the premodern era in Southeast Asia, Anthony Reid (1992) cites the constancy of warfare and its disruption of domestic life, which caused frequent shifts in residence as well as voluntary and forced migration. In Southeast Asia, as in the

Northwest Coast, Amazonia, and elsewhere, "rulers perceived their power in terms of human rather than territorial resources, their object in war was always to capture as many of the enemy as possible, to take home to populate their dominions" (A. Reid 1992, 461–62).

Junker focuses on captive taking and enslavement among the chiefdom-level societies of the Philippines during the twelfth to the sixteenth centuries (the following discussion is taken from Junker [2008] unless otherwise noted). Like Anthony Reid (1992), she emphasizes that the fragmented geography and low population levels of Southeast Asia created a demand for people rather than territory. "Political authority relied . . . on cultivating ties of personal loyalty, commanding productive labor, and expanding one's power base of followers through elaborate and continual ceremonial circulation of prestige goods" (Junker 2008, 115). In the Philippines, at least as early as the later part of the first millennium CE, chiefdom-level societies occupied the coast, while tribal-level swidden agriculturalists and mobile foragers called the uplands home. River-based trade, with trading relationships extending to mainland Southeast Asia as early as the tenth century CE, linked these disparate groups. Raiding and captive taking were an integral part of the relationships among Philippine societies, with the usual pattern being raids mounted by coastal chiefdoms against other chiefly polities or upland tribal groups, and occasionally even against groups outside the Philippine archipelago (Junker 2008, 115).

Status seeking, warfare, captive taking, and warrior ideology were fundamental aspects of Philippine chiefly polities (Junker 2008). High social status was accorded to successful warriors who accumulated large numbers of captives and other goods on raids. In epic stories presented in ceremonies that preceded raids, warrior heroes were valorized for their exploits and especially the taking of captives; captive taking was more highly valued than seizing booty or slaying the enemy. "The ideology of warrior prestige and supernatural power, as much as anticipated economic gain, helped flame male desire to participate in the endless raids against both neighbors and foreigners, and to concentrate their efforts on prestigious and economically lucrative slave-capture rather than human slaughter" (Junker 2008, 119).

Raiders captured women, children, and men from throughout the region and even from as far away as Vietnam, Thailand, or Sumatra (Junker 2008). Women were especially highly valued and were a common target of capture. After a raid they were divided among the participants of the raid and frequently became wives or secondary wives, as marriageable women were scarce in Philippines chiefly societies (Junker 2008, 122). These captive women might remain in slave status throughout their lives, but their offspring were generally considered full members of the society their mothers had joined. Foreignness and slave status could be erased in a single generation. After 1500 CE, "although slavery is an inescapable term for those newly captured or bought . . . it must be emphasized that this was an 'open' system of slavery which people moved in and out of almost imperceptibly" (A. Reid 1992, 480).

The labor of captives provided significant economic wealth to coastal chiefs and other aggrandizing males (Junker 2008, 120). Women commonly served as agricultural workers or in craft production. As in the Northwest Coast and Amazonia, the surplus goods produced by captive women were converted to social power by chiefs, who attracted warriors by sponsoring ritual feasts and distributing prestige goods to would-be adherents. Female captives produced many of the luxury goods used for elite consumption and trade, especially pottery and textiles. Captives created wealth and power in other ways. Like other goods, they could be used in the accumulation of bride price; the resulting marriages strengthened polities through the creation of affinal ties. Furthermore, female captives who became the wives or secondary wives of high-status males served as another source of status and wealth by increasing the population of the male's domestic lineages through reproduction.

Captives were wealth items and like other goods were traded extensively throughout Southeast Asia. As in many parts of the world, trading, raiding, and captive taking were related activities in Southeast Asia. Junker (2008, 115) links the rise of long-distance trading that began with the mid-first-millennium Chan polities of southern Vietnam with the rise of sea-based slave raiding. By the eleventh century extensive maritime raiding and trading routes had developed throughout the island and coastal mainland areas of Southeast Asia that extended from south China and Manila on the north to the Java Sea on the south (Junker 2008, 120, figure 5.3). Captives could be transported hundreds or even thousands of miles in this vast sea network. In the Sulu sultanate during the eighteenth and nineteenth centuries, captives (a large proportion of whom were from the Philippines) were the primary form of investment for the wealthy rulers and even served as a medium of exchange (Warren [1981] 1985, 201).

Small-scale societies could exhibit considerable social stratification, and captives, a distinctive and almost universal category of social person, were commonly found on the lowest rungs of these societies. Captives were important actors in the creation of power in the societies they joined, and this chapter evaluates how captives were used in the acquisition of power in small-scale societies. This section briefly summarizes the avenues toward the creation of power that captives opened and then explores the roles that captives may have played in the development of social complexity in the past. I do not argue that captives were the most important or even a major factor in the development of social complexity. In fact, it is clear that captive taking and enslavement could exist in captor societies for very long periods of time without transforming them; however, given the evidence presented above, I believe the role of captives should be considered in future archaeological studies of the development of social complexity.

Two major benefits that captives offered to captor society were increased population for captor households and labor that allowed for creation of surplus. In small-scale societies, aggrandizing males sought to increase the size of their households through incorporating kin, practicing polygyny, and siring many children. Captives represented an instant increase in household size, and the reproductive capacity of female captives promised further increase. Captives were also status markers, highlighting the power of their masters. As the three case studies demonstrate, in horticultural societies women's labor was especially important for crop production, and additional women may have permitted the production of surplus crops. In small-scale societies the competitive feast was often a route toward status and power, and surplus food could be produced by captive labor and processed into beer and other products that were integral to such feasts. Captives also made craft goods that could be traded or sold, increasing captor power. Captives themselves could be traded or sold. The costs of mounting a raid could be high in terms of danger to the raiders. If raiders were victorious, however, they achieved "unearned" wealth. While booty stolen on raids might be quickly dispersed or expended, captives constituted loot that kept on giving. Even in band-level societies in which raiding was uncommon, the appropriation of women and children as drudge laborers could allow their owners free time for the production of prestige or trade goods.

Archaeologists who study the development of social complexity, including the emergence of state-level societies, argue that power has several dimensions: economic, social or ideological, and political (Blanton et al. 1996; Earle 1997; Yoffee 1993). Political power refers to the ability of leaders to impose their will on a society. Leaders in small-scale societies have limited abilities to force other people to do their bidding. They work through persuasion, shaming, and calling on the obligations of kinship. The old saw "one word from the chief and everyone does as he pleases" aptly describes power in most small-scale societies.

Reciprocal social obligations and the ties of kinship can create significant limitations to the accrual of power. Young men who wish to marry may be forced to pay a hefty bride price for their wives and may incur lifelong labor obligations to her family. Kin-based leadership, such as that found especially in chiefdoms, means that when a chief calls upon kin for their labor— in building houses or canoes, stepping up their production of crops or craft goods so the chief can appropriate a surplus, standing by him in disputes with other lineages, going to war, or any of dozens of other situations—the chief has incurred social obligations. Kin may refuse to provide labor or services, but if they agree, they expect something in return—help with their own house or canoe-building project, a cut of products of the surplus food or craft production, a share in the spoils of war.

Archaeologists should consider Yoffee's (1993, 69) argument concerning requirements for a state to develop: "I suggest . . . that the most important necessary and sufficient condition that separates states from non-states is the emergence of certain socioeconomic and governmental roles that are emancipated from real or fictive kinship." Captives create ways for aggrandizing individuals to avoid the obligations of kinship. By taking captives, aggrandizing males could acquire wives without the payment of bride price or incurring future obligations to in-laws. Captives provided labor without any reciprocal obligations on the part of the master. Captives could not refuse to labor, nor did the master have to waste any time wheedling or cajoling the captive into doing the desired task. Captives increased the population of a household but without the restraints that come with kinship. Captive wives could not appeal to brothers or fathers if they were abused or overworked. The children that captive wives or concubines produced came with none of the entanglements to matrilineal kin that were common with native-born children. Captives were rarely able to scheme or connive with other members of the society against their masters. Captors could create a warrior class made up of captives who would have no divided loyalties.

Archaeologists who study the development of complex societies need a more sophisticated understanding of stratification in small-scale societies. Many of these groups had significant differences in social status. Archaeologists should consider the ways captives could allow aggrandizing individuals in prehistoric societies to build power outside the restrictions of kinship obligations. Such studies of small-scale and early state-level societies should help us come to a new understanding of the ways complex societies were created.

| Chapter Five

Captives, Social Boundaries, and Ethnogenesis

Captives are aliens who have crossed social boundaries, bringing the "enemy" into the heart of social life. This chapter focuses on those controversial social entities called "ethnic groups" and explores how ethnic boundaries are shaped and changed by the inclusion of captives. Captives arrive with a different set of cultural practices, but their often liminal role in captor society means that their ability to express either natal or captor ethnicity is a subject of constant negotiation. The chapter begins with a discussion of the concept of "ethnicity" as it is currently conceived in archaeology and as it relates to an understanding of captives and social boundaries. Archaeologists are well aware of the fluid nature of ethnic boundaries (although they sometimes ignore it); captives are an important element of this permeability. Rather than an exploration of how captive social identity is constructed *within* captor society (the subject of chapter 3) or of the contributions and transformations that captives can make *to* captor society (chapter 6), this chapter examines how the presence of captives affects the boundaries of a society—the ways captives help construct and maintain the imagined communities called "ethnic groups."[1]

The effects of captives on social boundaries are examined at both micro and macro scales (Lightfoot 1995; see also Scheiber and Mitchell 2010; Stein 2002, 2005a; Voss 2008c) using ethnographic and ethnohistoric examples. At the micro scale, intimate daily encounters between captives and their captors as well as captives' attempts at advantageous social positioning could strengthen social boundaries. At the macro scale, captives could at times form links among interacting societies that engaged in both violent and peaceful interactions. At other times, because the acquisition of captives often accompanies social unrest and demographic disruption, captives could be involved in processes of ethnogenesis or coalescence that resulted in the creation of new or transformed ethnic groups.

Captivity was a transformative process. Captives, who were aliens at the moment of capture, helped shape concepts of difference and similarity in captor culture, helped create a shared history, and in some cases helped shape or transform the traditions surrounding the expression of ethnic identity. Captives fit into and reacted against captor culture through processes with multitudes of contributing and interacting aspects. Some of these aspects are examined here.

The Nature of Ethnic Boundaries

Understanding the effect of captives on social boundaries requires knowledge of the sorts of boundaries captives may have crossed. Historically, ethnographers studied people as members of named ethnic groups (e.g., "the Nuer," "the Cubeo," "the Hopi") and archaeologists devised "archaeological cultures" (e.g., "the Anasazi," "the Wari") as similarly coherent groups defined through material traits (pottery designs, architectural styles, etc.) that have clear spatial and temporal patterning in the archaeological record.[2] Over the past several decades, however, the nature of ethnic boundaries, the sorts of groups they contain, and how such groups might be identified in the past have been the subject of considerable debate in archaeology (and other fields). This section briefly examines these arguments and recent conceptions of the "ethnic group" that are integral to understanding the role of captives in these social formations.

In the following discussion, ethnicity is considered separately from other social categories, such as gender or status/class, although these categories certainly intersect in complex ways with the situational expression of ethnic affiliation (Jones 1997, 85–86; Shortman 1989). Unlike gender or status/class (or other social classifications, such as race, nationality, or citizenship), ethnicity is a distinct way in which a social community is imagined (see also Voss 2008a, 28). Individuals, women and men, nonelite and elite experience and express ethnic affiliation differently. Because captives almost always enter captor society as subordinate individuals and because gender is such a crucial element in the selection and treatment of captives (see chapter 3), the intersection of gender, status/class, and ethnicity is especially important for the study of captives.

A particular consideration for small-scale societies is that kinship is often a more important structuring principle than ethnic group membership and reaches across ethnic boundaries to produce different and broader social formations. In small-scale societies, captives are outsiders because they are outside the kinship network of their captors. But as described in chapter 3, even kinship is an actively negotiated category. To show the problems with drawing social boundaries by using either kinship or ethnicity among the African Nuer, historians Brubaker and Cooper (2000, 21–25) point out that kinship relations could be extended beyond both types of boundaries by taking captive women as wives or incorporating other strangers through marriage, fictive kinship, or different methods such as blood brotherhood. They note, "In almost all societies, kinship concepts are symbolic and ideological resources, yet while they shape norms, self-understandings, and perceptions of affinity, they do not necessarily produce kinship 'groups'" (Brubaker and Cooper 2000, 24). The concept of "Nuer," they report, has similarly fuzzy boundaries.

While archaeologists today agree that ethnicity is self-referential, subjective, situational, often highly fluid, and possibly was absent prior to the development of modern nations (Goodby 1998; Jones 1997, 64; MacEachern 1998; Singleton 2006; Stahl 1991; Voss 2008a), many still tend to equate archaeological cultures with bounded ethnic groups in much of their day-to-day work. For example, the current effort in many parts of the world to reunite indigenous people with the bodies of their ancestors taken from archaeological excavations often assumes that contemporary indigenous groups existed as bounded social or ethnic groups centuries or even millennia ago. What we know of the development of historical social groups suggests that such lengthy continuity in social boundaries is unlikely, yet we seem to believe that for "people without history" (Wolf 1982) social boundaries are "timeless" (Stahl 1993).

Similarly, studies of migration often use material culture patterns assumed to be "typical" of certain geographically restricted archaeological cultures; when those same patterns are found in another location at a later period in time, a migration is presumed to have occurred (Cameron 2013; Clark 2001; Jones 1997, 27–28). Not only is such an essentialized concept of culture likely incorrect (Singleton 2006, 260), but an exclusive focus on the "origin" of objects ignores what may have been an extensive biography of use by people other than the objects' makers, including "hidden" people (Silliman 2010). Subordinate "others," like captives (although Silliman doesn't mention them), may have spent more time cooking with, washing, and handling pottery than the makers and owners of the pots themselves (see chapter 6), yet it is the makers whom we see most readily in the archaeological record.

The widespread practice of captive taking ensured porous group boundaries, and captives could have lasting effects on the boundaries they crossed. Rather than unchanging historical entities, ethnic groups are in a constant state of construction and change as individuals actively negotiate their social identity within a matrix of contested options. Perhaps most important for the study of captives, an especially salient aspect of group identification is the erection of social in-group/out-group boundaries (Barth [1969] 1998; Jones 1997, 84; Voss 2008a, 14). Identifying with the symbols, material culture, and daily practices of a particular ethnic group is, to some extent, a way of positioning oneself in opposition to others with different symbols, objects, and practices. Indeed, Barth's ([1969] 1998, 15–16) pioneering study of ethnic boundaries suggests that strong feelings of difference *between* ethnic groups are as important as shared cultural traits in delimiting ethnic group boundaries. He argues that in order for ethnic groups to persist, they must have procedures for dealing with

other groups that will channel interactions in ways that prevent ethnic modification.

Models of ethnic group formation, often dichotomized as "primordial" or "instrumentalist," do not work particularly well for understanding the effect of captive taking on ethnic boundaries (see Jones
1997, 65–72, for a discussion of primordial and instrumentalist approaches; see also Voss 2008a, 26–27). Primordial models see ethnicity as an essential part of human nature, a universal need for a feeling
of belonging. Our "blood," our language, the landscapes of our childhood, our cultural and religious practices, and so on create almost
immutable ties. Yet even a superficial reading of the many "captive
narratives" that resulted from the collision of European and indigenous cultures evokes serious questions about the immutability of
primordial kin bonds (Colley 2002, 2007; Demos 1994; Kestler 1990;
Meredith [1927] 2004; VanDerBeets 1973). Remarkably, captives can reconstruct their social identity in a new cultural context in a relatively short period of time.

"Instrumental" approaches, like that pioneered by Barth ([1969]
1998), see ethnic groupings as self-defining and subjective social entities and ethnicity as a way for individuals to further their economic
or political interests (see also Shortman 1989, on "salient social identities"). From the point of view of captives, instrumental explanations
are also problematic. Barth's social actors used their identity for purposes of improving their social position. The captives who form the
social actors in this book cross social and geographic boundaries unwillingly. As examples below illustrate, captives do attempt to situate
themselves in captor culture in personally beneficial ways, but their
liminal social position means they are generally far more limited in
actively pursuing advantageous ethnic expressions than a Barth-like
model suggests.

In her discussion of identity formation, ethnicity, and ethnogenesis, Voss (2008a, 27) distinguishes a useful interpretative gap between
primordialist and instrumentalist models of ethnicity. She suggests
growing consensus around a view of ethnicity as a consciousness of
difference based on a "combination of cultural difference, ideologies

of shared ancestry, history, and tradition. . . . Ethnicity thus consists of overlapping sets of loyalties and obligations that operate at multiple scales, 'a series of nesting dichotomizations of inclusiveness and exclusiveness'" (Voss 2008a, 27, citing R. Cohen 1978, 387). Understanding the formation of ethnic distinctions diachronically is particularly important for the study of captives. Neither primordialism nor instrumentalism can "explain how 'new' ethnicities—ones that might arise even in the course of a single lifetime—can generate emotional attachment, intragroup affinity, and intergroup antagonism" (Voss 2008a, 27; see also Santos-Granero 2002, 47–50). The boundary crossings experienced by captives provide an intriguing window into how and why such changes occur.

Captives, Multiethnic Societies, and Ethnogenesis

This section examines several interrelated phenomena in which captives can be key players in the maintenance or construction of ethnic boundaries. It represents only some of the ways (albeit significant ones) that captives affect social boundaries. The discussion uses historic and ethnohistoric data and focuses on social interactions. The ultimate goal, however, is to encourage archaeologists to recognize that captives may have been active players in the creation of the material record we use to reconstruct and study social groups in the past.

The remainder of the chapter explores four of the ways captives affect ethnic boundaries. First, they can be part of multiethnic societies in which several groups live in a single community yet maintain distinct ethnic affiliations. As the examples below illustrate, captives can function as "social opposites" in multiethnic societies, allowing captors to define themselves in contrast to their captives. Second, whether or not societies acknowledge and maintain multiethnic boundaries, for reasons of self-preservation or advancement captives may carefully adopt captor culture and actively participate in practices that strengthen captor ethnic boundaries. Third, at a macro scale, captives (especially women) can form central nodes that link disparate ethnic groups into larger, interacting social formations that defy essentialist notions of ethnic identities as social forms with unique combinations of language, culture, and genetics. Such links often result from the foregrounding of kin relations rather than ethnic identity in social interactions. Finally, captives can be involved in the process of ethnogenesis: either the transformation of identities or the formation of "neoteric" ethnicities, defined as social groups having no direct antecedents. Scholars now recognize that many historically known small-scale societies had short histories and were created by people of diverse ethnic origins, sometimes remnant populations that included captives (Sidbury and Cañizares-Esguerra 2011). Captives or former captives could be involved in the formation of "coalescent societies," generally entering as junior or subordinate members. Examples below illustrate the role of captives in each of these four processes.

Captives as Social Opposites

Captives can strengthen ethnic boundaries in captor society because they are a constant reminder of other, incorrect "ways of doing." In other words, captors calibrate the "correctness" of their behavior through comparison with the "incorrect" behavior of their captives. The role of captives as social opposites is especially prominent among groups in which captives are highly marginalized as slaves or other socially sanctioned people (see chapter 3).

Patterson (1982, 77–101) locates the relationship between master and slave in the concept of honor and shows the inextricable link between master and slave: the master's honor was demonstrated only in the slave's lack of honor and personal autonomy. He even argues that a third element of society was necessary—neither slaves nor masters but people who could observe interactions between slaves and masters and acknowledge the honor and prestige of the master (Patterson 1982, 99). Although one might substitute "power" for "honor" in Patterson's discussion (but see Patterson 1982, 80), he provides a framework for understanding how social boundaries are established or strengthened in multiethnic societies in which captives exist—through the expression of both power and powerlessness. The master was the opposite of the slave, not just in terms of power, honor, or autonomy but also in every other way, and these stark contrasts extended to other members of the master's social group and the groups from which captives were generally taken.

When certain groups were raided repeatedly for captives, a strong
in-group/out-group boundary could be established. These target societies were often considered subservient groups and even called "slave"
groups by the raiders. The identification of a particular group with
slave status is a common, worldwide pattern (Patterson 1982, 250). As
in the New World prior to the mid-nineteenth century, when people
from Africa or of African heritage came to be associated with a slave
status, Slavic people in medieval Europe were so often taken captive
and enslaved that that their ethnic label became the English word
slave. Similarly, many of the Amazonian groups that raided for and
enslaved captives considered their most common targets—or sometimes all neighbors—as inherently slavish (Santos-Granero 2009).

Slave-owning societies constructed the "otherness" of slaves in various ways. Most critically, captives were without kin in captor communities, an especially important aspect of their identity in societies
where kin relations were fundamental to social relations. Their appearance (clothing, hairstyle, body modification), cultural or religious
practices, ethnic origin, and behavior or moral qualities, as well as the
tasks they were forced to undertake—only a debased slave willingly
carried out such tasks—also stressed "otherness."

Karras (1988) found that the stereotype of the slave in medieval Scandinavia was a short, dark person who contrasted with the tall, blond
natives of the area, implying a different ethnic origin for slaves. This
was almost certainly a cultural construct; the Vikings' widespread
slave trade makes it difficult to determine exactly where slaves were obtained, but they undoubtedly included individuals of a variety of sizes
and complexions. Karras (1988, 57, 65) used ancient sagas to reconstruct
medieval Scandinavian slavery and found slave characters described
as ugly, dirty, and incompetent. Their degraded behavior or "mannerisms" easily identified them as slaves, in contrast to those of noble
birth. In the eastern part of Scandinavia, slaves were not explicitly described as foreigners, but sagas in Iceland depict many slaves as Irish.
Here slaves are distinguishable by their cowardliness and "ignoble"

character, rather than simply by their physical characteristics (Karras 1988, 59). They are also distinguished by the lowliness of their work (spreading manure, digging turf [Karras 1988, 60]). In discussing the saga *Rígspula*, Karras shows the importance of slaves in emphasizing the key characteristics of the nonslave population of Iceland (although the saga is not clearly Icelandic; Karras 1988, 61; T. Hill 1986): "The important point of the legend in Rígspula for its audience is that the nobleman is innately noble and the free man innately free. The slave's innate slavishness is only a foil for the other two. The description of the slave emphasizes by contrast the free man's role in bearing arms and managing the farm rather than doing the dirty work. The physical characteristics of the slave contrast with the healthy good looks of the ruddy free man" (Karras 1988, 63).

Santos-Granero (2009, 105) describes the ways captors in slave-owning societies in Amazonia and around the Caribbean constructed their captives as "alien, inferior, and subordinate, and hence not eligible for full membership in their society." Their worldviews often justified taking captives by considering people from other groups as less than human and thus potential slaves. These concepts are evident in the terms they applied to others, as well as in myths and similar oral accounts. Once taken, captors inscribed a slave's status on the captive's body by denying her clothing, ornaments, and other markers that would indicate humanity and full membership in the captor group; captors substituted other clothing, body marks, or mutilations that made captive status obvious at a glance (Santos-Granero 2005).

For example, the Tukano, horticultural peoples who lived along the Vaupes River in the eastern part of the Amazon Basin, consistently raided the forest-dwelling Makú (Santos-Granero 2009, 113–15). The Tukano considered the Makú completely opposite to themselves and not quite human. The characteristics of the Makú—their hunting-and-gathering way of life, simple dwellings, short stature, ugly features, unclean habits, lack of clothing and ornaments, awful language, and depraved marriage practices—contrasted completely with the sensible lifestyle, beautiful houses, clean and properly dressed bodies, and moral practices of the Tukano. Once they entered Tukano society, male

Makú captives were forbidden to wear the typical necklace and feather headdress of the Tukano men. The thought of marriage to Makú women repulsed Tukano men.

The Kalinago of the Lesser Antilles despised their neighbors, whom they raided frequently (Santos-Granero 2009, 107–10). After a violent entrance into the village of their captors, captive women and children had their hair cut as a sign of servitude and were henceforth called "female servant" or, for boys, "male servant" (or "my barbeque," a reference to their eventual roles in cannibalistic feasts). Captive boys were sometimes emasculated as an additional mark of their servile position. Female captives were denied the use of cotton leg bands that all Kalinago women wore as the ultimate sign of feminine beauty. Female captives also differed from other Kalinago women in being assigned heavy tasks that were not undertaken by native-born women.

In West Africa, the Fulani of the Upper Volta (now Burkina Faso) define themselves in opposition to others, especially their slaves, called *maccube*: "In Fulani eyes, it is among 'captives' or ex-slaves that one finds most clearly expressed everything that is the opposite of Fulani. . . . 'Captives' are black, fat, coarse, naïve, irresponsible, uncultivated, shameless, dominated by their needs and emotions. These qualities are innate and manifest in the servile condition. . . . A corollary of this attitude is that all the other blacks . . . already possess the principal attributes of slaves (Riesman 1977, 117)." Riesman's (1977) ethnography appeared long after the abolishment of slavery in the Upper Volta region, yet he still found strong concepts of difference between former slave and nonslave social groups in the region (see also Baldus 1977).

Perdue (1979) argues that among the Cherokees of North America slaves captured during warfare functioned as "social deviants." Slaves were people without kin, and by maintaining *atsi nahsa'i*, as slaves were called, Cherokees acknowledged their anomalous kinless situation, thereby strengthening the Cherokees' own kinship system. Perdue (1979, 17) also argues that *atsi nahsa'i* were important in bounding Cherokee group identity. The Cherokees valued individualism and lacked a strong centralized government. In daily interactions with *atsi nahsa'i* they strengthened their identity by proclaiming clearly who they were not (*atsi nahsa'i*).

Captives who were socially constructed as opposites (and often as slaves) were effective in maintaining social boundaries because they were in daily contact with their captors. They were not some remote "other" that might only be encountered during times of warfare but an intimate "other": an "other" by which one might calibrate one's behavior from moment to moment. This is a dominant-group view of the captive, however. The next section explores captives as engaged social actors who helped shape the matrix of domination in which they were enmeshed.

Captive Assimilation and Captive Agency

Captives might differ genetically or phenotypically from their captors, but they could become fluent in aspects of captor culture that defined membership (language, behavior, religion, dress) to the extent they were allowed or chose to. For reasons of self-preservation or self-promotion, captives could become not only careful followers but even assiduous replicators of captor social practices, in effect strengthening captor social boundaries. This was true of captives who became slaves and also of captives incorporated as kin into captor society, because they usually occupied a somewhat precarious social position. Newly recruited captives also became students as well as their captors' teachers in the recitation of the histories, traditions, loyalties, and obligations of captor society, reinforcing social norms for both captives and captors. Captives could proactively adopt captor social practices in societies that maintained multiple ethnicities as well as in those that downplayed or "forgot" multiethnic origins (see chapter 3).

Even in societies that incorporated many people from other cultures, dramatically changing the genetic makeup of captor society, captor social practices may have continued to be enforced by strong social sanctions that "encouraged" captives to adopt captor culture. Captives might actively embrace assimilation because of a psychological longing to be an accepted part of the community in which they found themselves and because cooperation meant survival as well as an improved or at least more comfortable social position. Highly marginalized captives could be prevented from full participation in the practices of captor society. But even captives who were integrated as kin, regardless of how well integrated they might appear, often remained somewhat marginal people with an incentive to "prove" their allegiance to the society in which they lived. In some cases, it is evident that captives who chose not to cooperate in their own assimilation did not survive.

Captors had the means to compel desired behavior from their captives, but a captive's performance of the behavior could be accomplished with a range of effort and a variety of attitudes (see Scott's [1990] "hidden transcripts," chapters 3 and 6). DeBoer (2008, 247–49) provides a number of examples from ethnohistoric accounts in North and South America of captives who made concerted efforts to replicate or promote captor culture, including daughters of captives who rigidly followed captor pottery styles, male captives who became warriors and fought against the society of their birth, and a captive who became a vocal booster of his captor's culture, even returning home to promote change in his natal society (see also Lathrap 1970, 182). Similarly, on the Northwest Coast, McIlwraith (1948, 633, cited in Donald 1997, 84) reports "a slave [among the Nuxalk tribe] completely assimilates attitudes and values of his owner's group and becomes very upset when visitors ignore local customs."

Yet in a study of slavery among indigenous people of tropical America, Santos-Granero (2009, 220, contesting arguments that slavery did not exist there because captives were well treated) observes that captives were treated well only when they complied unhesitatingly with their masters' wishes (see also Richter 1983, 533, for a similar observation in the Northeast). The following examples illustrate these contrasting motivations for captives' careful performance of captor social practices. Captive cooperation should not be conceived of as either voluntary or coerced, however, as it was almost certainly a product of the pressures of captors and the calculations of captives regarding which behaviors would promote survival and open a more comfortable social space for them in captor society.

Efforts to see "agency" in the actions of captives and slaves high-light some of the motivations for careful adherence to captor social norms. Miller (2007, 21), in the introduction to an edited volume on women and slavery in Africa and the Indian Ocean, sees such accom-modation to captor cultural practices as a strategy by women slaves for creating relatively protected spaces for themselves and their chil-dren within captor society. In the same volume, Campbell (2007) finds that women slaves in nineteenth-century Madagascar, rather than re-belling, attempted to forge links with their masters by acquiring their language and religion and passing on local belief and value systems to their own children (see also Campbell and Alpers 2005). These ef-forts would "ameliorate their working and living conditions and el-evate their status and that of their offspring" (Campbell 2007, 251).

Captive narratives offer another view of the reasons that captives might adopt, enforce, and promote social boundaries in captor society. In some cases, motivations take on the appearance of a "Stockholm syndrome," in which victims of capture identify strongly with their captors. McDougall (1998) recounts the life Fatma Barka, who, in the early twentieth century, became the slave and then the concubine of a wealthy merchant, Mohamed Barka, in North Africa. In telling an interviewer the story of her life, Fatma emphasized her strong connec-tion with the Barka family, saying that she was not a daughter—she had been purchased—yet that she was "mother" to the Barkas even though she had had no children with her master. Her relationship with the family continued long after she gained freedom. In the Americas, numerous captive narratives report Euro-American captives, often women, taken by indigenous Americans who seemed to be complete-ly integrated into the society of their captors and who refused to be "redeemed" when found by their natal families (Demos 1994; Ramsey 1990, 86–93). Some of these captives reported kind treatment by their captors and love for their indigenous husbands and mixed children as reasons for refusing to go "home." But as Brooks (2008) observes, the physical markings captives may have received, as well as the evi-dence of miscegenation that their children represented, made captives well aware that reintegration into natal societies would be difficult or impossible (see Biocca [1965] 1996 for a particularly poignant example, discussed in chapter 3). Furthermore, captive narratives represent "public transcripts" produced for the dominant culture and may inaccurately deny captive resistance or contestation of captor culture.

The contrasting influences of coercion and agency on captive assimilation are especially well illustrated in historic accounts of Iroquoian groups in the American Northeast, where war captives were extremely common, sometimes outnumbering the native-born. Scholars emphasize that captives could become fully functioning or even prominent members of Iroquoian society but at the same time remained in a precarious social location. The captives' own efforts to adopt captor culture and please their captors partly determined the completeness of their incorporation. Endemic warfare among Iroquoian groups existed long before the arrival of Europeans, but by the mid-seventeenth century the scale of warfare had increased dramatically and "mourning wars" became, at least in part, a means to replace people lost in epidemics or warfare (figure 8; Fox 2009; Richter 1983). The Iroquois believed that despair over a relative's death could make survivors mentally unstable and that warfare channeled grief in productive ways (Richter 1983, 531). By the late seventeenth century, warfare and captive taking had created a dramatic population turnover in Iroquois villages, with estimates of foreigner captives as high as two-thirds of the population (Richter1983, 541; see also Fox 2009, 66), evidence that captives were effectively trained into the practices of Iroquois society.

There is good evidence that captives participated fully in Iroquois culture. Young men might go to war against the society of their birth (Trigger 1969, 49) and they might become important leaders of their adopted village (Starna and Watkins 1991, 42). Women could be considered full sisters in their adopted family or even become head of their matrilineal lineage (Lafitau [1724] 1977, 171–72, cited in Donald 1997, 263; Trigger 1976, 831). But Starna and Watkins (1991) argue that captives actually lived more marginal lives than many Iroquois scholars acknowledge. They provide evidence from sixteenth-century Jesuit accounts that captives often escaped, that initial torture ceremonies (including cutting off fingers) left captives with permanent markers

8. Native American prisoner halter from the south Lake Erie region, late eighteenth century. The band encircled the prisoner's neck and was fitted with two long ropes by which the slave could be held. As with most such objects, it was made by a woman for a warrior in her community. "By looping an end so one rein could pass through it, she created a human choke collar that would fit across the throat and tighten if the slave tried to pull away" (Rushforth 2012:3). Courtesy the Colonial Williamsburg Foundation, Museum purchase, acc. no. 1996-816.

of a slave-like status, that captives could be sold or exchanged, and that captives, even after adoption, could be forced to undertake menial and degrading tasks not performed by "free" Iroquois (Starna and Watkins 1991, 42–50). Evidence shows that captives, even after many years in Iroquois society, remained subject to the ultimate sanction of death (Starna and Watkins 1991, 43).

It appears that captives among the Iroquois had some control over their social marginalization and that those who were most assiduous in their efforts to mimic captor culture became the most completely integrated. Richter (unpublished, cited in Starna and Watkins 1991, 42) has argued that individuals who appeared to function as slaves in Iroquois society were undergoing a probationary period during which they were assigned the most menial tasks in an effort to get them to imitate the ways of their captors. Captives who made an effort to please their new relatives could live long lives; those who did not were quietly killed (Richter 1983, 533). In other words, the social sanctions imposed on captives and the response of individual captives to those sanctions helped fix the social boundaries of the society.

This section and the previous one illustrate how captives and their captors engaged daily in practices that defined and strengthened the social boundaries of captor society. Captives could exemplify behavior antithetical to group norms or could (to the extent they were permitted) embrace and replicate group practices. Even where captives joined multicultural societies, strong social boundaries could be maintained by either excluding captives from membership in the dominant group or training them to become proficient group members. Captives had the option to comply eagerly or resist their assimilation. This section does not discuss those captives who resisted assimilation or who covertly maintained natal practices. Captives who actively resisted assimilation may have had short lives. Captives' attempts (whether covert or not) to continue natal practices are explored in chapter 6; captives not only brought with them practices that transformed captor society but may also have weakened or transformed captor ethnic boundaries in the process.

Captives as Social Nodes in Multiethnic Societies

Captives not only helped maintain ethnic boundaries but at a macro scale also functioned as social nodes that linked together alternatively peaceful and aggressive groups. This was especially true in areas where raiding and captive taking were elements of social relations that might also involve trading, noncoerced marriage, and other peaceful social interactions. Beckerman (2008, viii, following Verdier 1981), in a discussion of revenge taking in the Amazon, finds that the most aggressive type of warfare exists between the most socially distant groups. But groups at intermediate distance, who may be considered "in-laws," might engage in marriage as well as capturing women, and relations are always tenuous and contested. It is in these societies that women could be most effective as social intermediaries, as the three examples below from the New World illustrate. Transporting captive women over long distances greatly reduced their chances of continuing links with their natal society.

Scholars increasingly acknowledge that kinship is often a more important structuring principle than ethnic group membership for many small-scale societies and can result in multiethnic communities: "The social relations which linked tribes together were based primarily on ties of kinship and sodality. On the plains, as in other areas of North America . . . relationships did not exist on a random basis among anonymous social parties; they were always embedded in some kind of social nexus. Kinship was one of the constituting idioms through which multiple tribal groups were connected in wider, regional social formations" (Albers 1993, 98).

Captives typically occupy social locations that are either outside of captor kinship networks or marginally located in those networks, but nonetheless, their natal kin or their captors might use the captive to establish nonaggressive social relations between the two groups. In contrast to traditional conceptions of historic Plains tribes as distinct and bounded ethnic groups (Cheyennes, Crows, Kiowas, Blackfeet), social formations on the Great Plains actually consisted of multiethnic, overlapping regional groups created through processes of accommodation involving war, trade, intermarriage, adoption, and captive taking (Albers 1993, 1996). Hostile relations among tribes ensured the circulation of many captives; captive women and children could be items of trade, they could be retained to increase group numbers, and they could be used for their labor. Despite the violence surrounding their capture, captives often served as nodes for developing peaceful relationships between enemy groups that included visits from their natal family, gift giving, and trade (Albers 1993, 128). In other words, captives provided an opportunity for a variety of types of interactions among groups who might otherwise be at war, opening avenues for cooperation advantageous to both groups. Common interests produced different degrees of merger among Plains groups and in some cases the formation of neoteric groups (Albers 1996).

In Amazonia, social formations described as "tribes" or "language groups" have boundaries that are constantly crossed by captive women or formally obtained wives (Chernela 1992; see also Chernela 2003). Captive women create links between language groups: "In the highly common practice of mutual raiding, the roles of captive and captor alternate. The result over time is a residential unit with foreign captive women that . . . is thoroughly enmeshed in kin networks of both captives and captors" (Chernela 2011, 196). In short, interactions between captive-taking and captive-giving societies in Amazonia are structured through the idiom of kinship, focused on the captive, and result in "a multiethnic, cosmopolitan, society" (Chernela 2011).

James Brooks's (2002) *Captives and Cousins: Slavery, Kinship, and Community in the Southwest Borderlands* provides perhaps the most comprehensive description of the role of captives as key social nodes in the creation of multiethnic societies (see also Brooks 1998, 2000, 2009). In the post–Columbian Southwest Borderlands, women and children were violently wrenched from their homes during raids and warfare, but once incorporated into captor society, these same women served as (often multilingual) links among groups and opened opportunities for more peaceful interaction (for the contributions of such captives, see chapter 6). Spanish, Navajo, Comanche, Pueblo, and Ute communities all included people who originated in other cultures. Brooks provides rich examples from the historic record of captive women who maintained or reestablished ties with their natal groups and acted as intermediaries between natal and captor groups. As they were sold or traded, they could accumulate multiple languages and relationships that could be parlayed by the captive or employed by her captors to further economic, political, or social goals. Relations among the Southwest's indigenous inhabitants changed dramatically after European intrusion, but practices of captive taking existed among Southwest groups long before Europeans arrived, and pre-Columbian societies were likely similarly multiethnic.

Captives and the Process of Social Creation

Captives not only helped fix ethnic boundaries and served as social nodes for peaceful interactions between antagonistic groups, they also became key actors in restructuring or creating new social formations when old formations were disrupted or demolished. They could be involved in more routine processes of social construction as well, although it might be argued that violence and domination is never far from situations where new social formations develop. Ethnogenesis refers to the creation of novel or "neoteric" identities and is defined as "the general process by which members of a population form a shared meaning system and a related social order that transform them into a new, identifiable culture group" (Fennell 2007, 2). Some scholars describe ethnogenesis more explicitly as a form of subordinate resistance, a creative adaptation to violent change. In a study of colonial intrusion into the Americas, Jonathan D. Hill (1996b, 1) sees ethnogenesis as the result of "demographic collapse, forced relocations, enslavement, ethnic soldiering, ethnocide, and genocide." Voss (2008a, 35–36), in contrast, argues that ethnogenesis should also be conceptualized a means of asserting power and consolidating institutions of domination. In either situation, captives could be social actors.

A related concept, "coalescence," refers to the coming together of remnant groups into new social formations; the term "coalescent society" has been applied to the groups (including the Creeks, Choctaws, and Cherokees) that formed in the Southeast in the wake of severe population loss and social disruption resulting from European contact (Ethridge and Hudson 2002). Kowalewski (2006) explores the concept of the coalescent society for both prehistoric and postcontact societies and finds coalescence a common response to warfare and demographic decline or stasis. It involves the movement of refugees and other population remnants, abandonment of large tracks of land, and often the creation of larger towns or villages. Many of these responses have archaeological indicators (J. Brett Hill et al. 2004, 700–701), and coalescence is evident prehistorically in the American Plains and Southwest and in Mesoamerica (Kowalewski 2006). Coalescent groups often adopted the name and practices of a dominant or "host" group but also created new political institutions and ideologies that allowed the integration of disparate groups—pursuits that might otherwise be called ethnogenesis (Kowalewski 2006, 95).

The historically documented disruptions caused by the collision of European and indigenous societies gives us the best view of the role of captives in these processes of social creation. The problem for archaeologists is determining the extent to which postcontact changes provide useful analogies for precontact developments. Sidbury and Cañizares-Esguerra (2011, 182; see also critiques of the article in the same issue) argue that processes of ethnogenesis after contact were similar around the Atlantic world and urge scholars to "move beyond the labels that separate interpretations of the creole cultures of African-Americans, the hybrid cultures of Europeans, and the tribal cultures of Native Americans" and to explore the common processes that linked these groups. Although Sidbury and Cañizares-Esguerra (2011) do not apply their ideas to prehistoric periods, Kowalewski (2006) comfortably discusses common prehistoric and postcontact processes of coalescence. The cases presented below provide a starting place for exploring the role of captives in processes of ethnogenesis and coalescence in the past.

The importance of captives in ethnogenesis is most evident in the remarkable process of social creation that resulted in maroon societies composed of runaway slaves. Examples from the Caribbean show how a common history and common social practices developed among people with diverse ethnic origins. Seemingly more routine processes of cultural construction are found in Africa and in the creation of the Navajos in the American Southwest, although here, too, violence and captive taking lurk in the background. In the Southeast region of North America, extraordinary postcontact population decline and widespread slave raiding resulted in the virtual extinction of many chiefly societies, with remnant populations "coalescing" with more powerful survivors as subaltern members or virtual servant groups. In a perhaps more egalitarian process, the Quebec settlement of Kahnawake was formed during the seventeenth century by persons, including many former captives, displaced by violent warfare. Eventually the settlement took on the ethnic identity of its most common members, the Mohawks.

MAROON COMMUNITIES

In the violence of colonial encounters and the African slave trade, maroon communities in the New World, formed of escaped slaves, offer a fascinating view of the process of ethnogenesis directly undertaken by former captives (Jonathan D. Hill 1996a; R. Price [1973] 1996). Ethnogenesis among the Windward Maroons of Jamaica and the Aluku (Boni) of French Guiana and Surinam provides an example that explores both commonalities and differences in the process of ethnic creation (Bilby 1996). Both groups were formed in the seventeenth and eighteenth centuries of captives from diverse African origins who had survived transatlantic voyages, as well as creoles who had been born in the New World. Varying environmental and social factors resulted in somewhat different ethnic outcomes for each group, but commonalities are evident in the process by which individuals, who potentially had only violent capture and enslavement in common, established new ethnic identities. Both groups resulted from large-scale, global processes of colonization, capitalization, warfare, and slave raiding, and both created ethnic identities rooted in strongly held concepts of shared history and tradition.

The creation of the novel social identities represented by these two groups began with both biological and social reproduction (Bilby 1996). Military leaders who coordinated initial efforts to achieve freedom became important historical characters in maroon history. In addition, the original escaped female slaves played a crucial role in creating kin groups that eventually became the ancestral anchors that allowed maroons to see themselves as a large clan-like family related through descent from a common female ancestor. Birth into these ethnically defined social groups conferred community membership, including rights over land and resources and participation in traditional religion. Both the Windward Maroons of Jamaica and the Aluku of French Guiana and Surinam are well aware that their history extends back no more than 350 years, yet the ethnic identities of these two peoples are "profoundly rooted in the same sorts of seemingly primordial ties and sentiments that lend ethnic identities their affective power elsewhere in the world" (Bilby 1996, 137).

THE NAVAJOS

As with the Caribbean maroons, captive women were involved in the creation of the Navajos in the American Southwest. This example of ethnic emergence likely originated in violence. As reconstructed by archaeologist Richard Wilshusen (2010), migrations of Athapaskan peoples from far to the north along what is now the U.S.-Canadian border just prior to the entry of Europeans into the New World set in motion the process of Navajo ethnogenesis. Wilshusen (2010) uses linguistic data, early historic documents, Navajo oral traditions, and archaeological evidence to argue against scholars who assume that the Navajos arrived in the Southwest as an identifiable social group. Instead, he sees their emergence in the mid-seventeenth century as partly the result of adaptive responses to neighboring Pueblo and Spanish societies. Most interesting for the present study, Wilshusen (2010, 201) interprets the Navajo origin account called "the Gathering of the Clans" as indicating that some of the latest of these matrilineal clans to emerge to form the Navajos were the offspring of captives taken during warfare and taught to live like proper Navajos (see also Brooks 2002, 86–87). Alien women from Pueblo villages may not have experienced significant stigma during a time of fluid and ambiguous identities that must have characterized Navajo emergence. As in maroon communities of the Caribbean, these women seem to have played key roles as ancestral anchors for social groups that were developing a common history and shared identity.

AFRICA

In Africa, social creation was part of the usual development of social groups that routinely crumbled and re-formed (Kopytoff 1987; Stahl 1991). The intensity of the African slave trade means that violence must have been a common subtext to these processes. Kopytoff's (1987) now classic "internal African frontier" model for the development of African social groups sees ethnogenesis as a normal process of social creation in which slaves were subordinate actors. Rather than unitary groups with lengthy histories (partly a creation of European colonial administrators), most African "tribes" were composed of people with ancestors from multiple, diverse backgrounds. Like clouds, social formations in Africa constantly broke apart and re-formed (Kopytoff 1987, 11–12). A kin segment that struck out for the "frontier" gathered together not only other tribal members but also as many strangers and slaves as possible (Kopytoff 1987, 47). Strangers and slaves were the ancestral anchors for junior lineages that had far less power than the "first-comers" in the group.

Stahl's (1991, 2001) study of the Nafana in the Banda region of West Africa provides a microscale example of Kopytoff's model. West Africa underwent enormous cultural transformations as a result of the depredations of the slave trade (DeCorse 2001; Diouf 2003; Law 2004; Lovejoy [1983] 2000), and the process of ethnic transformation there resulted at least in part from the repositioning of remnant populations. Oral traditions of lineages, including lineages with captive or slave ancestors, show the diverse origins of the Nafana ethnic group. Banda is a "frontier society" located between forest and savannah, a place strategically located with regard to trade routes that is, as a result, ethnically and linguistically diverse. The Nafana expanded by assimilating people from other groups, at least some of whom were captives (Stahl 1991, 266; 2001, 44). The absorption of many people from diverse origins significantly affected marriage and funerary rites, propitiation rites related to a newly introduced yam festival, and guardianship roles for the land. While the proportion of captives who joined Nafana society is uncertain, they nevertheless are likely to have been involved in the transformation of Nafana culture. Furthermore, the "fluidity" in social boundaries evident over the past two hundred years in Banda likely characterized much more remote times in this region, as well as in other parts of West Africa (Stahl 1991, 268).

Coalescence involves creative adaptation to violent change. In times of severe social disruption, "coalescent" groups formed that included captives, refugees, and remnant populations that developed new social practices to allow disparate groups to live together. In some cases, these groups took on the attributes (name, language, cultural practices) of one of the merging groups and often created a hierarchy, with some elements claiming higher status and forcing others into secondary or subaltern status.

THE SOUTHEAST

The intrusion of Europeans into the American Southeast devastated indigenous cultures and created a "shatter zone" of fragmentary or reconstituted social groups as a result of epidemics, wars, enslavement, and the subsequent disintegration of indigenous political systems (Ethridge and Shuck-Hall 2009). Demographic collapse throughout North America after contact was stark (Cameron, Kelton, and Swedlund 2015) and especially pronounced in the Southeast, where a large and well-organized population existed before contact. A late seventeenth-century population estimated at almost two hundred thousand dropped by more than 50 percent in only thirty years partly because the European demand for labor and land instigated violent indigenous warfare and slave trading (Gallay 2002, 294–302; Wood 1989, 38–39). One response to living in the shatter zone was coalescence: "two or more relocated chiefdoms or splinter groups joined together into a new social formation that did not necessarily resemble preexisting chiefdoms" (Ethridge 2009, 38). Coalescent societies that developed during the colonial era in the Southeast included the Yamasees, Creeks, Catawbas, Chickasaws, Choctaws, and Caddos (Ethridge 2009, 38; for the Catawbas, see Beck 2009; Fitts and Heath 2009; for the Westos, see Bowne 2005, 2009; Meyers 2009; for the Seminoles, see Sattler 1996; for the Creeks, see Saunt 1999; see also articles in Gallay 2009; Snyder 2010).

Native Americans in the Southeast used captivity as a framework for incorporating entire groups of people, usually at the lowest levels of their society: "nations absorbed formerly independent polities just as lineages adopted formerly unrelated individuals" (Snyder 2010, 114). Some tribes became dominant through the absorption of broken groups (Snyder 2010, 114–22). The Creeks emerged in the Deep South after European diseases decimated the population and local chiefdoms collapsed (Saunt 1999, 18–19). People of diverse ethnicities who had fled warfare and destruction populated the newly formed

Creek towns (Snyder 2010, 114). The Natchez, after initially incorporating other groups in subservient positions, themselves became refugees after a devastating war in the early 1730s; these refugees became
slaves of the Chickasaws (Snyder 2010, 117–18). Although host groups
might call the weaker groups or refugees who joined them "worth-
less," "homeless," or "slave people" (Snyder 2010, 120), incorporation
of these troubled people was based on the concept that human identity was mutable and that foreigners could be transformed or "trained"
in new social practices (Snyder 2010, 126).

KAHNAWAKE—COMMUNITY OF REFUGEES

Somewhat intermediate between maroon communities of the Caribbean and coalescent communities of the Southeast, the settlement
of Kahnawake formed in seventeenth-century Quebec largely by displaced persons and former captives from different tribes. It was established by a Jesuit priest in 1667 and initially settled by French colonists
and a small number of Oneidas and members of other tribes after decades of devastating intertribal and intercolonial warfare involving the
French, English, and Native Americans (Demos 1994, 123). The settlement grew quickly and within a dozen years contained over six hundred people (Demos 1994, 127). Many of the settlers were refugees from
Mohawk villages in New York that had been destroyed by the French,
but many others had been captives among various Iroquois tribes.

An eyewitness said of the population of Kahnawake: "They . . . are
all coming from different Iroquois nations and are either natives of
that country or dwellers there as prisoners" (Demos 1994, 124). These
"marginal people" and "human flotsam" were the type most likely to
found a new settlement (Demos 1994, 124). The population also contained a number of Europeans who had been captured by the Iroquois and other groups, some of whom lived out the rest of their lives
at Kahnawake and adopted an indigenous identity (one such woman,
Eunice Williams, is the focus of Demos's [1994] study). The presence
of Jesuit priests provided a religious framework for the organization
of the settlement, but the disparate population must have struggled,
at least at the beginning, to develop a common social framework.

Interestingly, although the founding population was diverse, the community took on a Mohawk social identity and continues to identify as Mohawk today.

These case studies demonstrate the presence of captives at times and places where new ethnic groups were created or existing groups transformed. As the examples illustrate, captives could be members of remnant groups, they could be displaced persons who had escaped their captors or been "liberated" by the vagaries of war, or they could have been purchased or stolen to build the population of a newly developed social group. Captives should not necessarily be conceived of as distinct actors in processes of social creation, however. "Captive" is a transitory social role in which the captive, if spared death, is integrated into captor society in one of an array of social positions (see chapter 3). In transformed or new social formations, captive origins could be forgotten, distantly remembered, or used to create a hierarchy with captives and their descendants at the lowest levels of society. In other words, captives were individuals, like multiple others, who came together in a variety of ways to form new social groups. As demonstrated here, the fact that they had been taken violently and unwillingly from a natal society had a range of effects on their contribution to the creation of new societies.

Captives were involved in both the maintenance and creation of social boundaries. In daily interactions with their captors they could serve as social opposites, allowing captors to continually judge their social performance against that of marginalized people who originated in other social groups. When captives were permitted to copy captor social practices, they might become especially assiduous in their performances in an effort to curry favor with their captors and gain a somewhat better social standing for themselves. Captives might serve as nodes for social interaction that cut across ethnic boundaries, providing opportunities for both peaceful and violent encounters. The cross-cultural examples above suggest that these processes are common to small-scale societies in many parts of the world and likely occurred in the ancient societies studied by archaeologists.

In times of social disruption and population displacement, captives could become involved in processes of ethnogenesis or the formation of coalescent societies. The examples discussed here are largely postcontact, but they provide useful models for exploring the role of captives in cultural change in the precontact past. Ethnogenesis and coalescence almost certainly occurred in many parts of the world during pre-Columbian times, especially where warfare and captive taking decimated demographically small ethnic groups and created remnant populations.

| Chapter Six

Captives and Cultural Transmission

A substantial lacuna in archaeology surrounds the mechanisms by which cultural practices were transmitted between social groups. Archaeologists, at least those who study prehistory, have created largely broad-brush models of intercultural interaction that reference trade or migration. Studies of trade and exchange tend to focus on economic interactions between societies (however, see Bauer and Agbe-Davies 2010 for a new perspective) and method and theory in migration studies are just now beginning to explore the outcome of migration in destination areas (e.g., Clark 2001; Ortman and Cameron 2011; Stone 2003). Archaeologists have yet to develop detailed understandings of the ways that cultural practices were transmitted between groups and then adapted to a new social setting (see Kristiansen and Larsson 2005, 4–61, for a critique; see also Cameron 2011). This chapter explores the role of captives in cultural transmission. I argue that these marginalized people were one way in which cultural practices were transferred between groups. Captives, unwillingly or willingly, joined communities of practice in captor society, and their daily work could, in some cases, have long-term effects on the cultural practices of captor societies. Not only might captives bring with them new ways of doing, they could also affect processes of learning in existing communities of practice.

The chapter begins with a brief look at contemporary approaches to the study of cultural transmission, specifically intercultural interaction, and the need to evaluate factors surrounding the acceptance or rejection of novel cultural practices. It then evaluates the role captives may have played within frameworks of teaching and learning in captor society. We must rethink our assumption that craft learning was always warmly imparted from fond parent or trusted relative to receptive child. Instead, we should evaluate how knowledge might have been imparted to a low-status captive, the motivation of the captive to reproduce goods exactly as she is taught, and opportunities the captive might have to introduce new cultural practices. As social others, captives could form a unique part of learning frameworks (figure 9). The next section uses captive narratives to show that small-scale societies were often highly receptive to knowledge brought by outsiders. Even as captives were abused and humiliated, they were actively mined for useful knowledge and abilities. Finally, ethnohistoric and historic examples demonstrate that cultural practices, including craft skills, foodways, and religious practices, *were* moved from group to group through the agency of captives. There is no doubt that captives acted as a powerful avenue of cultural transmission.

Intercultural Interaction and Cultural Transmission

Cultural transmission has always been a central interest of archaeologists, even though the mechanics of this process were not explicitly examined until late in the twentieth century. Four recent edited volumes (O'Brien 2008; O'Brien and Shennan 2010; Shennan 2009; Stark, Bowser, and Horne 2008) and a number of articles signal strong current interest in the topic (O'Brien et al. 2014; Premo 2014; Rorabaugh 2014). These are only the most recent manifestation of the need for archaeologists to understand how social practices are created, maintained, and transformed. Our fundamental units of investigation are the people who operated within and between archaeologically constructed social boundaries; knowledge of how culture is transmitted, whether between generations or between groups, is central to our investigation of the past.

9. *Mujer conibo pintado ceramios* (Conibo woman painting pottery). Illustration by Paul Marcoy, who traveled through South America during the mid-1840s and illustrated what he observed. From Marcoy, *Viaje a través de América del Sur* (Lima: Instituto Francés de Estudios Andinos, 1875), 218.

Nineteenth-century anthropological pioneers recognized three mechanisms by which cultural practices were passed from generation to generation or were transferred between groups: (1) within groups through teaching and learning—in other words, through encultura-tion, the intergenerational transmission of group culture; (2) through trade or exchange with other groups that allowed the "diffusion" of cultural practices; and (3) through the migration of people into a new region (Lyman 2008, 10–11). For these early anthropologists and throughout much of the twentieth century, the fact of cultural trans-mission was simply assumed and there was no attempt to determine the mechanisms by which traits passed, the barriers to cultural trans-mission, or the most effective social pathways for transmitting cultural information. While archaeologists now have a far more sophisticated understanding of cultural transmission, research continues to follow these same three mechanisms (Lyman 2008, 11; O'Brien et al. 2008).

Processual and then postprocessual archaeology, both of which fo-cus on local developments within specific regions, swept away early efforts to examine and model processes of "diffusion" and migration (Kristiansen and Larsson 2005, 4–7). With few exceptions, intercultural interaction became the domain of studies of trade and exchange, with a strong focus on economic models for explaining how societies interacted with one another (although Agbe-Davies and Bauer [2010] have recently asked archaeologists to begin a reconsideration of trade as a social activity). Other modes of intercultural transmission were rarely examined. Ethnoarchaeological studies of craft production, especially the vast literature on ceramic ethnoarchaeology, should have alerted us to the complexity of processes of intercultural transmission. As Frank (1993, 387–88) observes concerning pottery production in Mali, "although tools and materials may appear to be rudimentary, the technical knowledge required to successfully form and fire is anything but simple. It is not a craft that someone could simply take up upon seeing a skilled potter work, much less upon being presented with the finished product."

Until recently, archaeologists (except historical archaeologists) have expended little effort to understand the mechanisms by which cultural practices are transmitted between cultures. Kristiansen and Larsson (2005) urge archaeologists to go beyond the spatial exploration of the "diffusion" of cultural "traits" to understand how cultural practices were accepted, recontextualized, and given meaning in the societies where they were introduced. They ask archaeologists to "attempt to trace the socially and culturally determined motives and incentives for individuals to travel and to adopt new values and behaviors. And in similar ways: the motives and incentives to resist change. As such social changes are played out by people, we need to identify those groups who had the capacity to adopt or to resist new values and behaviors" (Kristiansen and Larsson 2005, 14–15).

Of the three subfields of archaeology in which models of cultural transmission have been developed—evolutionary archaeology, ethnoarchaeology, and historical archaeology—historical archaeology is the only one that makes intercultural interaction a major focus (Mills 2008).[1] Ethnoarchaeologists, especially ceramic ethnoarchaeologists, have made detailed studies of how technological practices are transmitted between generations (as have evolutionary archaeologists, who are not discussed further here). Their studies are often framed within learning theory and use the concepts of "situated learning" and "communities of practice." As discussed below, we gain a great deal by considering how captives might have acted within their captors' communities of practice. Still, problems exist in the contrast between the short timescale represented by ethnoarchaeological studies and the long histories of cultural change that prehistoric archaeologists hope to understand (Mills 2008, 250).

Network analysis, a relatively new field of study (at least in archaeology), is also making contributions to our understanding of the transmission of cultural practices among social groups. Network analysis in archaeology focuses on relationships among entities in the past, including individuals, groups, and material culture (Collar et al. 2015, 10). Network models are criticized for ignoring individual decision making, but this is not always the case (Collar et al. 2015, 11–12). For example, a recent study of the development of Roosevelt Redware pottery during the thirteenth century in the American Southwest explores the identity and relationship of people who initially designed this style of pottery and those who first adopted it (Mills and Peeples, forthcoming). Of interest for the present study, the status of innovators and early adopters, as well as the network they maintained, was key to the spread of this influential pottery type.

While network analysis is fairly new, historical archaeology in the Americas has a long history of detailed studies of the process of cultural transmission. Operating under the rubric of "culture contact," most work focuses on interactions between a dominant elite—colonizers—and subordinate groups that generally consisted of indigenous people or transplanted African slaves. Early concepts such as acculturation, which posited a unidirectional, "top-down" transmission of traits from colonizer to colonized, have been replaced by concepts such as transculturation, creolization, hybridity, and ethnogenesis. These new concepts emphasize the cultural and genetic exchanges that occurred among indigenous New World populations and European and African newcomers (Armstrong 1998; Bhabha 1990, 1994; Deagan 1998;

Sidbury and Cañizares-Esguerra 2011; Singleton 1998; Stein 2005b, 16–17; Trouillot 2002; Voss 2008b).

Most important for the current study is that historic archaeologists study the factors that *condition* the transmission of cultural practices from one group to another, evaluating the circumstances surrounding the acceptance of some practices and the rejection of others. New cultural practices are not automatically adopted by societies exposed to them and there may be a variety of social or economic reasons for acceptance, partial acceptance, or rejection of new practices, including the status of the individual or group introducing the practice. In a study of colonial-era cuisine among the Zunis of the American Southwest, Mills (2008, 246–52), like Kristiansen and Larsson (2005; and in contrast to the models of biased transmission proposed by evolutionary archaeologists), emphasizes the importance of social impediments to the transmission process: powerful colonists imposed some practices; indigenous people rejected other practices because of their association with the brutality of colonization. The numbers of colonists in a region and their spatial relationship to indigenous people also affected the adoption of European practices.

Other factors also affect the transmission of cultural practices. Deagan's (1974, 1983) groundbreaking work at the site of St. Augustine in La Florida shows the importance of gender and social status in the use of Spanish-influenced versus indigenous material culture. She argues that Spanish colonists were largely unmarried military men who brought a reduced, male-oriented set of Spanish cultural traits with them. These men married indigenous women, who continued to use indigenous material culture in low-visibility, female-associated activities involved in food preparation and other domestic activities. Meanwhile, Spanish-derived traits were retained in public, male-associated, socially visible activities such as house construction or in weaponry characteristics. In a strong critique, Voss (2008c) points out that indigenous and African women living in Spanish colonial households in Florida and elsewhere in the Americas were *not* often wives but more often slaves, concubines, and servants, and that local goods such as utility pottery may actually have arrived in Spanish colonial homes primarily through macroscale labor regimes and distribution systems rather than through the agency of indigenous wives.

Scholars are increasingly aware that colonial encounters created arenas in which indigenous people played active roles in directing culture change. For example, a study of clothing and related items found in the graves of Seneca people (an Iroquoian group of the Northeast) interred between the early seventeenth and early nineteenth centuries shows that Seneca women adopted some European materials and used them to elaborate existing traditional decorative techniques (Kane 2014). The use of European materials released Seneca women from the labor of producing plant-fiber cloth and freed them to expand on their traditional designs: "Seneca people used European materials to become more Iroquois" (Kane 2014, 19). Furthermore, indigenous preferences for particular materials and designs required textile workers in England to reorient the types of materials they produced.

Traditional practices of indigenous people could take on new meanings in the colonial world. Indigenous workers at Rancho Petaluma, a large Mexican land-grant ranch in northern California, used European metal tools for their ranch work, but in domestic contexts they continued to make and use the stone tools characteristic of the precolonial period (Silliman 2001). Much of the stone came from distant sources and was likely procured through an indigenous exchange system. Silliman (2001) argues that stone tools (as well as the social network through which raw material was acquired and the technology of production) were active materializations of the native identity of these ranch workers.

Captives typically enter captor society as low-status individuals and with, we might assume, limited opportunity to accept or reject cultural practices, except through "hidden" resistance (L. Ferguson 1991; Scott 1990). Roux (2010, 224) argues that innovations are made by experts in a particular practice who are knowledgeable enough to experiment with new ways of doing. Roux (2010, 226) also cites Mendras (1984), who found peasants of historical periods especially resistant to change and determined that most innovations were made by the elite. But as described below, in small-scale societies captives were actively mined for any useful cultural practices they might

know. The possibility that productive industries in the state-level societies described by Roux were less open to innovation by social others than those in small-scale societies remains open to investigation.
Furthermore, the idea that elites are innovators has limited utility for
small-scale societies, in which elites often do not engage in productive activity (except social management) or work alongside their subordinate coresidents. In contrast to the tradition-bound peasants that
Mendras (1984) describes, captives would not be weighted down with
conventional ideas about how things should be done. Captives may
have been explicitly excluded from high-value captor practices, such as
religious observances or certain foodways, but captors had the option
of accepting or rejecting the cultural practices captives brought with
them. The next section explores the captive's role in communities of
practice in captor society and the factors that may have conditioned
the acceptance or rejection of captive-introduced cultural practices.

Situated Learning and the Captive

Captives entering captor societies were instantly immersed in a field
of social and economic activities that might be only minimally familiar, and their survival often depended on active and rapid learning
of their captors' cultural practices. In other words, the process of social learning for the captive, in contrast to that of most social learners, was usually one of coercion and could involve verbal or physical
abuse. The ability of captives to transmit cultural practices from their
natal society to that of their captors requires an understanding of how
they fit into captor learning frameworks. Because captives were generally marginal members of captor society, there is little documenta-
tion of their role in social learning. This section uses social learning
theory to explore how captives not only were incorporated into captor learning frameworks but may have affected learning in ways that
resulted in changes to captor culture.

Social learning is a topic of current interest for archaeologists and
anthropologists. There is widespread agreement that learning is situated in social contexts and that social actors, rather than simply
reproducing the behavior of generations above them (as traditional

anthropological theory assumed), constantly adjust their behavior in response to the social cues emanating from others around them, a process called "situated learning." A key concept in this theoretical approach is "communities of practice." A community of practice is a group of people who share a common interest in a particular activity or subject and who interact and share strategies, solutions, and innovations over an extended period of time (Lave and Wenger 1991; Wenger 1998). In communities of practice, learning is not just the rote transmission of information between individuals; instead, learners are motivated to achieve competency in a cultural practice as a way of signaling their membership in the group (Bowser and Patton 2008, 108). Gosselain (2008, 154) criticizes the emphasis by both evolutionary archaeologists and ethnoarchaeologists on *transmission* of cultural elements over acquisition and practice. He emphasizes the closely intertwined relationship between learning and practice. Individuals never cease learning as they engage in a particular practice, and both learning and practice contribute to the construction of the self.

Lave and Wenger (1991) describe learners as "legitimate peripheral participants," or newcomers to the group who initially occupy marginal positions and with time, practice, and involvement eventually gain competency and full group membership. Yet they identify a contradiction between the intergenerational continuity suggested by the communities of practice concept and the "displacement" that results as old practitioners are replaced by new ones. The dynamic tension newcomers create as they establish their own identities through practice is what causes change in cultural practices (Bowser and Patton 2008, 108). I suggest that the dynamic tension captives create affects captor communities of practice in ways that archaeologists should acknowledge in their studies of situated learning.

For most scholars studying communities of practice, legitimate peripheral participants are the young following a developmental cycle within communities of practice, moving through competency and eventually reaching senior group membership with specialized historical knowledge. As argued below, however, captives may be especially peripheral and may always be limited in their ability to become

full group members because they may be older when they join captor communities of practice and because, as outsiders, they create an
exceptionally potent dynamic tension.

Ethnoarchaeological studies of pottery production emphasize that
learning most often occurs between parent and child in traditional
potting communities, although the relationship between student and
teacher can be variable (Mills 2008, 250; Minar and Crown 2001; but
see Gosselain 2008, 151). Gosselain's (2008, 161) study of pottery production in Niger highlights the close relationship between student
and teacher, emphasizing that psychological closeness could be more
important than kin relations (see also Minar and Crown 2001). How
might a captive fit into this cozy picture of social learning? Wenger
(1998, 100–101) believes that newcomers must have some level of legit-
imacy and acceptance for learning to occur. Is this true for a despised
captive? How might our ideas about situated learning change if it is
reconceived as forced or coerced? Will captives be motivated to mimic exactly captor cultural practices in order to "fit in" and perhaps win
their captor's good opinion? Or at least avoid disapproval, censure, or
punishment? Or might they have more latitude for social expression?

Captives entering captor communities of practice are not only producers of captor material culture, they are actively involved in the
process of acquiring a new social identity and becoming "rehuman-
ized" in captor society. Gosselain (2011) argues that rather than experience an unbearable "social limbo" if they refuse to adopt the cultural
practices of their captors, captives would likely choose to acquire a
new social identity through active participation in group practices.
Evidence from Amazonia adds ethnographic breadth to Gosselain's
observations. Among the Conibo some captive women incorporated as wives became slavish reproducers of Conibo pottery designs
because their marginal position allowed them little latitude to challenge established conventions and introduce natal practices or their
own novel interpretations (DeBoer 1986, 238; 1990, 2011). Yet Bowser
(2008) challenges the idea that Amazonian captives would completely abandon the practices of pottery production they learned in the societies of their birth. She argues that captives would likely continue

to reproduce less obvious characteristics of pottery, for example, by using different technological steps or design styles (see also Cameron 1998, 2011; Carr 1995, 195–98; Clark 2001, 12–13; Duff 2002; Stark 1998).

The pressure on captives toward conformity may be like that on a young wife in a patrilineal society where, upon marriage, she must move to a distant and different community and learn the ways of her in-laws. Among the Luo of western Kenya, women learn pottery making from their mothers-in-law and in the style of the husband's local group (Herbich and Dietler 2008). Not unlike captives, young wives there (typically under age sixteen) go through a process of resocialization that requires them to unlearn practices from their childhood home and substitute local practices—recipes, plant knowledge, agricultural practices, rituals, styles, and so on (Herbich and Dietler 2008, 233). A young girl will not be taught pottery production prior to marriage but will learn from her mother-in-law or the senior co-wife. Yet learning pottery production is a life-long social process heavily influenced by interactions (both positive and negative) among the potter and her friends, co-wives, and others. These interactions result in stylistic differences in pottery that are not simply the results of one-on-one training (Herbich and Dietler 2008, 234). Nonetheless, local microstyles of pottery are routinely reproduced by women who came from outside the community in which they work.

If captives are always actively resocialized in captor society we should expect them rarely or never to have introduced new cultural practices, yet the examples that follow provide strong evidence that they did. To understand the role that captives might have played in cultural transmission, we need to recognize and explore the myriad of factors that affect the acceptance or rejection of novel practices. Such work already has been undertaken in ethnoarchaeology and culture contact studies. For example, some cultures are more receptive to social change than others and the role particular practices play in a society affects a group's willingness to consider introduced innovation.

An ethnoarchaeological study of pottery production in Cameroon links methods of teaching and learning to variability in receptiveness to innovation. Wallaert-Pêtre's (2001) study of several West

African groups found that those in which learning potting was primarily a process of observation were conservative and unlikely to incorporate innovation. Those in which learning was vocal and learners questioned and discussed the process were much more likely to incorporate new methods and styles. In the culture contact study from the American Southwest discussed above, residents of Zuni Pueblo initially rejected European wheat bread during the first violent centuries of colonization (Mills 2008). They continued to make the traditional and labor-intensive corn-based *hewe*, or paper bread, because of its role in a ceremonial complex introduced during the precontact period. Bread production practices changed in the late nineteenth century when growing wheat became economically profitable and baking wheat bread in outdoor ovens became a new way for Zuni people to meet and publicly demonstrate their fulfillment of ceremonial obligations.

An illustration of the ways captives may have interacted with communities of practice in captor society also comes from the Southwest and suggests that captives could continue aspects of their natal practices, blending them with captor cultural practices. Captive Navajo women held in Spanish homes in New Mexico during the eighteenth and nineteenth centuries made "slave blankets." The Navajos, who migrated to the Southwest about the same time as the Spanish, made textiles using cotton, adopted from the Pueblo Indians, and wool, adopted from the Spanish. The captive Navajo women made blankets using dyes provided them to by their captors and created designs often modeled on textiles made in Mexico. The women continued to use their indigenous upright loom, and their blankets are distinguished by "lazy lines," a Navajo spiritual symbol (Brooks 2002, 239; Mera 1938; see also Wheat 2003, 140–41, for problems with the identification of slave blankets). Reasons why the Spanish permitted their captives to use indigenous looms could involve the difficulty of access to European-style looms in remote colonial New Mexico (Wheat [2003, 30] reports fighting over control of European-style looms in the early seventeenth century) or admiration for the high quality of the tightly woven Navajo blankets (Brooks 2002, 239). The Spanish were likely ignorant of the significance of the "lazy lines" produced by their nominally Christianized captives. As the primary producers of textiles in Spanish homes, captive Navajos may have been more likely to interact with other Navajo weavers than with Spanish weavers. In that case, they were probably under little pressure to change their methods of manufacture; only their final product had to comply with captor demands, not the way it was made.

The role of captives in cultural transmission is complex, as DeBoer (2011) stresses in his Amazonian studies. At a micro level, discussed above, he found captive women among the Conibo so resocialized that they faithfully reproduced Conibo pottery designs. At the macro level (discussed below), however, he found evidence of female-linked material objects outside their normal area of distribution, suggesting that captive women in this region introduced cultural practices they had learned in their home villages. The contrast evident at these two scales of analysis highlights our lack of understanding about how various sorts of cultural knowledge are acquired and transmitted, the influence of trauma on such processes, and the effects of age and other human characteristics on capacities to learn new and unlearn old cultural information (DeBoer 2011, 95; see also Mills 2008, 250). The following section addresses some of these issues. It begins at the micro scale and uses captive narratives to show that captors saw their captives as valuable sources of extractable knowledge and skill. Then, at the macro scale, it provides evidence of some of the major forms of knowledge and skills introduced by captives in both state-level and small-scale societies.

Learning from the "Other"

Small-scale societies, as commonly conceived by archaeologists, are conservative social units in which change is slow and gradual. In fact, the term *diffusion* suggests a slow, almost imperceptible process. We must discard this view if we want to understand the process of intercultural transmission in these societies. While every culture differs in its openness to novelty and difference, ethnohistoric and historic data suggest that individuals in small-scale societies often saw interaction with foreigners as potentially advantageous as well as dangerous. Rather than reject outright other ways of doing, they might accept and reconfigure foreign practices to suit the needs of their group and the advancement of its leaders. Mary Helms (1988) long ago showed us the fascination that distant places and people held for ancient societies, and there is no doubt that indigenous people worldwide adopted aspects of European technology they found useful, such as metallurgy, guns, and horses. Like indigenous people elsewhere, Native Americans were interested in and open to many aspects of European technology and cultural practices. Historic accounts of the earliest European explorers in the Americas suggest that indigenous leaders immediately saw in these foreigners an opportunity for trade, alliance, and the acquisition of novel goods, skills, and knowledge (Ekberg 2010, 11; Foster 2003; Hudson 1997, 227; Rushforth 2003, 2012; Snyder 2007, 276).

While captives might be reviled and abused, the historic and ethnohistoric examples presented below and throughout this book emphasize that captors often valued and exploited captives' knowledge and skills. The most intimate accounts of captives in small-scale societies come from the historic period and especially from eighteenth- and nineteenth-century European captives who returned and wrote of their experiences. Problems with accuracy of the captive narrative in representing the social lives of indigenous people have been widely discussed. They include religious motivations for writing the accounts, plays to public sentiment against indigenous people, the youth of many captives, who may not have fully remembered their experience, and the fact that many narratives were written years after the captive returned (Gelo and Zesch 2003, 35; Toulouse 2007; VanDerBeets 1973, xi–xxxi). Furthermore, many nineteenth-century European captives spent their lives after redemption exploiting their experiences as a captive by selling written accounts or lecturing (Kestler 1990, 415; Mifflin 2009; Stewart 1987). Promoters often manipulated these former captives in these endeavors and may have affected the resulting narratives. We must also acknowledge the enormous disruption colonization caused in small-scale societies in the Americas and elsewhere. Still, captive narratives contain valuable evidence of how captives might have been incorporated into and contributed to communities of practice in prehistoric small-scale societies.

Reading captive narratives is disturbing. Women, children, and men watch as their family and friends are murdered. They are marched hundreds of miles over rugged terrain in freezing or blistering temperatures, often with minimal food, water, or clothing. They are beaten, starved, humiliated, and overworked. They are given the most difficult and menial tasks: gathering firewood and water, tending stock, packing up camp, and carrying burdens. Sometimes their indigenous "family" is kind to them, other times cruel. In either case, captors seem always on the lookout for useful information and skills they can extract from their captives. Captives may be at the lowest end of the social spectrum, but part of their value is the knowledge they carry. The following captive narratives from the Americas record attempts by captors to extract knowledge and skills from their captives.

Captive taking began almost the moment Columbus spied the island of Hispaniola; Europeans captured indigenous people and vice versa. One of the earliest and most detailed accounts by a European of his indigenous captivity is that of the sixteenth-century Spanish explorer Álvar Núñez Cabeza de Vaca, held for several years by peoples of the Gulf Coast. His experiences illustrate the common assumption among people in small-scale societies that foreigners have special powers. Cabeza de Vaca reported that his captors, certain that these newcomers had special medical abilities, demanded that he and his fellow captives cure illnesses. They brushed aside Cabeza de Vaca's protest that he lacked such expertise. Cabeza de Vaca and his companions prayed to "Our Lord God" and made the sign of the cross over the sick, but they also blew on them, combining both European and indigenous curing methods. They used these concocted medical skills to stay alive as they moved from group to group in their attempt to reach the safety of the Spanish colonies in central Mexico (Cabeza de Vaca [1542] 2003).

The same assumption that foreigners have special powers as curers or sorcerers is found in many other societies. In the Amazon, the Conibo who captured Cashibo and Campa, as well as the Turkanoans who captured and enslaved groups of Makú, believed that their despised captives were powerful sorcerers with access to potent forest medicines and poisons (DeBoer 2008, 249–50). In the mid-nineteenth century, Fanny Kelly, who spent five months as a captive of the Ogalala Sioux in what was then Dakota Territory, reported that the wounded chief of her captor's tribe wanted her to attend to him because of his "superstitious belief in the healing power of a white woman's touch" (Kestler 1990, 441).

Captives played important roles as cultural intermediaries, as Brooks (2002) skillfully reveals about the Southwest Borderlands (see chapter 5). Their competence in more than one language meant they could negotiate on behalf of their captors and, as Albers (1993) describes for Great Plains tribes, could serve as social nodes that encouraged trade and other sorts of interaction after a decrease in hostilities among adjacent groups (see chapter 5). Captors also valued the captives' other methods of communication. Fanny Kelly's Sioux captors admired her ability to read and write. She read to them from a book recovered from her family's ambushed wagon and it "interested them greatly" (Kestler 1990, 438). She also wrote a letter from her captor to a nearby army detail escorting an emigrant wagon train (Kestler 1990, 445). The chief, who hoped to convince the army captain to move on without attacking the Sioux camp, carefully monitored her composition of the letter. Fanny's captors also admired her ability to sing (presumably English songs) and urged her to do so as she worked (Kestler 1990, 444).

The account of John Jewitt's life among the Mowachahts of the Northwest Coast illustrates the value placed on captive craft knowledge, especially metallurgy. In 1803 the Mowachahts attacked Jewitt's ship and only Jewitt and one other crew member survived (Stewart 1987). Jewitt was the ship's armorer, and in the days before the attack visiting Indians had watched him work. During the attack the Mowachaht "chief" Maquinna protected Jewitt because of his skills and then enslaved him. Jewitt's narrative records the many items he made for Maquinna, for his wives, and for other village leaders: bracelets, daggers, and lances of copper and steel (Stewart 1987, 61, 110, 127–28) and iron fishhooks and ornaments, including nose ornaments (Stewart 1987, 67, 86, 90). Jewitt especially delighted Maquinna with a steel whaling harpoon, which was much sturdier than the native version. However,

Maquinna prevented Jewitt from making similar harpoons for other Mowachaht leaders, reserving this aspect of his slave's technological expertise for himself. When Maquinna decided to go to war, he required Jewitt to outfit the raiders with daggers and *cheetoolths* (war clubs). The other survivor of the massacre on Jewitt's ship had been the ship's sailmaker, who made a sail for Maquinna's canoe and clothing of European cloth, including a beautiful mantle pieced together of brightly colored vest patterns and ornamented with gilt buttons (Stewart 1987, 110–11). Other "ways of doing" also passed from these two European captives to their Mowachaht captors, including the practice of washing clothes instead of discarding them (Stewart 1987, 134). Captors assigned the actual washing, of course, to the captives.

Foreign clothing seems to have been especially readily adopted when indigenous societies interacted with Europeans. Catherine German, captured in 1874 by the Cheyennes, made clothes for her captors. "The Indian men and boys liked to have me make their shirts because I made button holes and put bone buttons on them, whereas the squaws had used sticks or string to fasten these garments" (Meredith [1927] 2004, 42). Mary Rowlandson, captive for over a year among the Algonquian tribes of the Northeast, knitted stockings and made shirts and caps for her indigenous family and others who demanded them (Kestler 1990, 32, 36, 37, 41, 45, 52, 55). These creative endeavors gave her no status among her captors, and she also carried burdens, fetched firewood and water, and often starved. Rowlandson does not report the types of garments she made for her captors, but one assumes she sewed and knit using techniques she had learned in her white home rather than in those of her captors. That her captors sought her out for garment making suggests that they valued European clothing styles (see also Kestler 1990, 49, for Indians "dressed in English apparel"; Kane 2014). The Algonquians were not receptive to all European practices, however. Rowlandson reports that she earned a piece of bear meat and a quart of peas for garments she made. She cooked the foods and invited her master and mistress to eat, but the mistress refused because the two ingredients had been boiled together, apparently in violation of indigenous cooking practices.

Other examples also highlight the interest of small-scale societies in new technologies. Helena Valero, captive of the Yanomamö in the Amazon (see chapter 3), angered her captors because she told them she was unable to make the metal tools they desired (Biocca [1965] 1996, 131; Tierney 2000, 245). Captors closely questioned Olive Oatman, a young girl held by a Mohave tribe in the mid-nineteenth century, about Anglo agricultural technology, including the use of the plow (figure 10). Her narrative portrays her captors as lazy and incompetent because of their casual attitude toward horticulture, yet they seem to have been interested in other production methods.

The examples above, although derived exclusively from accounts of Europeans held by Native Americans, suggest the extent to which small-scale societies were open to cultural practices introduced by foreigners, regardless of their status. These groups do not fit the highly conservative and conformist view archaeologists tend to have of them. We should recognize that these societies actively evaluated the cultural practices of other groups, adopting those that were useful and rejecting those that were not. The following section demonstrates the role of captives in this selection process. As common social persons in small-scale societies, captives acted as an avenue for the introduction of new cultural practices.

What Captives Contributed

Historic, ethnohistoric, and ethnographic data demonstrate that captives *could* be a source of innovation in the development of cultural practices. The following discussion is organized around several types of practices that captives are documented to have introduced: technology and craft production, food items and cuisine, and religious ideas and curing practices. The majority of this book focuses on small-scale societies, but this section discusses societies at all levels of social organization, including ancient Greece and Rome and the nations involved in the Atlantic slave trade. Captive contributions have been studied in much more detail in classical societies and especially in African diaspora studies. While cultural practices and the organization of labor in small-scale societies are quite different from those in state-level

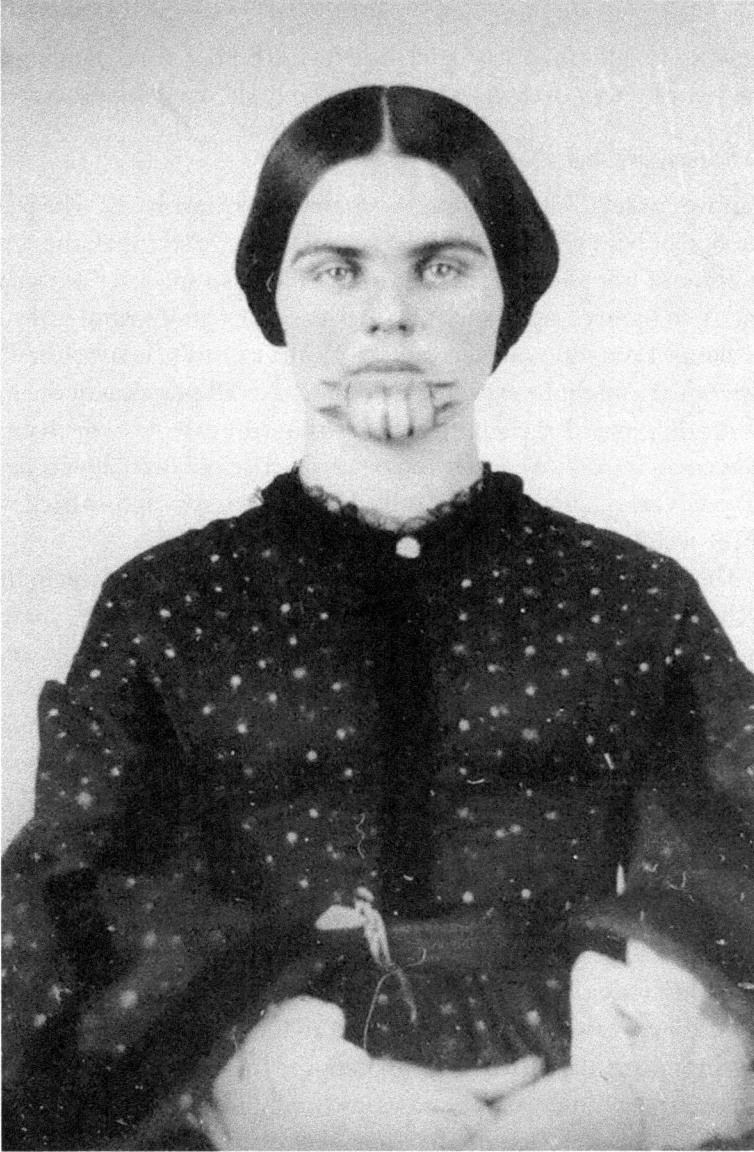

10. In 1851 fourteen-year-old Olive Oatman was captured by Yavapai Indians in what is now southern Arizona. She was traded to the Mohaves, who adopted her and tattooed her chin in the fashion of all Mohave women. Tintype portrait of Olive Ann Oatman courtesy Western Americana Collection, Beinecke Rare Book and Manuscript Library, Yale University.

societies, insights from state-level societies further our understanding of the contributions of captives to culture change in small-scale societies.

Technology and Craft Production

Captives in small-scale societies were frequently involved in the production of craft goods. In simpler societies, they undertook the production of household items but sometimes also specialty or ritual goods. In more complex societies, they produced goods whose sale or exchange brought wealth to captors. While captives, as subordinate individuals, might be expected to follow the craft practices of the societies they joined, the examples below show the extent to which captives could introduce new technologies, practices, or decorative styles. In some cases captors targeted skilled individuals for capture because of the technological or labor needs of captor society.

There is no doubt about the high value placed on skilled slaves in the earliest Western and Islamic societies (Patterson 1982, 179–80). Slaves in ancient Athens and Rome were often craft workers, making everything from the well-known Greek painted vases to the cut blocks of stone used to construct the temples and palaces of the cities of antiquity (Burford 1972; see also Fisher 1993; Joshel 2010; Thompson 2003). In Athens they labored "in the workshops at every kind and level of skilled work" (Burford 1972, 47). The lack of skilled workers in Athens could be overcome by buying slaves from elsewhere (Burford 1972, 58). After the second and first centuries BCE, increasing numbers of Greek and Oriental captives were returned to Italy to work in crafts and other activities (Burford 1972, 60). Roman entrepreneurs bought skilled slaves to work in handicraft and architectural industries (Westermann 1942). Slaves frequently apprenticed in workshops where they learned trades, and many workshops were staffed entirely by slaves (Burford 1972, 90). Despite the value of craftspeople to ancient societies, free citizens of Greece and Rome despised manual labor. Burford (1972, 29) attributes this to a lack of connection to the land by those who worked in crafts, but slavery's link to manual labor may also have been part of the reason (see Patterson 1982, 254–55; see also Fisher 1993, 52; Joshel 2010, 165).

North of the Roman empire, archaeological evidence reveals the presence of Roman captives apparently skilled in craft manufacture, in Germanic settlements prior to the fifth century CE (Lenski 2008, 90–91). Metal objects found as far north as Denmark suggest the capture and transport of skilled Roman metalsmiths. Objects including statuettes, drinking horns, and weapons found at archaeological sites in Germanic territory were apparently locally manufactured but with Mediterranean techniques and designs. Similarly, ceramics recovered in late-third-century settlements in Mainfranken indicate the presence of Roman potters among Germanic tribes. This pottery was locally made but with Roman methods (Lenski 2008, 90).

Beginning in the seventh century, Islamic armies conquered much of the eastern Mediterranean and beyond almost to India, including eastern and northern Africa and most of Spain. The thousands of slaves taken during these conquests introduced a myriad of novel cultural practices into the polyglot that became Islamic society. Samuel Haas (1942, iii) reports of Islamic slaves that "in the early development of Islam most of the crafts and skills which are so necessary for the development of any culture were performed by slaves. The members of this social group brought to Islam the trades of smithery, ceramics, mosaic work, carpentry, and painting. Other slaves supervised the construction of bridges, dams, and public buildings." To slaves also goes the credit for many developments in Islamic music and poetry, including the introduction of the Persian lute and the melodies and rhythms on which Muslim music is built (S. Haas 1942, iv).

During the seventeenth and eighteenth centuries, many British people who navigated the Mediterranean Sea became captives of Islamic societies located along the North African coast. Those captives with skills—medical practices, boat building, the making of armor, accounting, or the ability to speak multiple languages—were most highly valued (Colley 2002, 60). In fact, their value often excluded them from attempts at ransom.

Accounts from Africa and the Americas indicate that skilled craftspeople were often a focus of slave raids. Oral histories collected in northern Sierra Leone record that raids targeted blacksmiths for capture because of the great demand for their skills; female potters were also preferentially captured (DeCorse 1989, 137). Accomplished slaves were also valued in the trans-Atlantic trade. In the Lower Mississippi Valley in the early eighteenth century, French settlers imported many enslaved African people who originated in Senegal and the Bight of Benin (Usner 1992, 33). Most of the colonists of this region were occupied in farming, herding, hunting/gathering, fishing, trading, and transportation, and because skilled craftspeople were in short supply, some slaves were trained in craftwork. Other captive Africans brought different skills, including woodworking, weaving, and blacksmithing; they might even have been members of distinct occupational castes (Usner 1992, 55–56). While there is no evidence that slave raiders in Africa specifically targeted skilled individuals or castes, DeCorse's (1989, 137) observations above make it seem likely. Captive Africans were trained in a variety of new trades in the Americas, including house building, cabinetry, and the production of decorative metal elements (Genovese 1972, 395). Genovese (1972, 388–98) describes the strong influence of West African artistic styles on American crafts. This influence faded in the nineteenth century, presumably after the 1808 ban on importing slaves from Africa (although Genovese does not say this).

Small-scale societies also placed high value on captives' skills. Habicht-Mauche's (2008) study, described previously, found that plainware pottery in the Southern High Plains dating to the protohistoric period, though made locally, was technologically very similar to pottery from the adjacent Southwest. She argues that the bison hunters of the region needed women to prepare hides and raided their Pueblo neighbors for women in order to increase output. These captive women brought with them pottery-making abilities, which they apparently retained even though their daily life revolved around hide production. In Africa, Frank's (1993) study of potters living in villages in southern Mali reveals that the local potters were likely the daughters of slaves who had kept their profession alive, even though they had been removed to another region. Their foreign origin was evident in the technology of pottery production their mothers had learned elsewhere and passed on to them.

Captives made significant contributions to craftwork in small-scale societies, even in situations where they were not incorporated as slaves. In island Southeast Asia, from at least the twelfth through the late nineteenth centuries, large numbers of captives, especially women, were taken in raids by the most politically prominent and wealthy coastal chiefdoms (Junker 2008). These captives, whether retained as slaves or as wives, engaged in a variety of productive activities. Some were set to agricultural tasks, but many produced pottery, textiles, and other goods that created wealth for their masters. In the Philippines these women came with designs and other cultural elements they had learned in the small communities where they originated, and they used these elements in craftwork in their new homes (Junker 2008). Contrary to our assumption that cultural innovation occurs in major centers, here the direction of innovation went the other way.

Archaeologist Warren DeBoer (2011) takes a statistical approach to the investigation of the effects of captive taking on artifact distributions. Working in western Amazonia, he uses a material culture survey produced in the early twentieth century (Tessmann 1999) to explore the presence or absence of material goods, including weapons, utility objects, clothing, ornaments, and objects for body modification, among social groups located along the Ucayali River and its tributaries. The distribution of most objects shows a pattern consistent with a distance-decay model (fewer objects will be found as distance from the center of manufacture increases), but a number of similar female-linked objects are found in widely separated tributaries of the Ucayali. The matrilineal societies residing here would not likely pass women between groups as marriage partners. Instead this distribution of female-linked objects points to a consistent pattern of raiding for women (DeBoer 2011, 95). Although DeBoer does not discuss details of these female-linked objects, captive women in this region clearly introduced cultural practices they had learned in their original homes.

Foodways

There is no doubt that captives introduced food items and food preparation methods into the societies they joined, and these may have been among their most common contributions. Tracking these introductions can be difficult. Foods and food preparation methods, if adopted, can quickly become well accepted by the host society, and their origins, especially if contributed by a marginal or inferior group, may be readily forgotten (Andrews 1992). Captives were often women; because of women's roles in horticulture and food preparation, captive women likely introduced food items and cuisines. The horizontal transmission of novel foodways relies not only on the introduction of new foods but also on the mobility of cooks (Mills 2008).

The massive African diaspora of the sixteenth to nineteenth centuries is unparalleled in human history and is under intense study. The microscale processes through which plants, animals, agricultural techniques, and food preparation methods were transferred from Africa to the New Worlds are far less understood. Recently, Carney and Rosomoff (2009) have explored the movement of African foods and foodways in both Africa and to the New World. Their work shows that even the victims of the most restrictive systems of slavery implemented culture change on a large scale.

Long before the African diaspora, captives were instrumental in the movement of new plant varieties from sub-Saharan Africa to northern Africa (Carney and Rosomoff 2009, 28–30). Between the first millennium BCE and 500 CE, the Garamante culture was located along important caravan routes in southern Libya. Garamante farming communities used complex underground water-extraction systems to irrigate their fields, and this system required considerable labor. Slaves obtained from sub-Saharan farming communities and transported along established trade routes that originated in the area around Lake Chad met these labor demands. These slaves apparently introduced two drought-resistant crops: sorghum and pearl millet, both of which were originally domesticated in the Sahel. The new crops enabled a revolution in Garamante food production and expansion of their complex agricultural systems.

Because of Africans' subordinate position, their enormous contributions to New World agriculture and foodways have been largely ignored. African captives brought not only plants but also extensive knowledge of horticulture and animal husbandry and of processing tools and methods, as well as recipes appropriate to the use of African foods (Carney and Rosomoff 2009). Introduced African plants include rice, sorghum, millet, yams, bananas, okra, sesame, and many varieties of grasses. Slaves introduced horticultural methods that allowed these plants to flourish and preparation methods that turned them into valuable foods (Carney and Rosomoff 2009, 177–86). For example, displaced Africans brought to the New World, especially to the Caribbean, their traditional cultivation method of using a long-handled hoe to ridge and mound the soil (Carney and Rosomoff 2009, 117–18). European immigrants to the New World, often landless craft workers or traders, generally lacked farming skills. Furthermore, they came from the temperate zone, where flora was considerably different from that in the tropical climates of the New World where many settled. They turned to skilled African slaves to learn how to grow food: "The use of enslaved Africans as plantation laborers in the New World overwhelms the important consideration that many were expert tropical farmers or herders. Among immigrants to the Americas, only Africans came equipped with knowledge of raising food in the humid and semiarid tropics" (Carney and Rosomoff 2009, 105).

Africans were not only horticulturalists but also pastoralists with extensive knowledge of livestock. African livestock, including cattle, pigs, goats, sheep, and chickens, were purchased live to provide meat for slave ship crews (Carney and Rosomoff 2009, 157), but perhaps even more important were African grasses, which were loaded onto slave ships as fodder. African grasslands had coevolved over many millennia with grazing animals tended by pastoralists, a situation with no parallel in the New World (Carney and Rosomoff 2009, 166). The enormously successful introduction into the Americas of African forage species, such as cattle and goats, was key to the explosion of livestock that occurred there (Carney and Rosomoff 2009, 162). The knowledge captive African herders brought with them was essential to the success of the livestock business, however. Seventeenth-century accounts document the consistent demand for slaves from Senegambia, where cattle herding was the primary livelihood (Carney and Rosomoff 2009, 172). Tethering animals in fallow fields to allow their manure to act as fertilizer is an example of a traditional African practice introduced into the Caribbean and still used today (Carney and Rosomoff 2009, 174). Many American cattle-tending practices also derive from Africa, introduced by black cowboys in the eighteenth century (Holloway 2005, 55–56). Texas longhorn cattle are an African import, and the north-south migratory patterns and "open grazing" methods that once characterized the American cattle industry derived, according to Holloway, from similar patterns practiced by the Fulani of Africa.

The processes through which African plants, animals, and agricultural techniques were introduced cannot be known exactly. Carney and Rosomoff (2009) suggest that the remains of slave ship provisions, loaded in Africa and discarded in the New World at the end of the voyage, may have been one important method of introduction. African plantation slaves were generally required to grow their own food on small plots allotted to them in the yards around their houses (Carney and Rosomoff 2009, 108, 127). In this "shadow world of cultivation," enslaved Africans created a "little Guinea," growing African plants using traditional African methods (Carney and Rosomoff 2009, 125, 135). These plots not only allowed enslaved Africans to consume familiar foods from their homelands but are the source of the botanical legacy Africa gave to the Americas. African foods and African cuisine became "traditional" foods in the American South (rice and black-eyed peas [Hoppin' John], raw and boiled peanuts, peanut brittle, sorghum molasses, and okra-based gumbo): "Among the millions of Africans forcibly dispersed to these regions were members of specialist ethnic groups and people skilled as herders, farmers, blacksmiths, dyers and spinners of textiles, and diverse craftspersons. The complex of knowledge they held was neither trifling nor incidental. It spanned vast categories of human endeavor, having produced in many of these vocations matchless levels of expertise. In the New World, Africans and African knowledge made indelible contributions to the shaping of landscapes where they lived and labored" (Carney and Rosomoff 2009, 176).

The impact of captives on foodways is clear and compelling in African diaspora studies, but it was likely no less important in other historic and prehistoric societies. The role of captives in the spread of domesticates, novel crops, food production methods, and recipes should be considered by archaeologists in many parts of the world.

Religious Innovations and Curing Practices

While captives could be marginalized and reviled, their position as outsiders to captor culture meant that captives sometimes played unique roles. In particular, captives were not infrequently involved with the introduction of new religions concepts and, as noted above, they were often required to act as curers. In Europe, Lenski (2008, 104) reports, the Germanic peoples who attacked the Roman Empire in its decline converted to Christianity between the fourth and sixth centuries, and in many cases the conversion seems to have been initiated by Roman captives. For example, the first Gothic bible was translated by a descendant of captives whose family and other Christian captives had begun the process of converting the Goths.

Some of the religious vodun cults in the West African slaving port of Ouidah (in the modern state of Bénin) were introduced by slaves captured from the interior (Law 2004, 90). For example, a shrine to Azili, a female water spirit, is said to have been founded by an enslaved woman captured by the Dohomian army and taken to Ouidah. Later, ex-slaves returned from Brazil introduced Islam into Ouidah (Law 2004, 91). In the Kingdom of Dahomey a palace woman (many palace women were captives) introduced Islam into one of the royal lineages when she became part of the royal household (Bay 1983, 347). A slave woman who also became integrated into palace society introduced another vodun cult into Dahomey (Bay 1983).

In small-scale societies, captives were also involved in the introduction of religious practices. During battles between Northwest Coast groups, a warrior who killed the owner of a song, dance, or ritual could claim these prerogatives for himself (Donald 1997, 112), but not all such ritual specialists were slain; some were captured and enslaved, bringing their ritual knowledge with them. For example, Bellabella slaves introduced house-building potlatches to the Haidas (Murdock 1965, 267). On the rare occasions when slaves managed to return to their homes, they might return with cultural practices learned during their enslavement (Ruby and Brown 1993, 34). In the American Southwest, Hopi oral accounts of the attack in 1700 CE on the village Awatovi by neighboring pueblos describe the destruction of most of the Awatovi population. The few women saved were members of religious societies and knew special ceremonies (Malotki 1993, 405–7). A few others with special knowledge of the cultivation of peaches (a European introduction), sweet corn, and pottery making were also reported to have been saved because of their skills.

There are other reports from the Americas of captives acting as vectors of novel religious or curing practices, including the introduction of the False Face Society into the Iroquois by Huron captives and curing practices into Neural settlements by their Mascouten captives (DeBoer 2008, 249). In the Amazon, captive-taking groups including Tukanoans and Conibo held extremely low opinions of the groups from whom they took captives, yet they nonetheless believed these people had strong powers that could be used in curing or sorcery (DeBoer 2008, 249–50).

Despite considerable interest in processes of cultural transmission, prehistoric archaeologists have been slow to develop models of how cultural practices are transmitted between cultures. Even the term *diffusion* has largely dropped out of usage, and archaeologists have been satisfied with vague references to trade, exchange, or "interaction." Historic archaeologists *have* developed useful models for explaining processes of intercultural interaction and it is clear that colonial encounters provide a fertile ground for such research. But these models have rarely been adopted by scholars of prehistory. This chapter contends that the activities of captives were one way by which cultural practices were transferred between cultures. I suggest that learning theory, especially as employed by ethnoarchaeologists, as well as the studies of historic archaeologists can help us understand the ways captives affected and contributed to the cultures of their captors.

This chapter examines the way archaeologists have engaged with situated learning and the concept of communities of practice (Lave and Wenger 1991). By considering how captives may have fit into communities of practice we begin to understand their contributions to captor society. The concept of communities of practice conjures up images of affectionate parents or teachers imparting knowledge to eager "legitimate peripheral learners," usually children. I ask archaeologists to consider how captors might engage with captives they are training. Especially important is recognizing that, as discussed in chapter 5, marginal people such as captives can significantly affect social boundaries. How does the presence of captives impact the replication or modification of cultural practices in captor society? This chapter is only a beginning, and I urge archaeologists to consider the different relationships that may develop between teacher and learner, including coercion and abuse, and what those relationships imply for cultural transmission in small-scale societies.

Captive narratives provide evidence that foreign knowledge and skills are often welcomed in small-scale societies. Most of the examples presented above come from colonial periods, but we should anticipate that foreign knowledge and skills were equally valued in prehistory. Rather than rigidly defending the social practices that defined their group, people in ancient small-scale societies were open to opportunities to improve their situation, whether by adopting new technological, religious, social, or nutritional practices. The capture of other people had many benefits, and the knowledge and skills captives brought were important ones. The acceptance of new cultural processes was selective, however. The factors that led captors to accept or reject particular cultural practices are not addressed in detail here but should be considered in future work (see also Cameron 2011).

In the final part of this chapter, examples from societies of all social levels show that captives made contributions to the societies they joined. This is a fact that will come as no surprise to historians or many cultural anthropologists. I hope this chapter and the remainder of the book ensures that archaeologists also recognize the presence of captives in prehistoric societies and investigate their role in culture change.

| Chapter Seven

Captives in Prehistory

Captive taking has been an almost universal practice in human history. The captive is a constant presence in human society, almost as common as the nuclear family or the incest taboo. This book was written for archaeologists who study the past, but captive taking goes on today—as the quotes that open the book attest, another indication of the universal nature of this practice. Orlando Patterson (1982, 334–42) has called slavery "human parasitism." This is an apt description of the motivations for captive taking: the use of a fellow human being to improve one's own situation. The ubiquitous taking of women may even suggest a biological imperative—men gathering more women than are available in their own society in order to improve their genetic fitness. This is a question that I will leave to biological anthropologists. Instead, this book focuses on how, in important ways, the presence of captives changed and shaped the groups they joined. I urge archaeologists to consider the role of captives in culture change. Even though change through time is a fundamental objective of archaeological analysis (see chapter 6), we have neglected to identify mechanisms for culture change. I argue that captive taking constituted one of those mechanisms.

This chapter summarizes and discusses the results of my study. I believe that the broad-scale and cross-cultural methods I use are appropriate for beginning a conversation on the role of captives in prehistory. The next step is to use this general knowledge of captives in more systematic examinations of captive taking and its effects on particular societies and regions of the world. I have begun this process for my own area of study, the American Southwest (Cameron 2013).

Whenever I describe my study of captives to archaeologists, friends, or acquaintances, the first question is usually, "How can you see captives in the archaeological record?" The second section of this chapter addresses this question by reviewing the methods archaeologists have recently begun to develop for seeing captives in the past. The final section of the chapter returns to chapter 1 and the consideration of human trafficking today as part of the long history of captive taking. Our rather selective recognition of warfare, slavery, and captive taking in ethnographically known groups has, until recently, prevented us from seeing these activities clearly in the time before historic records.

Captives as Invisible Agents of Culture Change

The book began by identifying captives as a common category of social person in the past whose origin was generally in warfare or kidnapping. Archaeologists recognize that "archaeological cultures" are created to order collections of artifacts in space and time; such cultures likely did not represent clearly bounded social groups in the past, even when the use of these cultures often implies that such boundaries existed. Chapter 1 emphasized the permeability of social boundaries and showed that the landscape of captive taking entangled societies at a variety of social scales and could move people over great distances. Captive taking is one of many reasons to doubt that genes, language, and culture are a package that moves and evolves as a unit.

Chapter 1 explained the methods used in the book. My methods were broadly comparative and followed a theoretical trend in archaeology toward cross-cultural comparison (Michael Smith and Peregrine 2012; Trigger 2003). Chapter 2 described the eight regions of the world in which I have found ethnohistoric, historic, or ethnographic accounts of captive taking and the lives of captives. There are problems and limitations with the use of analogy and cross-cultural comparison (addressed in chapter 1), especially the fact that when one sets out to find similarities, one generally does find them ("After all, the outcome of comparative projects is, I suspect, somewhat predictable" [Hodson 2011, 231]). Further complicating such analyses is the selective manner in which traits are pulled from their cultural context in order to compare them to similarly disembodied traits pulled from other cultures. But I argue that identifying patterns common to captive taking around the world can help us as we incorporate captives into our understanding of the social lives of small-scale societies. The patterns identified here are a first step in what I hope will result in increased recognition of the presence of subordinate individuals in most small-scale societies.

Four chapters compose the body of the book. Chapter 3 provided a microscale look at how captives become incorporated into captor society, the social roles offered them, and how the characteristics of the captured individual have a determinative effect on captives' ultimate social location in captor society. The ease of incorporating reproductive-aged women as wives or concubines, as well as their sexuality, made them the most prized captives in most groups. Children were also favored because they could be so readily enculturated. In most (but not all) small-scale societies, captives could use their skills and intelligence to improve their situation, although only some of them may have made such efforts. I categorized the degree to which captives were integrated into captor society as wives, slaves, drudge wives, concubines, and so on, but I admit that we have little evidence of how well-incorporated captives themselves might have felt.

Moving to a larger scale, chapter 4 explored captive-captor relationships. In his worldwide comparison of slavery, Patterson (1982) characterized the master-slave relationship as one based on honor. The slave was fundamentally a dishonored person and the slave's mere existence created honor for the master. While a great admirer of Patterson's study, I find the concept of honor problematic in considering the relationship between a female captive and her captor. Did Patterson think of women when he analyzed the master-slave relationship? (He certainly did later; see Patterson 1991.) In chapter 4 I substituted "power" for honor and argued that captives were a potent source of power for their captors. Their presence and degraded condition emphasized the status and control exercised by their captors. They increased their captors' number of followers. They provided labor through which the captors gained wealth. As items of trade, they created additional wealth. Archaeologists should investigate the role of captives in the creation of complex societies. They may find that captives were not a small part of the many factors that fostered complexity.

The last two chapters pulled the focus of analysis back to the boundaries of captor society in order to explore how captives affected those boundaries. As chapter 5 explained, archaeologists create "archaeological cultures" from bundles of archaeological traits located in time and space. As any archaeologist will acknowledge, archaeological cultures are some of our most basic elements of analysis. But much of our interpretive use of archaeological cultures treats them as entities with solid boundaries that are crossed rarely, if at all. The recognition that captives frequently crossed social boundaries in the past means that we need to reassess what our archaeological cultures really mean. Captives can, in a number of different ways, reinforce social boundaries, even as they mix with genetically unrelated people. The chapter also emphasized the fluidity of small-scale groups that continually break up and re-form in different configurations. I argue that archaeologists need to wean themselves from the view of social groups as entities with lengthy histories—a view that today permeates contemporary indigenous politics (see also Cameron 2013). Otherwise our reconstructions of the past are bound to be incorrect.

Exploring the practices that captives transported across the boundaries of captor culture (chapter 6) was the most important but also the most difficult portion of the book to develop. We have few firsthand accounts of captives in small-scale societies, significantly limiting our understanding of contributions captives made. I used situated learning theory and the concept of communities of practice to evaluate how captives may have become involved in captor technological production and other activities. Within communities of practice, technology is transferred from approving teachers to eager learners (legitimate peripheral participants). But captives' training is unlikely to have fit this model, and their learning may have been accompanied by coercion and abuse. We need to consider how captives fit into communities of practice and what skills and practices they might be able to introduce into captor society despite their alien status. Using accounts of whites held captive by Native Americans in the eighteenth and nineteenth centuries, I showed that small-scale societies welcomed useful technological, medical, and religious knowledge that foreigners might bring. Accounts from state-level societies showed that captives *did* introduce a multitude of different practices into the societies of their captors, ranging from technology to foodways to ideology. Identifying the contributions of captives to small-scale societies in the past will be more difficult, but once we acknowledge that they existed, we can begin to link them to cultural changes we see in the archaeological record.

Finding Captives in the Archaeological Record

Finding captives in the archaeological record is a challenge for studying their influence on past cultures. As archaeologist Ann Stahl (2008, 38) wonders with regard to Africa, "How will we know slavery when we dig it up?" Archaeologists are beginning to address this concern. For each of the regions considered in this study, a brief overview of archaeological evidence for prehistoric captive taking was presented (chapter 2). Here I summarize these and other lines of evidence and discuss large-scale projects that are beginning to provide us with the tools we need not only to find captives in the past but to evaluate their impact.

Prehistoric violence can be used as a basis for inference of captive taking because warfare and raiding are almost always accompanied by captive taking in ethnographic accounts. Despite arguments to the contrary (see chapter 1), Keeley's (1996, 39) worldwide study of warfare in small-scale societies found that "warfare is documented in the archaeological record of the past 10,000 years in every well-studied region." Archaeological indicators of warfare include defensively positioned sites, weapons of war, and sometimes evidence of a "no-man's land" between settled groups. But the most compelling evidence of warfare is human remains with trauma, suggesting a violent death.

Human remains are also our best line of evidence for the presence of captives in cultures before historic records. Evidence from human remains that suggests the presence of captives includes skewed sex ratios (Cybulski 1990; Kohler and Turner 2006); different burial practices or lack of formal burial for certain members of society; evidence of ongoing abuse to subsets of society (especially women; see Martin 2008); and genetic, trace element, or craniometric studies that detect nonlocal individuals (Hallgrimsson et al. 2004; Ortman 2010; T. Price, Blos, and Burton 2006; Schillaci and Stojanowski 2000, 2002).

Debra Martin of the University of Nevada, Las Vegas, and her students are undertaking studies of violence in the past, including the identification of captives (Martin, Harrod, and Fields 2010; Martin, Harrod, and Pérez 2012). She has developed a list of signatures on human skeletal remains that can indicate whether the individual may have suffered captivity and enslavement. These include healed cranial fractures, injury recidivism (indicating repeated beatings), and fractures to the arms and other limbs (Martin 2008, table 1). In her analysis of the human remains from the La Plata region of the northern Southwest, Martin (2008) found a subset of women whose healed fractures on their heads and forearms suggest systematic abuse and efforts by victims to protect themselves. In addition, these women were not given the types of formal burial typical of other individuals in the group. Martin (2008, 174) suggests they may have been captives. Harrod (2012), also working in the northern Southwest, found a similar group of abused women at the Chacoan site of Kin Bineola whom he believes were captives.

Sex ratios in burial populations can provide a strong line of evidence for captive taking. In a normal burial population, the number of males and females should be approximately equal because males and females occur in relatively equal numbers in living populations. Significantly more female than male remains can indicate populations that took captive women, while more men than women might indicate a source for female captives. Kohler and Turner's (2006) analysis of a large population of human remains in the northern Southwest dating between 600 and 1300 CE had precisely these characteristics. The large centers of Chaco Canyon and Aztec Ruins had more women than expected, while small sites in the region had fewer women, which suggests they were the source of the captive women found in the large centers. In the Northwest Coast, Cybulski (1990) examined human remains recovered from excavations in the Prince Rupert harbor and dating as early as two thousand years ago. He found far more males than females and argued that enslaved females had not been given formal burials and therefore were unrepresented in the population. A mass grave found by archaeologists at the Crow Creek site in South Dakota dating to the early fourteenth century contained more than five hundred scalped and mutilated men, children, and women, but far fewer young women than there should have been. The missing women were likely taken captive (Keeley 1996, 68).

The presence of nonlocal individuals in a population can result from a variety of factors (intermarriage, migration, long-term visiting, etc.), but one of these is the presence of captives. Genetic studies and the analysis of isotopes in human bone have been successful in identifying nonlocal people in populations of human remains. Genetic studies of the contemporary population of Iceland suggest that the founding population was made up largely of Scandinavian males and females from the British Isles (Helgason et al. 2000). This is consistent with historic records for Viking raiding and captive taking in Ireland (Jóhannesson 2013; Walvin 2006, 27–28). In Mexico, individuals exhumed from a sixteenth- to seventeenth-century cemetery in the city of Compache had dental mutilations characteristic of practices in West Africa. An isotopic study confirmed that these likely were some of the first of the millions of African people forcibly exported to the Americas (T. Price, Blos, and Burton 2006).

A number of other lines of evidence can also be used, especially in conjunction with human remains and evidence of warfare, to identify captives in the archaeological record. Captives are sometimes seen in prehistoric iconography, such as the kneeling captive figurine found at the Spiro Mound site in Oklahoma with an armed warrior looming over him (likely made in Cahokia; Dye 2004, figure 16a–b; figure 2). More mundane sorts of artifacts can also be used to identify captives in the past. For example, female-linked intrusive traits at a site, such as pottery and hearth style, and a lack of male-linked intrusive traits (the style of religious architecture or projectile points) could signal the presence of female captives (see Cameron's 2011 interpretation of Lowell 2007). Regional-scale distributions of gender-linked artifact types have been suggested as indicators of raiding for women in the Amazon (DeBoer 2011) and in the American Northeast (Trigger 1976, 159–61).

Words for captives or slaves in indigenous languages that appear to be ancient are also a useful line of evidence suggesting captives in the past, as discussed in chapter 2 for the Northeast (Rushforth 2012; Starna and Watkins 1991) and the Northwest Coast (Donald 1997, 205–9). Oral traditions that include captives or slaves as social actors are important indicators of the practice of captive taking (Averkieva [1941] 1966, cited in Donald 1997, 45). Among the Philippian chiefdoms the heroes of epic tales are elite warriors who returned from battle with many captives; bringing other goods was secondary (Junker 2008, 119).

Reports of the presence of captives or slaves in the accounts of the earliest European explorers are particularly valuable as they confirm that the practice existed prior to colonial intrusion. Columbus heard about Kalinago raiders on his first voyage, and on his second he met some of their victims, who described canoes that traveled long distances to plunder and take captives (Santos-Granero 2009, 49). Francisco Vásquez de Coronado, the first European to explore the Southwest, found captives from Plains tribes living among the Pueblo people, including a tattooed woman whom one of his lieutenants took as a concubine (Brooks 2002, 47). Other explorers made similar reports.

Existing archaeological methods should allow us to infer or identify captives in the archaeological record, but identification is just the first step. We also must develop methods for exploring the roles captives played in captor society and their involvement in culture change in studies of practices in particular regions. This will be considerably more difficult, but my hope is that this book provides some avenues

for analysis, including the use of ethnohistoric and ethnographic accounts as analogy. The work of historical archaeologists also contains
a wealth of material that can be used to model how captives might
have operated in captor society and what the limits and potentials of
their lives might have been.

From the Past to the Future

The quote that opens this book describes the capture of over two hundred Nigerian schoolgirls by Islamic extremists. More than a year later,
it seems the Nigerian girls are largely forgotten, at least by the Western media. A few escaped, but most of the rest are assumed to be lost,
likely forever. Every day throughout the world, the lives of girls and
sometimes boys and women as well as men are stolen. It is an experience that may be as old as the formation of the modern human mind.

Captive taking and enslavement likely will never be completely eradicated, but if current trends continue, the number of people caught in
the brutality of human trafficking or born into a debt slavery they cannot escape may decrease. Our modern, highly connected world makes
it possible to track and find victims. The Boko Haram case demonstrates that, beyond simply identifying where captives and slaves are
held, states must have the political power and will to fight for their
freedom. Education, especially for women, is important for developing a world population that sympathizes across boundaries of race,
class, ethnic group, and political affiliation. Groups such as the United
Nations Office on Drugs and Crime and the Walk Free Foundation—
both of which work to bring the issues of slavery and trafficking into
the open—are working to reduce captive taking and slave numbers.
Books such as Kevin Bales's (2005, 2007, [1999] 2012) *Disposable People*
and Nicholas Kristof and Sheryl WuDunn's (2009) *Half the Sky* expose
slavery and other abuses against women around the world.

This volume looks at captive taking and enslavement in the context of world prehistory. I did not write the book with the intent of
affecting the horrors of modern trafficking, but I hope that a better
understanding of the deep history and patterns of captive taking and
enslavement will inform efforts to end the practice today. I take heart

in the knowledge that we have gone from a time in which a large proportion of the world's inhabitants lived in bondage to one in which it is illegal everywhere—and this in only two hundred years. But "illegal" and eradicated are very different things. Today only one-half of 1 percent of the world's population lives in slavery. That figure may seem small but it translates to thirty-six million people whose lives are lost to toil and abuse. We can only imagine what contributions they might make if they lived free in an equal society.

By ignoring captives, a class of people who made up a substantial proportion of some small-scale societies, archaeologists may overlook significant social stratification in groups they label "egalitarian." One might counter that egalitarian societies are almost always stratified by age and sex and since most captives are women and children, they simply represent additional elements in that stratification. But that ignores the importance of social boundaries that all societies maintain. With time, captives could become more or less integrated into their captors' society, but their alien origins were rarely forgotten. Captives, simply by their presence, raised the status of their captors; and the products of their labor, appropriated by their captors, were another avenue for the creation of status. The drudge-filled lives of captive wives differed from those of native-born women. The presence of captives might be the most important factor in creating more comfortable lives for native women. Can we really label a society "egalitarian" when as much as one-tenth to one-quarter of the group cannot participate fully in societal membership?

Captives have affected the construction of social groups through time. As part of a web of relationships that encompassed every member of a society, and through daily activities and interactions with other persons, places, and things, captives changed not only their social place in the captor society but almost certainly the society's basic conceptions of self and other. This was as true in the small-scale societies of the Amazon as in the early nineteenth-century American South.

Captives are "invisible" people and difficult to see in the past. But archaeologists may not only mischaracterize small-scale societies by ignoring captives, they also ignore a strong influence on those material entities we call "archaeological cultures." Captives were influential bearers of culture and likely changed captor culture in ways we cannot ignore. I hope this book helps in the development of a new field of study of these forgotten, stolen people.

| Notes

3. The Captive as Social Person

1. That is, except in cases where the goal of captive taking was trade, ransom, or use in sacrifice; from the viewpoint of the captive herself, however, and that of her birth family, the state of captivity might extend for years. See, for example, Demos 1994.

5. Captives, Social Boundaries, and Ethnogenesis

1. Brubaker and Cooper (2000) argue that the concept of *identity* is vague and overused and has little analytic power.

2. Archaeological cultures are bundles of archaeological traits located in time and space. In the area of the northern Southwest, the "Ancestral Pueblo" culture is represented by black-on-white pottery, stone buildings of particular configurations, flexed burials, and a myriad of other details gleaned from over one hundred years of excavation. The focus of a majority of archaeological investigation is explaining the changes that can be seen over time in the remains of the archaeological cultures under study.

6. Captives and Cultural Transmission

1. Theory developed in evolutionary archaeology, like that in ethnoarchaeology, focuses primarily on intergenerational teaching and learning within groups, rather than intercultural transmission. Evolutionary anthropologists recognize intercultural interaction as one aspect of "horizontal transmission" (Cavalli-Sforza and Feldman 1981; horizontal transmission can also refer to transmission among generational peers within a society), but in general they believe this form of cultural transmission is rare (Tehrani and Collard 2002; VanPool, Palmer, and Van-Pool 2008, 77; see also Gosselain 2008, 151). Evolutionary anthropologists largely ignore the social mechanisms through which culture is transmitted between groups (Gosselain 2008, 151). Instead, they debate the extent to which cultural evolution is the result of phylogenesis, in which the transmission of cultural traits is similar to the transmission of genetic material in biological phylogenesis, and ethnogenesis, in which cultural evolution is the result of interaction, borrowing, blending, and trade/exchange of ideas and practices among populations. See Tehrani and Collard 2002, 443–44.

References

Agbe-Davies, Anna S., and Alexander A. Bauer. 2010. "Rethinking Trade as a Social Activity: An Introduction." In *Social Archaeologies of Trade and Exchange: Exploring Relationships among People, Places, and Things*, edited by Alexander A. Bauer and Anna S. Agbe-Davies, 13–28. Walnut Creek CA: Left Coast Press.

Albers, Patricia. 1993. "Symbiosis, Merger, and War: Contrasting Forms of Intertribal Relationship among Historic Plains Indians." In *The Political Economy of North American Indians*, edited by John H. Moore, 94–132. Norman: University of Oklahoma Press.

———. 1996. "Changing Configurations of Ethnicity in the Northeastern Plains." In *Culture, Power, and History: Ethnogenesis in the Americas*, edited by Jonathan Hill, 90–118. Iowa City: University of Iowa Press.

Alexander, J. 2001. "Islam, Archaeology, and Slavery in Africa." *World Archaeology* 33(1): 44–60.

Alpers, Edward A. 1983. "The Story of Swema: Female Vulnerability in Nineteenth-Century East Africa." In *Women and Slavery in Africa*, edited by Claire C. Robertson and Martin A. Klein, 185–99. Madison: University of Wisconsin Press.

———. 2003. "Soldiers, Slaves, and Saints: An Overview of the African Presence in India." *Kenya Past and Present* 34(1): 47–54.

Alt, Susan. 2008. "Unwilling Immigrants: Culture, Change, and the 'Other' in Mississippian Societies." In *Invisible Citizens: Captives and Their Consequences*, edited by Catherine M. Cameron, 205–22. Salt Lake City: University of Utah Press.

Ames, Kenneth M. 2001. "Slaves, Chiefs and Labour on the Northern Northwest Coast." *World Archaeology* 33(1):1–17.

———. 2008. "Slavery, Household Production, and Demography on the Southern Northwest Coast: Cables, Tacking, and Ropewalks." In *Invisible Citizens: Captives and Their Consequences*, edited by Catherine M. Cameron, 138–58. Salt Lake City: University of Utah Press.

Ames, Kenneth M., and Herbert D. G. Maschner. 1999. *Peoples of the Northwest Coast: Their Archaeology and Prehistory*. London: Thames and Hudson.

Anderson, David G. 1994. *The Savannah River Chiefdoms: Political Change in the Late Prehistoric Southeast*. Tuscaloosa: University of Alabama Press.

Andrews, Jean. 1992. "The Peripatetic Chili Pepper: Diffusion of the Domesticated Capsicums since Columbus." In *Chilies to Chocolate: Food the Americas Gave the World*, edited by Nelson Foster and Linda S. Cordell, 81–94. Tucson: University of Arizona Press.

Arkush, Elizabeth N., and Mark W. Allen, eds. 2006. *The Archaeology of Warfare: Prehistories of Raiding and Conquest*. Gainesville: University Press of Florida.

Armstrong, Douglas V. 1998. "Cultural Transformation within Enslaved Laborer Communities in the Caribbean." In *Studies in Culture Contact: Interaction, Culture Change, and Archaeology*, edited by James G. Cusick, 378–401. Carbondale IL: Center for Archaeological Investigations.

Averkieva, Julia. (1941) 1966. *Slavery among the Indians of North America*. Translated by G. R. Elliot. Victoria BC: Victoria College.

Baier, Stephen, and Paul E. Lovejoy. 1977. "The Tuareg of the Central Sudan: Gradations in Servility at the Desert Edge (Niger and Nigeria)." In *Slavery in Africa: Historical and Anthropological Perspectives*, edited by Suzanne Miers and Igor Kopytoff, 391–414. Madison: University of Wisconsin Press.

Baldus, Bernd. 1977. "Responses to Dependence in a Servile Group: The Cachube of Northern Benin." In *Slavery in Africa: Historical and Anthropological Perspectives*, edited by Suzanne Miers and Igor Kopytoff, 435–58. Madison: University of Wisconsin Press.

Bales, Kevin. (1999) 2012. *Disposable People: New Slavery in the Global Economy*. Berkeley: University of California Press.

———. 2005. *Understanding Global Slavery: A Reader*. Berkeley: University of California Press.

———. 2007. *Ending Slavery: How We Free Today's Slaves*. Berkeley: University of California Press.

Barnes, R. H. 1999. "Marriage by Capture." *Journal of the Royal Anthropological Institute* 5(1): 57–73.

Barr, Juliana. 2007. *Peace Came in the Form of a Woman: Indians and Spaniards in the Texas Borderlands*. Chapel Hill: University of North Carolina Press.

Barth, Fredrik. (1969) 1998. *Ethnic Groups and Boundaries: The Social Organization of Culture Difference*. Long Grove IL: Waveland Press.

Bauer, Alexander A., and Anna S. Agbe-Davies. 2010. "Trade and Interaction in Archaeology." In *Social Archaeologies of Trade and Exchange: Exploring Relationships among People, Places, and Things*, edited by Alexander A. Bauer and Anna S. Agbe-Davies, 29–48. Walnut Creek CA: Left Coast Press.

Bay, Edna. 1983. "Servitude and Worldly Success in the Palace of Dahomey." In

Women and Slavery in Africa, edited by Claire C. Robertson and Martin A. Klein, 340–67. Madison: University of Wisconsin Press.

Beck, Robin A., Jr. 2009. "Catawba Coalescence and the Shattering of the Carolina Piedmont, 1540–1675." In *Mapping the Mississippian Shatter Zone: The Colonial Indian Slave Trade and Regional Instability in the American South*, edited by Robbie Ethridge and Sheri M. Shuck-Hall, 115–41. Lincoln: University of Nebraska Press.

Beckerman, Stephen. 2008. "Revenge: An Overview." In *Revenge in the Cultures of Lowland South America*, edited by S. Beckerman and P. Valentine, 1–9. Gainesville: University of Florida Press.

Bellwood, Peter. 1992. "Southeast Asia before History." In *The Cambridge History of Southeast Asia*, vol. 1, *From Early Times to c. 1800*, edited by Nicholas Tarling, 55–136. Cambridge: Cambridge University Press.

Bhabha, Homi K. 1990. "The Third Space." In *Identity, Community Culture, Difference*, edited by Jonathan Rutherford, 207–21. London: Lawrence and Wishart.

———. 1994. *The Location of Culture*. London: Routledge.

Bilby, Kenneth. 1996. "Ethnogenesis in the Guianas and Jamaica: Two Maroon Cases." In *History, Power, and Identity: Ethnogenesis in the Americas, 1492–1992*, edited by Jonathan D. Hill, 119–41. Iowa City: University of Iowa Press.

Biocca, Ettore. (1965) 1996. *Yanoáma: The Story of Helena Valero, a Girl Kidnapped by Amazonian Indians*. New York: Kodansha International.

Bishop, Charles A., and Victor Lytwyn. 2007. "Barbarism and Ardour of War from the Tenderest Years: Cree-Inuit Warfare in the Hudson Bay Region." In *North American Indigenous Warfare and Ritual Violence*, edited by R. Chacoan and R. Mendoza, 30–57. Tucson: University of Arizona Press.

Blanton, Richard, Gary Feinman, Stephen Kowalewski, and Peter Peregrine. 1996. "A Dual-Processual Theory for the Evolution of Mesoamerican Civilization." *Current Anthropology* 37(1): 1–14, 47–86.

Bloch, Marc. (1947) 1975. *Slavery and Serfdom in the Middle Ages*. Translated by William R. Beers. Berkeley: University of California Press.

Bonnassie, Pierre. 1991. *From Slavery to Feudalism in Southwestern Europe*. Cambridge: Cambridge University Press.

Bourne, Edward Gaylord. 1904. *Narratives of the Career of Hernando de Soto*. New York: A. S. Barnes.

Bowne, Eric E. 2005. *The Westo Indians: Slave Traders of the Early Colonial South*. Tuscaloosa: University of Alabama Press.

———. 2009. "'Caryinge Away their Corne and Children': The Effects of Westo Slave Raids on the Indians of the Lower South." In *Mapping the Mississippian Shatter Zone: The Colonial Indian Slave Trade and Regional Instability in the American South*, edited by R. Ethridge and S. M. Shuck-Hall, 104–14. Lincoln: University of Nebraska Press.

Bowser, Brenda J. 2008. "Captives in Amazonia: Becoming Kin in a Predatory Landscape." In *Invisible Citizens: Captives and Their Consequences*, edited by Catherine M. Cameron, 262–82. Salt Lake City: University of Utah Press.

Bowser, Brenda J., and John Q. Patton. 2008. "Learning and Transmission of Pottery Style: Women's Life Histories and Communities of Practice in the Ecuadorian Amazon." In *Cultural Transmission and Material Culture: Breaking down Boundaries*, edited by Miriam T. Stark, Brenda J. Bowser, and Lee Horne, 105–29. Tucson: University of Arizona Press.

Boyd, R. 1990. "Demographic History, 1774–1874." In *Northwest Coast*, edited by W. Suttles, 135–48. Handbook of North American Indians, vol. 7. Washington DC: Smithsonian Institution.

Bromber, Katrin. 2007. "Mjakazi, Mpambe, Mjoli, Suria: Female Slaves in Swahili Sources." In *Women and Slavery*, vol. 1, *Africa, the Indian Ocean World, and the Medieval North Atlantic*, edited by Gwyn Campbell, Suzanne Miers, and Joseph C. Miller, 111–28. Athens: Ohio University Press.

Brooks, James F. 1998. "Amerindian Societies." In *Macmillan Encyclopedia of World Slavery*, edited by Paul Finkelman and Joseph C. Miller, 1:52–55. London: Simon & Schuster and Prentice Hall International.

———. 2000. "Served Well by Plunder: La Gran Ladronería and Producers of History Astride the Río Grande." *American Quarterly* 52(1): 23–58.

———. 2002. *Captives and Cousins: Slavery, Kinship, and Community in the Southwest Borderlands*. Chapel Hill: University of North Carolina Press.

———. 2008. "Captive, Concubine, Servant, Kin: A Historian Divines Experience in Archaeological Slaveries." In *Invisible Citizens: Captives and Their Consequences*, edited by Catherine M. Cameron, 262–82. Salt Lake City: University of Utah Press.

———. 2009. "'We Betray Our Own Nation' Indian Slavery and Multi-ethnic Communities in the Southwest Borderlands." In *Indian Slavery in Colonial America*, edited by Alan Gallay, 319–52. Lincoln: University of Nebraska Press.

Brown, Carolyn A. 2003. "Memory as Resistance: Identity and the Contested History of Slavery in Southeastern Nigeria, an Oral History Project." In *Fighting the Slave Trade: West African Strategies*, edited by Sylviane A. Diouf, 219–25. Athens: Ohio University Press.

Brown, Michael F., and Eduardo Fernandez. (1992) 1999. "Tribe and State in a Frontier Mosaic: The Asháninka of Eastern Peru." In *War in the Tribal Zone: Expanding States and Indigenous Warfare*, 2nd ed., edited by Brian Ferguson and Neil Whitehead, 175–98. Santa Fe NM: School of American Research Press.

Brubaker, Rogers, and Frederick Cooper. 2000. "Beyond 'Identity.'" *Theory and Society* 29(1): 1–47.

Brugge, David M. (1968) 2010. *Navajos in the Catholic Church Records of New Mexico, 1694–1875.* Santa Fe, NM: School for Advanced Research Press. Originally published as Research Section Reports 1 (Window Rock AZ: Navajo Nation Parks and Recreation Department).

———. 1979. "Early 18th Century Spanish-Apachean Relations." In *Collected Papers in Honor of Bertha Pauline Dutton*, edited by Albert H. Schroeder, 103–22. Albuquerque NM: Albuquerque Archaeological Society Press.

———. 1993a. "Eighteenth-Century Fugitives from New Mexico among the Navajos." In *Papers from the Third, Fourth, and Sixth Navajo Studies Conferences*, edited by June-el Piper, 279–83. Window Rock AZ: Navajo Nation Historic Preservation Department.

———. 1993b. "The Spanish Borderlands: Aboriginal Slavery." In *Encyclopedia of the North American Colonies*, edited by Jacob Ernest Cooke, 91–101. New York: Charles Scribner's Sons.

Burford, Alison. 1972. *Craftsmen in Greek and Roman Society.* Ithaca NY: Cornell University Press.

Busby, Cecilia. 1997. "Permeable and Partible Persons: A Comparative Analysis of Gender and Body in South India and Melanesia." *Journal of the Royal Anthropological Institute* 3: 261–78.

———. 2000. *The Performance of Gender: An Anthropology of Everyday Life in a South Indian Fishing Village.* Somerset NJ: Transaction Publishers.

Cabeza de Vaca, Álvar Núñez. (1542) 2003. *The Narrative of Cabeza de Vaca.* Edited and translated by Rolena Adorno and Patrick Charles Pautz. Lincoln: University of Nebraska Press.

Cameron, Catherine M. 1998. "Coursed Adobe Architecture, Style, and Social Boundaries in the American Southwest." In *The Archaeology of Social Boundaries*, edited by Miriam T. Stark, 183–207. Washington DC: Smithsonian Institution Press.

———. 2008a. "Introduction: Captives in Prehistory as Agents of Social Change." In *Invisible Citizens: Captives and Their Consequences*, edited by Catherine M. Cameron, 1–24. Salt Lake City: University of Utah Press.

———, ed. 2008b. *Invisible Citizens: Captives and Their Consequences.* Salt Lake City: University of Utah Press.

———. 2011. "Captives and Culture Change: Implications for Archaeology." *Current Anthropology* 52(2): 169–209.

———. 2013. "How People Moved among Ancient Societies: Broadening the View." *American Anthropologist* 115(2): 218–31.

———. 2015. "The Effects of Warfare and Captive-Taking on Indigenous Mortality in Post-Contact North America." In *Beyond Germs: Exploration of Native Depopulation in North America*, edited by Catherine M. Cameron, Paul Kelton, and Alan C. Swedlund, 174–97. Tucson: University of Arizona Press.

Cameron, Catherine M., Paul Kelton, and Alan C. Swedlund, eds. 2015. *Beyond Germs: Exploration of Native Depopulation in North America*. Tucson: University of Arizona Press.

Campbell, Gwyn. 2007. "Female Bondage in Imperial Madagascar, 1820–95." In *Women and Slavery*, vol. 1, *Africa, the Indian Ocean World, and the Medieval North Atlantic*, edited by Gwyn Campbell, Suzanne Miers, and Joseph C. Miller, 237–58. Athens: Ohio University Press.

Campbell, Gwyn, and Edward A. Alpers. 2005. "Introduction: Slavery, Forced Labour and Resistance in Indian Ocean Africa and Asia." In *Slavery and Resistance in Africa and Asia*, edited by Edward Alpers, Gwyn Campbell, and Michael Salman, 1–19. New York: Routledge.

Campbell, Gwyn, Suzanne Miers, and Joseph C. Miller, eds. 2007. *Women and Slavery*, vol. 1, *Africa, the Indian Ocean World, and the Medieval North Atlantic*. Athens: Ohio University Press.

———. 2008. *Women and Slavery*, vol. 2, *The Modern Atlantic*. Athens: Ohio University Press.

———. 2009. *Children in Slavery through the Ages*. Athens: Ohio University Press.

Carneiro, Robert L. 1991. "The Nature of the Chiefdom as Revealed by Evidence from the Cauca Valley of Colombia." In *Profiles in Cultural Evolution: Papers from a Conference in Honor of Elman R. Service*, edited by A. Terry Rambo and Kathleen Gillogly, 167–90. Ann Arbor: Anthropological Papers, Museum of Anthropology, University of Michigan.

Carney, J., and R. N. Rosomoff. 2009. *In the Shadow of Slavery: Africa's Botanical Legacy in the Atlantic World*. Berkeley: University of California Press.

Carocci, Max, and Stephanie Pratt, eds. 2012. *Native American Adoption, Captivity, and Slavery in Changing Contexts*. New York: Palgrave Macmillan.

Carr, Christopher. 1995. "A Unified Middle-Range Theory of Artifact Design." In *Style, Society, and Person: Archaeological and Ethnological Perspectives*, edited by Christopher Carr and Jill Neitzel, 171–258. New York: Plenum Press.

Cavalli-Sforza, L. L, and M. W. Feldman. 1981. *Cultural Transmission and Evolution: A Quantitative Approach*. Monographs in Population Biology, 16. Princeton NJ: Princeton University Press.

Chacon, Richard J., and David H. Dye, eds. 2007. *The Taking and Displaying of Human Body Parts as Trophies by Amerindians*. New York: Springer.

Chacon, Richard J., and Ruben G. Mendoza, eds. 2007a. "Ethical Considerations and Conclusions Regarding Indigenous Warfare and Ritual Violence in Latin America." In *Latin American Indigenous Warfare and Ritual Violence*, edited by Richard J. Chacon and Ruben G. Mendoza, 234–48. Tucson: University of Arizona Press.

———. 2007b. *Latin American Indigenous Warfare and Ritual Violence*. Tucson: University of Arizona Press.

Chagnon, Napoleon. 1992. *Yanomano: The Last Days of Eden*. San Diego CA: Harcourt Brace Jovanovich.

———. 1988. "Life Histories, Blood Revenge, and Warfare in a Tribal Population." *Science* 239: 985–92.

Chatterjee, Indrani, and Richard M. Eaton, eds. 2006. *Slavery and South Asian History*. Bloomington: Indiana University Press.

Chernela, Janet M. 1992. "Social Meanings and Material Transaction: The Wanano-Tukano of Brazil and Columbia." *Journal of Anthropological Archaeology* 11(2): 111–24.

———. 2003. "Language Ideology and Women's Speech: Talking Community in the Northwest Amazon." *American Anthropologist* 105(4): 794–806.

———. 2011. "Comment on 'Captives and Culture Change: Implications for Archaeology.'" *Current Anthropology* 52(2): 196.

Clark, Jeffery J. 2001. *Tracking Prehistoric Migrations: Pueblo Settlers among the Tonto Basin Hohokam*. Anthropological Papers of the University of Arizona, 65. Tucson: University of Arizona Press.

Cobb, Charles R. 2005. "Archaeology and the 'Savage Slot': Displacement and Emplacement in the Premodern World." *American Anthropologist* 107(4): 563–74.

Cobb, Charles R., and Brian M. Butler. 2002. "The Vacant Quarter Revisited: Late Mississippian Abandonment of the Lower Mississippi Valley." *American Antiquity* 67(4): 625–41.

Cohen, David William. 1978. "Trends in African Historical Studies." *American Anthropologist* 80: 101–5.

Cohen, Ronald. 1978. "Ethnicity: Problem and Focus in Anthropology." *Annual Review of Anthropology* 7: 379–403.

Collar, Anna C. F., Fiona Coward, Tom Brughmans, Barbara J. Mills. 2015. "Networks in Archaeology: Phenomena, Abstraction, Representation." *Journal of Archaeological Method and Theory* 22(1): 1–32.

Colley, Linda. 2002. *Captives: The Story of Britain's Pursuit of Empire and How Its Soldiers and Civilians Were Held Captive by the Dream of Global Supremacy, 1600–1850*. New York: Pantheon Books.

———. 2007. *The Ordeal of Elizabeth Marsh: A Woman in World History*. New York: Pantheon Books.

Comaroff, John L., and Jean Comaroff. 2001. "On Personhood: An Anthropological Perspective from Africa." *Social Identities* 7(2): 267–83.

Cooper, Frederick. 1979. "The Problem of Slavery in African Studies." *Journal of African History* 20: 103–25.

Copley, Esther. (1839) 1960. *History of Slavery, and Its Abolition.* Detroit: Negro History Press.

Coquery-Vidrovitch, Catherine. 2007. "Women, Marriage, and Slavery in Sub-Saharan Africa in the Nineteenth Century." In *Women and Slavery,* vol. 1, *Africa, the Indian Ocean World, and the Medieval North Atlantic,* edited by Gwyn Campbell, Suzanne Miers, and Joseph C. Miller, 43–61. Athens: Ohio University Press.

Cordell, Linda S. 2006. "Rio Grande Glaze Paint Ware in Southwestern Archaeology." In *The Social Life of Pots: Glaze Wares and Cultural Dynamics in the Southwest, AD 1250–1680,* edited by Judith Habicht-Mauche, Suzanne Eckert, and Deborah Huntley, 253–72. Tucson: University of Arizona Press.

Cordell, Linda S., and Maxine E. McBrinn. 2012. *Archaeology of the Southwest,* 3rd ed. Walnut Creek CA: Left Coast Press.

Costin, Cathy, and Rita Wright, eds. 1998. *Craft and Social Identity.* Archaeological Papers of the American Anthropological Association, 8. Arlington VA: American Anthropological Association.

Croucher, Sarah K. 2015. *Capitalism and Cloves: An Archaeology of Plantation Life on Nineteenth-Century Zanzibar.* New York: Springer-Verlag.

Curtin, Philip, Steven Feierman, Leonard Thompson, and Jan Vansina. 1995. *African History: From Earliest Times to Independence.* New York: Longman Group.

Cybulski, Jerome S. 1990. "Human Biology." In *Northwest Coast,* edited by Wayne Suttles, 52–59. Handbook of North American Indians, vol. 7. Washington DC: Smithsonian Institution Press.

———. 1992. *A Greenville Burial Ground: Human Remains and Mortuary Elements in British Columbia Prehistory.* Hull QC: Canadian Museum of Civilization.

———. 1994. "Culture Change, Demographic History, and Health and Disease on the Northwest Coast." In *In the Wake of Contact: Biological Responses to Conquest,* edited by C. S. Larsen, 75–85. New York: Wiley-Liss.

Dannin, Robert. 1982. "Forms of Huron Kinship and Marriage." *Ethnology* 21(2): 101–10.

David, Nicholas, and Carol Kramer. 2001. *Ethnoarchaeology in Action.* Cambridge: Cambridge University Press.

Davies, Norman. 1996. *Europe: A History.* Oxford: Oxford University Press.

Davis, David Brion. 1966. *The Problem of Slavery in Western Culture.* Ithaca NY: Cornell University Press.

Deagan, Kathleen. 1974. "Sex, Status, and Role in the Mestizaje of Spanish Colonial Florida." PhD diss., University of Florida, Gainesville.

———. 1983. *Spanish St. Augustine: The Archaeology of a Colonial Creole Community*. New York: Academic Press.

———. 1998. "Transculturation and Spanish American Ethnogenesis: The Archaeological Legacy of the Quincentenary." In *Studies in Culture Contact: Interaction, Culture Change, and Archaeology*, edited by James G. Cusick, 23–43. Carbondale IL: Center for Archaeological Investigations.

DeBoer, Warren R. 1981. "Buffer Zones in the Cultural Ecology of Aboriginal Amazonia: An Ethnohistorical Approach." *American Antiquity* 46(2): 384–77.

———. 1986. "Pillage and Production in the Amazon: A View through the Conibo of the Ucayali Basin, Eastern Peru." *World Archaeology* 18(2): 231–46.

———. 1990. "Interaction, Imitation, and Communication as Expressed in Style: The Ucayali Experience." In *The Uses of Style in Archaeology*, edited by Margaret W. Conkey and Christine A. Hastorf, 82–104. Cambridge: Cambridge University Press.

———. 2008. "Wrenched Bodies." In *Invisible Citizens: Captives and Their Consequences*, edited by Catherine M. Cameron, 233–61. Salt Lake City: University of Utah Press.

———. 2011. "Deep Time, Big Space: An Archaeologist Skirts the Topic at Hand." In *Ethnicity in Ancient Amazonia: Reconstructing Past Identities from Archaeology, Linguistics, and Ethnohistory*, edited Alf Hornborg and Jonathan D. Hill, 75–98. Boulder: University Press of Colorado.

DeCorse, Christopher R. 1989. "Material Aspects of Limba, Yalunka, and Kuranko Ethnicity: Archaeological Research in Northeastern Sierra Leone." In *Archaeological Approaches to Cultural Identity*, edited by S. Shennan, 125–40. London: Unwin Hyman.

———. 2001. *West Africa during the Atlantic Slave Trade: Archaeological Perspectives*. London: Leicester University Press.

Demos, John. 1994. *The Unredeemed Captive*. London: Papermac.

Deutsch, Jan-Georg. 2007. "Prices for Female Slaves and Changes in their Life Cycle: Evidence from German East Africa." In *Women and Slavery*, vol. 1, *Africa, the Indian Ocean World, and the Medieval North Atlantic*, edited by Gwyn Campbell, Suzanne Miers, and Joseph C. Miller, 129–46. Athens: Ohio University Press.

Diouf, Sylviane A., ed. 2003. *Fighting the Slave Trade: West African Strategies*. Athens: Ohio University Press.

Donald, Leland. 1997. *Aboriginal Slavery on the Northwest Coast of North America*. Berkeley: University of California Press.

Dornberg, John. 1996. *Western Europe*. International Government and Politics Series. Phoenix: Oryx Press.

Drennan, Robert D., Timothy Earle, Gary M. Feinman, Roland Fletcher, Michael J. Kolb, Peter Peregrine, Christian E. Peterson, Carla Sinopoli, Michael E. Smith, Monica L. Smith, Barbara L. Stark, and Miriam T. Stark. 2012. "Comparative Archaeology: A Commitment to Understanding Variation." In *The Comparative Archaeology of Complex Societies*, edited by Michael E. Smith, 1–3. Cambridge: Cambridge University Press.

Driver, Harold E. 1966. "Geographical-Historical versus Psycho-Functional Explanations of Kin Avoidances." *Current Anthropology* 7: 131–60.

Drucker, Philip. 1965. *Cultures of the North Pacific Coast*. Scranton PA: Chandler.

Duff, Andrew I. 2002. *Western Pueblo Identities: Regional Interaction, Migration, and Transformation*. Tucson: University of Arizona Press.

Dye, David H. 2004. "Art, Ritual, and Chiefly Warfare in the Mississippian World." In *Hero, Hawk, and Open Hand: American Indian Art of the Ancient Midwest and South*, edited by R. V. Sharp, 190–205. New Haven CT: Art Institute of Chicago and Yale University Press.

Earle, Timothy. 1997. *How Chiefs Come to Power: The Political Economy in Prehistory*. Palo Alto CA: Stanford University Press.

Edwards, Paul, ed. 1967. *Equiano's Travels: The Interesting Narrative of the Life of Olaudah Equiano or Gustavus Vassa the African*. New York: Frederick A. Praeger.

Ekberg, Carl J. 2010. *Stealing Indian Women: Native Slavery in the Illinois Country*. Urbana: University of Illinois Press.

Engerman, Stanley, Seymour Drescher, and Robert Paquette, eds. 2001. *Slavery*. New York: Oxford University Press.

Ethridge, Robbie. 2009. Introduction to *Mapping the Mississippian Shatter Zone: The Colonial Indian Slave Trade and Regional Instability in the American South*, edited by Robbie Ethridge and Sheri M. Shuck-Hall, 1–62. Lincoln: University of Nebraska Press.

Ethridge, Robbie, and Charles Hudson, eds. 2002. *The Transformation of the Southeastern Indians, 1540–1760*. Jackson: University Press of Mississippi.

Ethridge, Robbie, and Sheri M. Shuck-Hall, eds. 2009. *Mapping the Mississippian Shatter Zone: The Colonial Indian Slave Trade and Regional Instability in the American South*. Lincoln: University of Nebraska Press.

Fennell, Christopher C. 2007. *Crossroads and Cosmologies: Diasporas and Ethnogenesis in the New World*. Gainesville: University Press of Florida.

Fenton, William N. 1978. "Northern Iroquoian Culture Patterns." In *Northeast*, edited by Bruce G. Trigger, 296–321. Handbook of North American Indians, vol. 15. Washington DC: Smithsonian Institution.

Ferguson, Leland. 1991. "Struggling with Pots in Colonial South Carolina." In *The Archaeology of Inequality*, edited by Randall H. McGuire and Robert Paynter, 28–39. Oxford: Basil Blackwell.

———. 1992. *Uncommon Ground: Archaeology and Early African America, 1650–1800*. Washington DC: Smithsonian Institution Press.

Ferguson, R. Brian. 2006. "Archaeology, Cultural Anthropology, and the Origins and Intensifications of War." In *The Archaeology of Warfare*, edited by Elizabeth N. Arkush and Mark W. Allen, 470–523. Gainesville: University Press of Florida.

———. 2013. "Pinker's List: Exaggerating Prehistoric War Mortality." In *War, Peace, and Human Nature: The Convergence of Evolutionary and Cultural Views*, edited by Douglas P. Fry, 112–31. Oxford: Oxford University Press.

Ferguson, R. Brian, and Neil L. Whitehead, eds. (1992) 1999. *War in the Tribal Zone: Expanding States and Indigenous Warfare*. 2nd ed. Santa Fe NM: School of American Research Press.

Finley, Moses. 1964. "Between Slavery and Freedom." *Comparative Studies in Society and History* 6: 233–49.

———. 1980. *Ancient Slavery and Modern Ideology*. New York: Viking Press.

Fisher, N. R. E. 1993. *Slavery in Classical Greece*. London: Bristol Classical Press.

Fitts, Mary Elizabeth, and Charles L. Heath. 2009. "'Indians Refusing to Carry Burdens': Understanding the Success of Catawba Political, Military, and Settlement Strategies in Colonial Carolina." In *Mapping the Mississippian Shatter Zone: The Colonial Indian Slave Trade and Regional Instability in the American South*, edited by Robbie Ethridge and Sheri M. Shuck-Hall, 142–62. Lincoln: University of Nebraska Press.

Flannery, Kent, and Joyce Marcus. 2012. *The Creation of Inequality: How Our Prehistoric Ancestors Set the Stage for Monarchy, Slavery, and Empire*. Cambridge MA: Harvard University Press.

Foster, William H. 2003. *The Captor's Narrative: Catholic Women and Their Puritan Men on the Early American Frontier*. Ithaca NY: Cornell University Press.

Fowler, Chris. 2004. *The Archaeology of Personhood: An Anthropological Approach*. London: Routledge.

———. 2010. "From Identity and Material Culture to Personhood and Materiality." In *The Oxford Handbook of Material Culture Studies*, edited by Mary C. Beaudry and Dan Hicks, 352–85. Oxford: Oxford University Press.

Fox, William A. 2009. "Events as Seen from the North: The Iroquois and Colonial Slavery." In *Mapping the Mississippian Shatter Zone: The Colonial Indian Slave Trade and Regional Instability in the American South*, edited by Robbie Ethridge and Sheri M. Shuck-Hall, 63–80. Lincoln: University of Nebraska Press.

Frank, Barbara E. 1993. "Reconstructing the History of an African Ceramic Tradition: Technology, Slavery and Agency in the Region of Kadiolo (Mali)." *Cahiers d'Etudes Africaines* 131: 381–401.

Gallay, Alan. 2002. *The Indian Slave Trade: The Rise of the English Empire in the American South, 1670–1717.* New Haven CT: Yale University Press.

———. 2009. Introduction to *Indian Slavery in Colonial America*, edited by Allan Gallay, 1–32. Lincoln: University of Nebraska Press.

Gelo, Daniel J., and Scott Zesch. 2003. "'Every Day Seemed to Be a Holiday': The Captivity of Bianca Babb." *Southwestern Historical Quarterly* 107(1): 34–67.

Genovese, Eugene D. 1972. *Roll Jordan Roll: The World the Slaves Made.* New York: Pantheon Books.

Golitko, Mark, and Lawrence H. Keeley. 2007. "Beating Ploughshares Back into Swords: Warfare in the Linearbandkeramik." *Antiquity* 81(312): 332–42.

Goodby, Robert G. 1998. "Technological Patterning and Social Boundaries: Ceramic Variability in Southern New England, AD 1000–1675." In *The Archaeology of Social Boundaries*, edited by Miriam T. Stark, 161–82. Washington DC: Smithsonian Institution Press.

Goody, Jack. 1971. *Technology, Tradition, and the State in Africa.* Oxford: Oxford University Press.

Gosselain, Oliver P. 2008. "Mother Bella Was Not a Bella: Inherited and Transformed Traditions in Southwestern Niger." In *Cultural Transmission and Material Culture: Breaking down Boundaries*, edited by Miriam T. Stark, Brenda J. Bowser, and Lee Horne, 150–77. Tucson: University of Arizona Press.

———. 2011 "Comment on 'Captives and Culture Change: Implications for Archaeology.'" *Current Anthropology* 52(2): 197.

Gould, Richard A., and Patty Jo Watson. 1982. "A Dialogue on the Meaning and Use of Analogy in Ethnoarchaeological Reasoning." *Journal of Anthropological Archaeology* 1: 355–81.

Greer, Allan, ed. 2000. *The Jesuit Relations: Natives and Missionaries in Seventeenth-Century North America.* Boston MA: Bedford/St. Martin's.

Guilaine, Jean, and Jean Zammit. 2005. *The Origins of War: Violence in Prehistory*, translated by Melanie Hersey. Malden MA: Blackwell.

Gutiérrez, Ramón A. 1991. *When Jesus Came, the Corn Mothers Went Away.* Palo Alto CA: Stanford University Press.

Guyer, Jane I., and Samuel M. Eno Belinga. 1995. "Wealth in People, Wealth in Knowledge: Accumulation and Composition in Equatorial Africa." *Journal of African History* 36: 91–120.

Gwynne, Samuel C. 2010. *Empire of the Summer Moon: Quanah Parker and the*

Rise and Fall of the Comanches, the Most Powerful Indian Tribe in American History. New York: Scribner.

Haas, J., and W. Creamer. 1993. *Stress and Warfare among the Kayenta Anasazi of the Thirteenth Century AD.* Fieldiana Anthropology (New Series), 21. Chicago: Field Museum of Natural History.

Haas, Mary. 1943. "The Linguist as a Teacher of Languages." *Language* 19: 203–8.

Haas, Samuel S., Jr. 1942. "The Contributions of Slaves to and Their Influence upon the Culture of Early Islam." PhD diss., Princeton University.

Habicht-Mauche, Judith. 2008. "Captive Wives? The Role and Status of Non-local Women on the Protohistoric Southern High Plains." In *Invisible Citizens: Captives and Their Consequences*, edited by Catherine M. Cameron, 181–204. Salt Lake City: University of Utah Press.

Hajda, Yvonne P. 2005. "Slavery in the Greater Lower Columbia Region." *Ethnohistory* 52(3): 563–88.

Hallgrimsson, B., B. O. Donnabha, G. B. Walters, D. Cooper, D. Guobjartsson, and K. Stefansson. 2004. "Composition of the Founding Population of Iceland: Biological Distance and Morphological Variation in Early Historic Atlantic Europe." *American Journal of Physical Anthropology* 124: 257–74.

Hämäläinen, Pekka. 2008. *The Comanche Empire.* New Haven CT: Yale University Press.

Harrod, Ryan P. 2012. "Centers of Control: Revealing Elites among the Ancestral Pueblo during the 'Chaco Phenomenon.'" *International Journal of Paleopathology* 2(2–3): 123–35.

Hayden, Brian. 1996. "Feasting in Prehistoric and Traditional Societies." In *Food and the Status Quest: An Interdisciplinary Perspective*, edited by Polly Wiessner and Wulf Schiefenhovel, 127–48. Providence RI: Berghahn Books.

Heckenberger, Michael J. 2002. "Rethinking the Arawakan Diaspora: Hierarchy, Regionality, and the Amazonian Formative." In *Comparative Arawakan Histories: Rethinking Language Family and Culture Area in Amazonia*, edited by Jonathan D. Hill and Fernando Santos-Granero, 99–122. Urbana: University of Illinois Press.

Helgason, Agnar, Sigrún Sigurðardóttir, Jayne Nicholson, Bryan Sykes, Emmeline W. Hill, Daniel G. Bradley, Vidar Bosnes, Jeffery R. Gulcher, Ryk Ward, and Kári Stefánsson. 2000. "Estimating Scandinavian and Gaelic Ancestry in the Male Settlers of Iceland." *American Journal of Human Genetics* 67: 697–717.

Helms, Mary W. 1988. *Ulysses' Sail: An Ethnographic Odyssey of Power, Knowledge, and Geographical Distance.* Princeton NJ: Princeton University Press.

Herbich, Ingrid, and Michael Dietler. 2008. "The Long Arm of the Mother-in-Law: Learning, Postmarital Resocialization of Women, and Material Culture

Style." In *Cultural Transmission and Material Culture: Breaking Down Boundaries*, edited by Miriam T. Stark, Brenda J. Bowser, and Lee Horne, 223–44. Tucson: University of Arizona Press.

Hill, J. Brett, Jeffery J. Clark, William H. Doelle, and Patrick D. Lyons. 2004. "Prehistoric Demography in the Southwest: Migration, Coalescence, and Hohokam Population Decline." *American Antiquity* 69(4): 689–716.

Hill, Jonathan D., ed. 1996a. *History, Power, and Identity: Ethnogenesis in the Americas, 1492–1992.* Iowa City: University of Iowa Press.

———. 1996b. "Introduction: Ethnogenesis in the Americas: 1492–1992." In *History, Power, and Identity: Ethnogenesis in the Americas, 1492–1992*, edited by Jonathan D. Hill, 1–19. Iowa City: University of Iowa Press.

Hill, Thomas D. 1986. "Rígspula: Some Medieval Christian Analogues." *Speculum* 61(1): 79–89.

Hochschild, Adam. 2005. *Bury the Chains: Prophets and Rebels in the Fight to Free an Empire's Slaves.* Boston: Houghton Mifflin.

Hodson, Christopher. 2011. "Weird Science: Identity in the Atlantic World." *William and Mary Quarterly* 68(2): 227–32.

Holloway, Joseph E. 2005. "'What Africa Has Given America': African Continuities in the North American Diaspora." In *Africanisms in American Culture*, edited by Joseph E. Holloway, 82–110. Bloomington: Indiana University Press.

Holsoe, Svend E. 1977. "Slavery and Economic Response among the Vai (Liberia and Sierra Leone)." In *Slavery in Africa: Historical and Anthropological Perspectives*, edited by Suzanne Miers and Igor Kopytoff, 287–304. Madison: University of Wisconsin Press.

Homer. 1898. *The Iliad.* Translated by Samuel Butler. Project Gutenberg ebook. http://www.gutenberg.org/files/2199/2199-h/2199-h.htm.

Hruby, Zachary, and Rowan Flad, eds. 2007. *Rethinking Craft Specialization in Complex Societies: Archaeological Analyses of the Social Meaning of Production.* Archaeological Papers of the American Anthropological Association, 17. Arlington VA: American Anthropological Association.

Hudson, Charles M. 1976. *The Southeastern Indians.* Knoxville: University of Tennessee Press.

———. 1997. *Knights of Spain, Warriors of the Sun: Hernando de Soto and the South's Ancient Chiefdoms.* Athens: University of Georgia Press.

Isaacman, Barbara, and Allan Isaacman. 1977. "Slavery and Social Stratification among the Sena of Mozambique: A Study of the Kaporo System." In *Slavery in Africa: Historical and Anthropological Perspectives*, edited by Suzanne Miers and Igor Kopytoff, 105–20. Madison: University of Wisconsin Press.

Jackson, Jason Baird, and Raymond D. Fogelson. 2004. Introduction to *Southeast,* edited by Raymond D. Fogelson and William Sturtevant, 1–13. Handbook of North American Indians, vol. 14. Washington DC: Smithsonian Institution.

Jeter, Marvin D. 2012. "Ripe for Colonial Exploitation: Ancient Traditions of Violence and Enmity as Preludes to the Indian Slave Trade." In *Native American Adoption, Captivity, and Slavery in Changing Contexts*, edited by Max Carocci and Stephanie Pratt, 23–46. New York: Palgrave Macmillan.

Jóhannesson, Guðni T. 2013. *The History of Iceland*. Santa Barbara CA: Greenwood, ABC-CLIO.

Jones, Siân. 1997. *The Archaeology of Ethnicity: Constructing Identities in the Past and Present*. London: Routledge.

Jorgensen, Joseph G. 1980. *Western Indians: Comparative Environments, Languages, and Cultures of 172 Western American Indian Tribes*. San Francisco: W. H. Freeman.

Joshel, Sandra R. 2010. *Slavery in the Roman World*. New York: Cambridge University Press.

Junker, Laura L. 2008. "The Impact of Captured Women on Cultural Transmission in Contact Period Philippine Slave-Raiding Chiefdoms." In *Invisible Citizens: Captives and Their Consequences*, edited by Catherine M. Cameron, 110–37. Salt Lake City: University of Utah Press.

Kan, Sergei. 1989. *Symbolic Immortality: The Tlingit Potlatch of the Nineteenth Century*. Washington DC: Smithsonian Institution Press.

Kane, Maeve. 2014. "Covered with Such a Cappe: The Archaeology of Seneca Clothing, 1615–1820." *Ethnohistory* 61(1): 1–25.

Karras, Ruth Mazo. 1988. *Slavery and Society in Medieval Scandinavia*. New Haven CT: Yale University Press.

Keeley, Lawrence H. 1996. *War before Civilization: The Myth of the Peaceful Savage*. Oxford: Oxford University Press.

Keim, Curtis A. 1983. "Women in Slavery among the Mangbetu c. 1800–1910." In *Women and Slavery in Africa*, edited by Claire C. Robertson and Martin A. Klein, 144–59. Madison: University of Wisconsin Press.

Kestler, Frances Roe. 1990. *The Indian Captivity Narrative: A Woman's View*. New York: Garland.

Klein, Martin A. 1977. "Servitude among the Wolof and Sereer of Senegamia." In *Slavery in Africa: Historical and Anthropological Perspectives*, edited by Suzanne Miers and Igor Kopytoff, 335–66. Madison: University of Wisconsin Press.

———. 1983. "Women in Slavery in the Western Sudan." In *Women and Slavery in Africa*, edited by Claire C. Robertson and Martin A. Klein, 67–88. Madison: University of Wisconsin Press.

———. 2007. "Sex, Power, and Family Life in the Harem: A Comparative Study."

In *Women and Slavery*, vol. 1, *Africa, the Indian Ocean World, and the Medieval North Atlantic*, edited by Gwyn Campbell, Suzanne Miers, and Joseph C. Miller, 63–82. Athens: Ohio University Press.

Kohler, Timothy A., and Kathryn Kramer Turner. 2006. "Raiding for Women in the Prehispanic Northern Pueblo Southwest? A Pilot Examination." *Current Anthropology* 47: 1035–45.

Kopytoff, Igor. 1982. "Slavery." *Annual Review of Anthropology* 11: 207–30.

———. 1987. "The Internal African Frontier: The Making of African Political Culture." In *The African Frontier*, edited by Igor Kopytoff, 3–87. Bloomington: Indiana University Press.

Kopytoff, Igor, and Suzanne Miers. 1977. "Introduction: African 'Slavery' as an Institution of Marginality." In *Slavery in Africa: Historical and Anthropological Perspectives*, edited by Suzanne Miers and Igor Kopytoff, 3–81. Madison: University of Wisconsin Press.

Kowalewski, Stephen A. 2006. "Coalescent Societies." In *Light on the Path: The Anthropology and History of the Southeastern Indians*, edited by T. J. Pluckhahn and R. Ethridge, 94–122. Tuscaloosa: University of Alabama Press.

Kristiansen, Kristian, and Thomas B. Larsson. 2005. *The Rise of Bronze Age Society: Travels, Transmissions and Transformations*. Cambridge: Cambridge University Press.

Kristof, Nicholas D., and Sheryl WuDunn. 2009. *Half the Sky: Turning Oppression into Opportunity for Women Worldwide*. New York: Vintage Books.

Kusimba, Chapurukha M. 2004. "Archaeology of Slavery in East Africa." *African Archaeological Review* 21(2): 59–88.

Lafitau, Joseph-Francois. (1724) 1977. *Customs of the American Indians Compared with the Customs of Primitive Times*. Vol. 1. Translated by William N. Fenton and Elizabeth L. Moore. Toronto: Champlain Society.

Lass, Barbara. 1998. "Crafts, Chiefs, and Commoners: Production and Control in Precontact Hawai'i." In *Craft and Social Identity*, edited by Cathy Lynne Costin and Rita P. Wright, 19–30. Archaeological Papers of the American Anthropological Association, 8. Arlington, *VA*: American Anthropological Association.

Lathrap, Donald W. 1970. *The Upper Amazon*. New York: Praeger.

Lave, Jean, and Etienne Wenger. 1991. *Situated Learning, Legitimate Peripheral Participation*. Cambridge: University of Cambridge Press.

Law, Robin. 2004. *Ouidah: The Social History of a West African Slaving "Port," 1727–1892*. Athens: Ohio University Press.

LeBlanc, Steven A. 1998. "Settlement Consequences of Warfare during the Late Pueblo III and Pueblo IV Period." In *Migration and Reorganization: The Pueblo*

IV Period in the American Southwest, edited by Katherine A. Spielmann, 115–35. Anthropology Papers, 51. Tempe: Arizona State University.

———. 1999. *Prehistoric Warfare in the American Southwest.* Salt Lake City: University of Utah Press.

———. 2002. "Conflict and Language Dispersal: Issues and a New World Example." In *Examining the Farming/Language Dispersal Hypothesis*, edited by Peter Bellwood and Colin Renfrew, 357–65. Cambridge: McDonald Institute for Archaeological Research.

LeBlanc, Steven A., and Katherine E. Register. 2003. *Constant Battles: Why We Fight.* New York: St. Martin's Press.

Legros, Dominique. 1985. "Wealth, Poverty, and Slavery among 19th Century Tutchone Athapaskans." *Research in Economic Anthropology* 7: 37–64.

Lekson, Stephen H. 2002. "War in the Southwest, War in the World." *American Antiquity* 67(4): 607–24.

———. 2011. "Chaco as Altepetl: Secondary States." *The Southwest in the World.* July 22. http://stevelekson.com/2011/07/22/what-was-chaco/.

Lenski, Noel. 2008. "Captivity, Slavery, and Cultural Exchange between Rome and the Germans from the First to the Seventh Century CE." In *Invisible Citizens: Captives and their Consequences*, edited by Catherine M. Cameron, 80–109. Salt Lake City: University of Utah Press.

———. Forthcoming. "Framing the Question: What Is a Slave Society?" In *What Is a Slave Society*, edited by Noel Lenski and Catherine M. Cameron. Cambridge University Press.

Lightfoot, Kent G. 1995. "Culture Contact Studies: Redefining the Relationship between Prehistoric and Historical Archaeology." *American Antiquity* 60(2): 199–217.

Lovejoy, Paul E. (1983) 2000. *Transformations in Slavery: A History of Slavery in Africa.* 2nd ed. Cambridge: Cambridge University Press.

Lovisek, Joan A. 2007. "Aboriginal Warfare on the Northwest Coast: Did the Potlatch Replace Warfare?" In *North American Indigenous Warfare and Ritual Violence*, edited by Richard J. Chacon and Ruben G. Mendoza, 58–73. Tucson: University of Arizona Press.

Lowell, Julia C. 2007. "Women and Men in Warfare and Migration: Implications of Gender Imbalance in the Grasshopper Region of Arizona." *American Antiquity* 72(1): 95–124.

Lyman, R. Lee. 2008. "Cultural Transmission in North American Anthropology and Archaeology, ca. 1895–1965." In *Cultural Transmission and Archaeology: Issues and Case Studies*, edited by Michael J. O'Brien, 10–20. Washington DC: Society for American Archaeology.

MacEachern, Scott. 1998. "Scale, Style and Cultural Variation: Technological Traditions in the Northern Mandara Mountains." In *The Archaeology of Social Boundaries*, edited by Miriam Stark, 107–31. Washington DC: Smithsonian Institution Press.

———. 2001. "State Formation and Enslavement in the Southern Lake Chad Basin." In *West Africa during the Atlantic Slave Trade: Archaeological Perspectives*, edited by Christopher R. DeCorse, 131–51. London: Leicester University Press.

MacGaffey, Wyatt. 1977. "Economic and Social Dimensions of Kongo Slavery (Zaire)." In *Slavery in Africa: Historical and Anthropological Perspectives*, edited by Suzanne Miers and Igor Kopytoff, 235–60. Madison: University of Wisconsin Press.

Malotki, Ekkehart. 1993. *Hopi Ruin Legends*. Lincoln: University of Nebraska Press.

Martin, Debra L. 2008. "Ripped Flesh and Torn Souls: Skeletal Evidence for Captivity and Slavery from the La Plata Valley, New Mexico, AD 1100–1300." In *Invisible Citizens: Captives and Their Consequences*, edited by Catherine M. Cameron, 159–80. Salt Lake City: University of Utah Press.

Martin, Debra L., Ryan P. Harrod, and M. Fields. 2010. "Beaten Down and Worked to the Bone: Bioarchaeological Investigations of Women and Violence in the Ancient Southwest." *Landscapes of Violence* 1(1): 1–19.

Martin, Debra L., Ryan P. Harrod, and Ventura R. Pérez. 2012. *The Bioarchaeology of Violence*. Gainesville: University Press of Florida.

Maschner, Herbert D. G., and Katherine L. Reedy-Maschner. 1998. "Raid, Retreat, Defend (Repeat): The Archaeology and Ethnohistory of Warfare on the North Pacific Rim." *Journal of Anthropological Archaeology* 17(1): 19–51.

McCormack, Edward Michael. 1977. *Slavery on the Tennessee Frontier*. Knoxville: Tennessee American Revolution Bicentennial Commission.

McDonald, John, and G. D. Snooks. 1986. *Domesday Economy: A New Approach to Anglo-Norman History*. New York: Clarendon Press.

McDougall, E. Ann. 1998. "A Sense of Self: The Life of Fatma Barka." *Canadian Journal of African Studies* 32(2): 285–315.

McIlwraith, Thomas Forsyth. 1948. *The Bella Coola Indians*. Vol. 1. Toronto: University of Toronto Press.

McLennan, J. F. 1865. *Primitive Marriage: An Inquiry into the Original of the Form of Capture in Marriage Ceremonies*. Edinburgh: Black.

Meillassoux, Claude. 1983. "Female Slavery." In *Women and Slavery in Africa*, edited by Claire C. Robertson and Martin A. Klein, 49–66. Madison: University of Wisconsin Press.

———. 1991. *The Anthropology of Slavery: The Womb of Iron and Gold*. Chicago: University of Chicago Press.

Mendras, H. 1984. *La fin des paysans: Suivi d'une reflexion sur la fin des paysans vingt ans après*. Arles: Actes-Sud.

Mera, H. P. 1938. *The "Slave Blanket."* Santa Fe NM: Royal Press.

Meredith, Grace E. (1927) 2004. *Girl Captives of the Cheyennes: A True Story of the Capture and Rescue of Four Pioneer Girls, 1874*. Mechanicsburg PA: Stackpole Books.

Meyers, Maureen. 2009. "From Refugees to Slave-Traders: The Transformation of the Westo Indians." In *Mapping the Mississippian Shatter Zone: The Colonial Indian Slave Trade and Regional Instability in the American South*, edited by R. Ethridge and S. M. Shuck-Hall, 84–103. Lincoln: University of Nebraska Press.

Miers, Suzanne, and Igor Kopytoff, eds. 1977. *Slavery in Africa: Historical and Anthropological Perspectives*. Madison: University of Wisconsin Press.

Mifflin, Margot. 2009. *The Blue Tattoo: The Life of Olive Oatman*. Lincoln: University of Nebraska Press.

Miller, Joseph C. 2007. "Women as Slaves and Owners of Slaves: Experiences from Africa, the Indian Ocean World, and the Early Atlantic." In *Women and Slavery*, vol. 1, *Africa, the Indian Ocean World, and the Medieval North Atlantic*, edited by Gwyn Campbell, Suzanne Miers, and Joseph C. Miller, 1–40. Athens: Ohio University Press.

Mills, Barbara J. 2008. "Colonialism and Cuisine: Cultural Transmission, Agency, and History at Zuni Pueblo." In *Cultural Transmission and Material Culture: Breaking Down Boundaries*, edited by Miriam T. Stark, Brenda J. Bowser, and Lee Horne, 245–62. Tucson: University of Arizona Press.

Mills, Barbara J., and Matthew A. Peeples. Forthcoming. "Reframing Diffusion through Social Network Theory." In "Social Networks in the American Southwest." Manuscript to be submitted to University Press of Colorado.

Milner, George R. 2007. "Warfare, Population, and Food Production in Prehistoric Eastern North America." In *North American Indigenous Warfare and Ritual Violence*, edited by R. J. Chacon and R. G. Mendoza, 182–201. Tucson: University of Arizona Press.

Minar, C. Jill, and Patricia L. Crown. 2001. "Learning and Craft Production." *Journal of Anthropological Research* 57(4): 369–80.

Mitchell, Donald. 1984. "Predatory Warfare, Social Status, and the North Pacific Slave Trade." *Ethnology* 23(1): 39–48.

Morey, Nancy K. C. 1975. "Ethnohistory of the Colombian and Venezuelan Llanos." PhD diss., University of Utah.

Morrissey, M. 1984. "Migrantness, Culture, and Ideology." In *Ethnicity, Class, and Gender in Australia*, edited by G. Bottomley and M. de Lepervanche, 72–81. Sydney: George Allen and Unwin.

Murdock, George Peter. 1965. *Culture and Society*. Pittsburg: University of Pittsburg Press.

Murdock, George Peter, and Douglas R. White. 1969. "Standard Cross-Cultural Sample." *Ethnology* 8(4): 329–69.

Myers, Thomas P. 1974. "Spanish Contacts and Social Change on the Ucayali River, Peru." *Ethnohistory* 21(2): 135–57.

Nieboer, H. J. 1910. *Slavery as an Industrial System: Ethnological Researches*. 2nd ed. The Hague: Martinus Nijhoff.

———. 1900. *Slavery as an Industrial System*. The Hague: Martinus Nijhoff.

Nwachukwu-Ogedengbe, K. 1977. "Slavery in Nineteenth-Century Aboh (Nigeria)." In *Slavery in Africa: Historical and Anthropological Perspectives*, edited by Suzanne Miers and Igor Kopytoff, 133–54. Madison: University of Wisconsin Press.

Oberg, Kalervo. 1973. *The Social Economy of the Tlingit Indians*. Seattle: University of Washington Press.

O'Brien, Michael J., ed. 2008. *Cultural Transmission and Archaeology: Issues and Case Studies*. Washington DC: Society for American Archaeology Press.

O'Brien, Michael J., Matthew T. Boulanger, Briggs Buchanan, Mark Collard, R. Lee Lyman, and John Darwent. 2014. "Innovation and Cultural Transmission in the American Paleolithic: Phylogenetic Analysis of Eastern Paleoindian Projectile Point Classes." *Journal of Anthropological Archaeology* 34: 100-119.

O'Brien, Michael J., R. Lee Lyman, Mark Collard, Clare J. Holden, Russell D. Gray, and Stephen J. Shennan. 2008. "Transmission, Phylogenetics, and the Evolution of Cultural Diversity." In *Cultural Transmission and Archaeology: Issues and Case Studies*, edited by Michael J. O'Brien, 77–90. Washington DC: Society for American Archaeology Press.

O'Brien, Michael J., and Stephen J. Shennan, eds. 2010. *Innovation in Cultural Systems: Contributions from Evolutionary Anthropology*. Cambridge MA: MIT Press.

Ogundiran, Akinwumi, and Toyin Falola, eds. 2007. *Archaeology of Atlantic Africa and the African Diaspora*. Bloomington: Indiana University Press.

Ortman, Scott G. 2010. "Genes, Language, and Culture in Tewa Ethnogenesis, AD 1150–1400." PhD diss., Arizona State University.

Ortman, Scott G., and Catherine M. Cameron. 2011. "A Framework for Controlled Comparisons of Ancient Southwestern Movement." In *Movement, Connectivity and Landscape Change in the American Southwest*, edited by Margaret Nelson and Coleen Strawhacker, 233–52. Boulder: University Press of Colorado.

Patterson, Orlando. 1977. "The Structural Origins of Slavery: A Critique of the Nieboer-Domar Hypothesis from a Comparative Perspective." *Annals of the New York Academy of Science* 292: 12–33.

———. 1982. *Slavery and Social Death: A Comparative Study*. Cambridge MA: Harvard University Press.

———. 1991. *Freedom in the Making of Western Culture*. New York: Basic Books.

———. 2008. "Slavery, Gender, and Work in the Pre-modern World and Early Greece: A Cross-Cultural Analysis." In *Slave Systems: Ancient and Modern*, edited by Enrico Dal Lago and Constantina Katsari, 3-32. Cambridge: Cambridge University Press.

Perdue, Theda. 1979. *Slavery and the Evolution of Cherokee Society, 1540–1866*. Knoxville: University of Tennessee Press.

Peregrine, Peter N. 2001. "Cross-Cultural Comparative Approaches in Archaeology." *Annual Review of Anthropology* 30: 1–18.

———. 2008. "Social Death and Resurrection in the Western Great Lakes." In *Invisible Citizens: Captives and Their Consequences*, edited by Catherine M. Cameron, 223–31. Salt Lake City: University of Utah Press.

Piot, Charles. 1996. "Of Slaves and the Gift: Kabre Sale of Kin during the Era of the Slave Trade." *Journal of African History* 37(1): 31–49.

Premo, Luke S. 2014. "Cultural Transmission and Diversity in Time-Averaged Assemblages." *Current Anthropology* 55(1): 105–14.

Price, Richard. (1973) 1996. *Maroon Societies: Rebel Slave Communities in the Americas*. 3rd ed. Baltimore: Johns Hopkins University Press.

Price, T. Douglas, Vera Tiesler Blos, and James Burton. 2006. "Early African Diaspora in Colonial Campeche, Mexico: Strontium Isotopic Evidence." *American Journal of Physical Anthropology* 130(4): 485–90.

Ramsey, Jack C. 1990. *The Story of Cynthia Ann Parker: Sunshine on the Prairie*. Austin TX: Eakin Press.

Ray, V. F. 1938. *Lower Chinook Ethnological Notes*. Publications in Anthropology, 7. Seattle: University of Washington.

Reichel-Dolmatoff, Gerardo. 1971. *Amazonian Cosmos: The Sexual and Religious Symbolism of the Turkano Indians*. Chicago: University of Chicago Press.

Reid, Anthony, ed. 1983. *Slavery, Bondage and Dependency in Southeast Asia*. New York: St. Martin's Press.

———. 1992. "Economic and Social Change, c. 1400–1800." In *The Cambridge History of Southeast Asia*, vol. 1, *From Early Times to c. 1800*, edited by Nicholas Tarling, 460–507. Cambridge: Cambridge University Press.

Reid, Anthony, and Jennifer Brewster. 1983. "Introduction: Slavery and Bondage in Southwest Asian History." In *Slavery, Bondage, and Dependency in Southeast Asia*, edited by Anthony Reid, 1–43. New York: St. Martin's Press.

Reid, Richard J. 2012. *Warfare in African History*. New York: Cambridge University Press.

Richter, Daniel K. 1983. "War and Culture: The Iroquois Experience." *William and Mary Quarterly* 40(4): 528–59.

———. 2011. *Before the Revolution: America's Ancient Pasts*. Cambridge MA: Belknap Press of Harvard University Press.

Riesman, Paul. 1977. *Freedom in Fulani Social Life: An Introspective Ethnography*. Chicago: University of Chicago Press.

Rivaya-Martínez, Joaquín. 2006. "Captivity and Adoption among the Comanche Indians, 1700–1875." PhD diss., University of California, Los Angeles.

———. 2012. "Becoming Comanches: Patterns of Captive Incorporation into Kinship Networks, 1820–1875." In *On the Borders of Love and Power: Families and Kinship in the American West*, edited by David Wallace Adams and Crista DeLuzio, 47–70. Berkeley: University of California Press.

Robertshaw, Peter. 1999. "Women, Labor, and State Formation in Western Uganda." In *Complex Polities in the Ancient Tropical World*, edited by E. A. Bacus and L. J. Lucero, 51–66. Archaeological Papers of the American Anthropological Association, 9. Arlington VA: American Anthropological Association.

Robertshaw, Peter, and William L. Duncan. 2008. "African Slavery: Archaeology and Decentralized Societies." In *Invisible Citizens: Captives and Their Consequences*, edited by Catherine M. Cameron, 57–79. Salt Lake City: University of Utah Press.

Robertson, Claire C., and Martin A. Klein, eds. 1983a. *Women and Slavery in Africa*. Madison: University of Wisconsin Press.

———. 1983b. "Women's Importance in African Slave Systems." In *Women and Slavery in Africa*, edited by Claire C. Robertson and Martin A. Klein, 3–25. Madison: University of Wisconsin Press.

Robertson, Claire C., and Marsha Robinson. 2008. "Remodeling Slavery as If Women Mattered." In *Women and Slavery*, vol. 2, *The Modern Atlantic*, edited by Gwyn Campbell, Suzanne Miers, and Joseph C. Miller, 253–83. Athens: Ohio University Press.

Rohner, Ronald P., and Evelyn C. Rohner. 1970. *The Kwakiutl: Indians of British Columbia*. New York: Holt, Rinehart and Winston.

Rorabaugh, Adam N. 2014. "Impacts of Drift and Population Bottlenecks on the Cultural Transmission of a Neutral Continuous Trait: An Agent Based Model." *Journal of Archaeological Science* 49: 255–64.

Ross, Alexander. (1849) 1969. *Adventures of the First Settlers on the Columbia River*. New York: Citadel Press.

Roux, Valentine. 2010. "Technological Innovations and Developmental Trajectories: Social Factors as Evolutionary Forces." In *Innovation in Cultural Systems:*

Contributions from Evolutionary Anthropology, edited by Michael J. O'Brien and Stephen J. Shennan, 217–33. Cambridge MA: MIT Press.

Ruby, Robert H., and John A. Brown. 1993. *Indian Slavery in the Pacific Northwest*. Spokane WA: Arthur H. Clark.

Rushforth, Brett. 2003. "'A Little Flesh We Offer You': The Origins of Indian Slavery in New France." *William and Mary Quarterly* 60(4): 777–809.

———. 2006. "Slavery, the Fox Wars, and the Limits of Alliance." *William and Mary Quarterly* 63(1): 53–80.

———. 2012. *Bonds of Alliance: Indigenous and Atlantic Slaveries in New France*. Chapel Hill: University of North Carolina Press.

Santos-Granero, Fernando. 2002. "The Arawakan Matrix: Ethos, Language, and History in Native South America." In *Comparative Arawakan Histories: Rethinking Language Family and Culture Area in Amazonia*, edited by Jonathan D. Hill and Fernando Santos-Granero, 25–50. Urbana: University of Illinois Press.

———. 2005. "Amerindian Torture Revisited: Rituals of Enslavement and Markers of Servitude in Tropical America." *Tipiti* 3(2): 42–69.

———. 2009. *Vital Enemies: Slavery, Predation, and the Amerindian Political Economy of Life*. Austin: University of Texas Press.

Sattler, Richard. 1996. "Remnants, Renegades, and Runaways: Seminole Ethnogenesis Reconsidered." In *History, Power, and Identity: Ethnogenesis in the Americas, 1492–1992*, edited by Jonathan D. Hill, 36–69. Iowa City: University of Iowa Press.

Saunt, Claudio. 1999. *The New Order of Things: Property, Power, and the Transformation of the Creek Indians, 1733–1816*. Cambridge: Cambridge University Press.

Schaafsma, Polly. 2000. *Warrior, Shield, and Star: Imagery and Ideology of Pueblo Warfare*. Santa Fe, NM: Western Edge Press.

Scheiber, Laura L., and Mark D. Mitchell, eds. 2010. *Across a Great Divide: Continuity and Change in Native North American Societies, 1400–1900*. Amerind Studies in Archaeology. Tucson: University of Arizona Press.

Scheidel, Walter. 2012. "Slavery." *The Cambridge Companion to the Roman Economy*, edited by Walter Scheidel, 89–113. Cambridge: Cambridge University Press.

Schillaci, Michael A., and Christopher M. Stojanowski. 2000. "Postmarital Residence and Biological Variation at Pueblo Bonito." *American Journal of Physical Anthropology* 120(1): 1–15.

———. 2002. "A Reassessment of Matrilocality in Chacoan Culture." *American Antiquity* 67(2): 343–56.

Schurr, Mark R. 1992. "Isotopic and Mortuary Variability in a Middle Mississippian Population." *American Antiquity* 57(2): 300–320.

Scott, James C. 1990. *Domination and the Arts of Resistance: Hidden Transcripts.* New Haven CT: Yale University Press.

Seaver, Kristen A. 2007. "Thralls and Queens: Female Slavery in the Medieval Norse Atlantic." In *Women and Slavery*, vol. 1, *Africa, the Indian Ocean World, and the Medieval North Atlantic*, edited by Gwyn Campbell, Suzanne Miers, and Joseph C. Miller, 147–67. Athens: Ohio University Press.

Segal, Ronald. 2001. *Islam's Black Slaves: The Other Black Diaspora.* New York: Farrar, Straus, and Giroux.

Service, E. R. 1971. *Primitive Social Organization: An Evolutionary Perspective.* New York: Random House.

Shennan, Stephen J., ed. 2009. *Pattern and Process in Cultural Evolution.* Berkeley: University of California Press.

Shimada, Izumi, ed. 2007. *Craft Production in Complex Societies: Multicraft and Producer Perspectives.* Salt Lake City: University of Utah Press.

Shortman, Edward M. 1989. "Interregional Interaction in Prehistory: The Need for a New Perspective." *American Antiquity* 54(1): 52–65.

Sidbury, James, and Jorge Cañizares-Esguerra. 2011. "Mapping Ethnogenesis in the Early Modern Atlantic." *William and Mary Quarterly* 68(2): 181–208.

Silliman, Stephen W. 2001. "Agency, Practical Politics, and the Archaeology of Culture Contact." *Journal of Social Archaeology* 1(2): 190–209.

———. 2010. "Indigenous Traces in Colonial Spaces: Archaeologies of Ambiguity, Origin, and Practice." *Journal of Social Archaeology* 10(1): 28–58.

Singleton, Theresa A. 1998. "Cultural Interaction and African American Identity in Plantation Archaeology." In *Studies in Culture Contact: Interaction, Culture Change, and Archaeology*, edited by James G. Cusick, 172–88. Carbondale IL: Center for Archaeological Investigations.

———. 2006. "African Diaspora Archaeology in Dialogue." In *Afro-Atlantic Dialogues: Anthropology in Diaspora*, edited by Kevin A. Yelvington, 249–88. Santa Fe NM: School of American Research Press.

Smith, Marian W. 1940. *The Puyallup-Nisqually.* Columbia University Contributions to Anthropology, 32. New York: AMS Press.

Smith, Michael E., ed. 2012. *The Comparative Archaeology of Complex Societies.* Cambridge: Cambridge University Press.

Smith, Michael E., and Peter Peregrine. 2012. "Approaches to Comparative Analysis in Archaeology." In *The Comparative Archaeology of Complex Societies*, edited by Michael E. Smith, 21–43. Cambridge: Cambridge University Press.

Snyder, Christina. 2007. "Conquered Enemies, Adopted Kin, and Owned People: The Creek Indians and Their Captives." *Journal of Southern History* 73: 255–88.

———. 2009. "The Lady of Cofitachequi: Gender and Political Power among

Native Southerners." In *South Carolina Women: Their Lives and Times*, edited by Joan Johnson, Valinda Littlefield, and Marjorie Spruill, 11–25. Athens: University of Georgia Press.

———. 2010. *Slavery in Indian Country: The Changing Face of Captivity in Early America*. Cambridge MA: Harvard University Press.

Socolow, Susan Migden. 1992. "Spanish Captives in Indian Societies: Cultural Contact along the Argentine Frontier, 1600–1835." *Hispanic American Historical Review* 72(1): 73–99.

Spielmann, Katherine A. 1998. "Ritual Craft Specialists in Middle Range Societies." In *Craft and Social Identity*, edited by Cathy Lynne Costin and Rita P. Wright, 153–60. Archaeological Papers of the American Anthropological Association, 8. Arlington, VA: American Anthropological Association.

Stahl, Ann B. 1991. "Ethnic Style and Ethnic Boundaries: A Diachronic Case Study from West-Central Ghana." *Ethnohistory* 38(3): 250–75.

———. 1993. "Concepts of Time and Approaches to Analogical Reasoning in Historical Perspective." *American Antiquity* 58(2): 235–60.

———. 1999. "Perceiving Variability in Time and Space: The Evolutionary Mapping of African Societies." In *Beyond Chiefdoms: Pathways to Complexity in Africa*, edited by Susan K. McIntosh, 39–55. Cambridge: Cambridge University Press.

———. 2001. "Historical Process and the Impact of the Atlantic Trade on Banda, Ghana, c. 1800–1920." In *West Africa during the Atlantic Slave Trade: Archaeological Perspectives*, edited by Christopher R. DeCorse, 38–58. New Approaches to Anthropological Archaeology. Leicester, UK: Leicester University Press.

———. 2008. "The Slave Trade as Practice and Memory: What Are the Issues for Archaeologists?" In *Invisible Citizens: Captives and Their Consequences*, edited by Catherine M. Cameron, 25–56. Salt Lake City: University of Utah Press.

Stark, Miriam T., ed. 1998. *The Archaeology of Social Boundaries*. Washington DC: Smithsonian Institution Press.

Stark, Miriam, Brenda J. Bowser, and Lee Horne, eds. 2008. *Cultural Transmission and Material Culture: Breaking Down Boundaries*. Tucson: University of Arizona Press.

Starna, William A., and Ralph Watkins. 1991. "Northern Iroquoian Slavery." *Ethnohistory* 38(1): 34–57.

Stein, Gil J. 2002. "From Passive Periphery to Active Agents: Emerging Perspectives in the Archaeology of Interregional Interaction." *American Anthropologist* 104(3): 903–16.

———, ed. 2005a. *The Archaeology of Colonial Encounters: Comparative Perspectives*. Santa Fe NM: School of American Research Press.

————. 2005b. "Introduction: The Comparative Archaeology of Colonial Encounters." In *The Archaeology of Colonial Encounters: Comparative Perspectives*, edited by Gil J. Stein, 3–32. Santa Fe NM: School of American Research Press.

Steward, Julian H., and Alfred Métraux. 1948. "Tribes of the Peruvian and Ecuadorian Montana." In *Handbook of South American Indians*, vol. 3, *The Tropical Forest Tribes*, edited by Julian H. Steward, 535–656. Washington DC: U.S.
Government Printing Office.

Stewart, Hilary. 1987. *The Adventures and Sufferings of John R. Jewitt: Captive of
Maquinna*. Seattle: University of Washington Press.

Stone, Tammy T. 2003. "Social Identity and Ethnic Interaction in the Western
Pueblos of the American Southwest." *Journal of Archaeological Method and
Theory* 10: 31–67.

Strathern, Marilyn. 1988. *The Gender of the Gift: Problems with Women and Problems with Society in Melanesia*. Berkeley: University of California Press.

Taylor, Timothy. 2001. "Believing the Ancients: Quantitative and Qualitative Dimensions of Slavery and the Slave Trade in Later Prehistoric Eurasia." *World
Archaeology* 33(1): 27–43.

————. 2005. "Ambushed by a Grotesque: Archaeology, Slavery, and the Third
Paradigm." In *Warfare, Violence, and Slavery in Prehistory: Proceedings of a
Prehistoric Society Conference at Sheffield University*, edited by Michael Park-
er Pearson and I. J. N. Thorpe, 25–233. Oxford, UK: Archaeopress.

Tehrani, Jamshid, and Mark Collard. 2002. "Investigating Cultural Evolution
through Biological Phylogenetic Analyses of Turkmen Textiles." *Journal of
Anthropological Archaeology* 21: 443–63.

Tessmann, Gunter. 1930. *Die Indianer Nordost-Perus*. Hamburg: Frederichsen, De
Gruyter.

————. 1999. *Los indigenas del Peru Oriental: Investigaciones fundamentals para un
studio sistematico de la cultura*. Quito: Abya-Yala.

Thompson, F. Hugh. 2003. *The Archaeology of Greek and Roman Slavery*. London: Duckworth.

Thornton, John K. 1983. "Sexual Demography: The Impact of the Slave Trade on
Family Structure." In *Women and Slavery in Africa*, edited by Claire Robertson and Martin Klein, 39–48. Madison: University of Wisconsin Press.

————. 1998. "The African Experience of the '20 and Odd Negroes' Arriving in
Virginia in 1619." *William and Mary Quarterly* 55: 421–34.

————. (1999) 2003. *Warfare in Atlantic Africa 1500–1800*. London: Routledge.

Thwaites, Reuben Gold. (1896–1901) 1959. *The Jesuit Relations and Allied Documents: Travel and Explorations of the Jesuit Missionaries in New France, 1610–
1791*. 73 vols. New York: Pageant.

Tierney, Patrick. 2000. *Darkness in El Dorado: How Scientists and Journalists Devastated the Amazon*. New York: Norton.

Toulouse, Teresa A. 2007. *The Captive's Position: Female Narrative, Male Identity, and Royal Authority in Colonial New England*. Philadelphia: University of Pennsylvania Press.

Trigger, Bruce G. 1969. *The Huron: Farmers of the North*. New York: Holt, Rinehart and Winston.

———. 1976. *The Children of Aataentsic I: A History of the Huron People to 1660*. Montreal: McGill-Queen's University Press.

———. 1978a. Introduction to *Northeast*, edited by Bruce G. Trigger, 1–3. Handbook of North American Indians, vol. 15. Washington DC: Smithsonian Institution.

———, ed. 1978b. *Northeast*. Handbook of North American Indians, vol. 15. William C. Sturtevant, general editor. Washington DC: Smithsonian Institution.

———. 2003. *Understanding Early Civilizations: A Comparative Study*. New York: Cambridge University Press.

Trouillot, Michel-Rollph. 2002. "Culture on the Edges: Caribbean Creolization in Historical Context." In *From the Margins: Historical Anthropology and Its Futures*, edited by Brian Keith Axel, 189–210. Durham NC: Duke University Press.

Ubelaker, Douglas H. 2006. "Population Size, Contact to Nadir." In *Environment, Origins, and Population*, edited by Douglas H. Ubelaker, 694–701. Washington DC: Smithsonian Institution Press.

United Nations Office of Drugs and Crime. 2012. *Global Report on Trafficking in Persons*. Vienna. https://www.unodc.org/documents/data-and-analysis/glotip/Trafficking_in_Persons_2012_web.pdf.

Usner, Daniel H., Jr. 1992. *Indians, Settlers, and Slaves in a Frontier Exchange Economy: The Lower Mississippi Valley before 1783*. Chapel Hill: University of North Carolina Press.

VanDerBeets, Richard, ed. 1973. *Held Captive by Indians: Selected Narratives, 1642–1836*. Knoxville: University of Tennessee Press.

VanPool, Todd L., Craig T. Palmer, and Christine S. VanPool. 2008. "Horned Serpents, Traditions, and the Tapestry of Culture: Culture Transmission in the American Southwest." In *Cultural Transmission and Archaeology: Some Fundamental Issues*, edited by M. J. O'Brien, 77–90. Washington DC: Society for American Archaeology.

Verdier, Raymond. 1981. "Le système vindicatoire: Esquisse théorique." In *La vengeance: Etudes d'ethnologie, d'histoire et de philosophie*, vol. 1, edited by Raymond Verdier, 12–42. Paris: Éditions Cujas.

Voss, Barbara L. 2008a. *The Archaeology of Ethnogenesis: Race and Sexuality in Colonial San Francisco*. Berkeley: University of California Press.

———. 2008b. "Domesticating Imperialism: Sexual Politics and the Archaeology of Empire." *American Anthropologist* 110(2): 191–203.

———. 2008c. "Gender, Race, and Labor in the Archaeology of the Spanish Colonial Americas." *Current Anthropology* 49(5): 861–93.

Voss, Barbara L., and Robert A. Schmidt, eds. 2000. *Archaeologies of Sexuality.* London: Routledge.

Walk Free Foundation. 2015. http://www.walkfreefoundation.org/.

Wallaert-Pêtre, Helene. 2001. "Learning How to Make the Right Pots: Apprenticeship Strategies and Material Culture: A Case Study in Handmade Pottery from Cameroon." *Journal of Anthropological Research* 57: 471–93.

Walvin, James. 2006. *Atlas of Slavery.* Harlow, UK: Pearson and Harlow.

Warren, James F. (1981) 1985. *The Sulu Zone: 1768–1898.* Quezon City, Philippines: New Day Publishers.

———. 2002. *Iranun and Balangingi: Globalization, Maritime Raiding, and the Birth of Ethnicity.* Singapore: Singapore University Press.

Watson, James L. 1980. "Slavery as an Institution, Open and Closed Systems." In *Asian and African Systems of Slavery*, edited by James L. Watson, 1–15. Berkeley: University of California Press.

Weltfish, Gene. 1965. *The Lost Universe.* With a closing chapter on *The Universe Regained.*" New York: Basic Books.

Wenger, Etienne. 1998. *Communities of Practice: Learning, Meaning, and Identity.* Cambridge: Cambridge University Press.

Westermann, William L. 1942. "Industrial Slavery in Roman Italy." *Journal of Economic History* 2: 149–63.

Wheat, Joe Ben. 2003. *Blanket Weaving in the Southwest.* Edited by Ann Lane Hedlund. Tucson: University of Arizona Press.

White, Richard. 1991. *The Middle Ground: Indians, Empires, and Republics in the Great Lakes Region, 1650–1815.* Cambridge: Cambridge University Press.

Wilshusen, Richard H. 2010. "The Dine at the Edge of History: Navajo Ethnogenesis in the Northern Southwest, 1500–1750." In *Across a Great Divide: Continuity and Change in Native North American Societies, 1400–1900*, edited by Laura L. Scheiber and Mark D. Mitchell, 192–211. Amerind Studies in Archaeology. Tucson: University of Arizona Press.

Witthoft, John. 1959. "Reminiscences of Susquehannock Archaeology." In *Susquehannock Miscellany*, edited by John Witthoft and W. Fred Kinsey III, 148–54. Harrisburg: Pennsylvania Historical and Museum Commission.

Wobst, H. Martin. 1978. "The Archaeo-ethnography of Hunter-Gatherers, or The Tyranny of the Ethnographic Record in Archaeology." *American Antiquity* 43: 303–9.

Wolf, Eric R. 1982. *Europe and the People without History.* Berkeley: University of California Press.

Wood, Peter H. 1989. "The Changing Population of the Colonial South: An Overview by Race and Region, 1685–1790." In *Powhatan's Mantle: Indians in the Colonial Southeast*, edited by Peter H. Wood, Gregory A. Waselkov, and M. Thomas Hatley, 35–103. Lincoln: University of Nebraska Press.

Wood, Peter H., Gregory A. Waselkov, and M. Thomas Hatley. 1989. *Powhatan's Mantle: Indians in the Colonial Southeast.* Lincoln: University of Nebraska Press.

Woolf, Alex. 1997. "At Home in the Long Iron Age: A Dialogue between Households and Individuals in Cultural Reproduction." In *Invisible People and Processes: Writing Gender into European Archaeology*, edited by Jenny Moore and Eleanor Scott, 68–74. London: Leicester University Press.

Wright, Marcia. 1993. *Strategies of Slaves and Women: Life-Stories from East/Central Africa.* New York: Lilian Barber Press.

Wylie, Alison. 1985. "The Reaction against Analogy." *Advances in Archaeological Method and Theory* 8: 63–111.

Yoffee, Norman. 1993. "Too Many Chiefs? (or Safe Texts for the '90s)." In *Archaeological Theory: Who Sets the Agenda*, edited by Norman Yoffee and Andrew Sherratt, 60–78. Cambridge: Cambridge University Press.

Index

Page numbers in italic indicate illustrations

Africa: captives selection and social location in, 48–49, 58, 59–60, 62, 63, 64, 65, 67–68, 70; captor worldview in social construct of captives in, 54; cultural transmission in, 143–44, 153, 154, 156–59; ethnogenesis in, 126–28; gender in, 37–38, 46, 48, 52, 59–60, 62, 63, 64, 65, 67–68, 82, 86; Islamic slave trade in, 37, 39, 89; kinship systems in, 48–49, 58, 70, 107, 126–27; pottery making in, 143–44; slavery in, 8, 9, 17, 37–39, 46, 47, 48, 58, 59–60, 62, 63, 64, 65, 67–68, 70, 82, 85, 86, 89, 159; social personhood in, 54, 58; women as captives in, 37–38, 48, 62, 63, 64, 67–68, 70, 82, 86, 153–54
African diaspora: cultural transmission and, 37, 156–59
Agbe-Davies, Anna, 133, 136
agricultural production: captive labor and, 6, 64, 65, 86–87, 97, 100, 101–2, 150, 156, 157–58
Albers, Patricia, 148
Algonquians, 21, 23, 149
Aluku (Boni) maroon society, 125
Amazonia. *See* South America
Ames, Kenneth, 89, 90, 93, 94
Arawakans, 82
"archaeological cultures," 106, 107, 108, 164, 166, 172–73, 175n2
archaeological record: captive taking in the, 167–71
archaeology, 2, 135–38, 164; and ethnoarchaeology, 136–37, 141, 142, 143–44, 160, 175n1; and evolutionary archaeology, 136–37, 138, 141, 175–76n1; and historical archaeology, 136, 137–38, 160, 171; network analysis in, 137
assimilation: captives and, 47, 57, 61, 64, 110, 115–20, 130. *See also* social boundaries; social location
Atlantic slave trade, 8, 17, 37, 38, 39, 89, 150, 153–54
atsi nahsa'i (Cherokee word for slave), 114–15

Bales, Kevin, 171
Banda society, 127
Barth, Fredrik, 108–9
Bauer, Alexander, 136
Beckerman, Stephen, 120
Bellabella slaves, 159–60
Bloch, Marc, 17
Boko Haram kidnappings, 1–2, 16, 171
Bonnassie, Pierre, 49
Bowser, Brenda, 36, 52, 82, 142–43
Brooks, James, 30, 68, 89, 117–18, 122, 148
Brown, Carolyn, 17
Brubaker, Rogers, 107, 175n1
Brugge, David, 29–30
Burford, Alison, 152
Busby, Cecilia, 62

Cabeza de Vaca, Álvar Núñez, 147
Caddos, 128
Cahokia, 25, *28*
Cameroon, 143–44
Campbell, Gwyn, 38, 117
Cañizares-Esguerra, Jorge, 124
cannibalism, 24, 61, 114
captive defined, 9
captive narratives: cultural transmission and, 146–50, 161, 167
captive-taking: analogy for study of, 4, 11–14, 20, 41, 164–65, 170–71
Carney, J., 156, 158
Catawbas, 128
Catholic Church, 17, 40
Cauca Valley, 46, 89
Chernela, Janet, 36
Cherokees, 26, 56, 114–15, 123
Cheyennes, 121, 149
Chickasaws, 128, 129

chiefdoms, 3; and power in kin-based leadership, 102; and social stratification, 79–80; in South America, 89, 95; in the Southeast, 25–26, 27, 102, 128; in Southeast Asia, 9, 40–41, 98, 99–101, 155, 170

children as captives: in Africa, 58, 59–60, 62; and captive selection and social location, 6, 59–60, 62, 82; among Comanches, 30–31, 60–61; among Conibos, 96–97, 98; in contemporary human trafficking, 17; and creation of power, 81, 82, 102; enculturation of, 165; in Northwest Coast, 86, 90, 91; and power and personhood among Kabres, 58; as sought after through time, 2, 4; in South America, 8, 52, 55, 61–62, 96–97, 98, 114; in Southeast, 51, 60–61

Chinooks, 93–94

Chisi-Ndjurisiye-Sichyajungas, 60

Choctaws, 123, 128

coalescent groups, 106, 111, 123–24, 127–28, 129, 131

Columbus, Christopher, 35–36, 147, 170

Comanches, 7, 30–31, 51, 56, 60–61, 63, 68, 122

Comaroff, John L., and Jean, 54

"communities of practice," 133, 137, 140, 141–42, 144, 146–47, 160–61, 166–67

competitive feasts, 87, 97–98, 102

concubines, 9, 48, 50, 57, 61, 63–64, 85, 96, 97, 98, 103, 117, 138–39, 165, 170

Conibos, 61, 65, 87, 94–98, 95, 135, 142–43, 145, 147–48, 160

Cooper, Frederick, 87, 107, 175n1

Coronado, Francisco Vásquez de, 170

craft knowledge of and production by captives, 43, 66–67, 87–88, 100–102, 148–49, 150, 152–55

Creeks, 123, 128–29

cross-cultural approach in study of warfare and captive taking, 2, 11–15, 163–65

cultural change. See cultural transmission and change

cultural transmission and change: in Africa, 143–44, 153, 154, 156–59; and acceptance or rejection of practices, 138–40, 143–46, 161; captive narratives in, 146–50, 161, 167; captives as agents of, 3, 14–15, 16, 133, 134, 143, 148, 150, 160, 163, 164–67; clothing and, 139, 149; and "communities of practice," 133, 137, 140, 141–42, 144, 146–47, 160–61, 166–67; in Conibo society, 142–43, 145, 147–48, 160; contemporary approaches to, 134–40; in culture contact studies, 137, 143, 144; "diffusion" in, 135–36, 145, 160; ethnoarchaeology in study of, 136–37, 141, 142, 143–44, 160,

175n1; evolutionary archaeology in study of, 136, 138, 141, 175–76n1; foodways in, 3, 134, 140, 155–59, 167; historical archaeology in study of, 137–38, 160; "horizontal transmission" of, 156, 175n1; and learning from the "Other," 145–50; mechanisms of, 135–36; Navaho weavers and, 144–45; network analysis in, 137; in Northeast, 139, 149, 160; in Northwest Coast, 148–49, 159–60; pottery making and, 136, 142–44, 145, 154; religious practices in, 3, 134, 140, 150, 159–60, 161, 167; situational learning theory and, 140–45, 160–61, 165–66; in South America, 142–43, 145, 147–48, 155, 160; in Southeast, 138–39, 148; in Southwest, 137, 138, 144–45, 154, 160; in state-level societies, 14, 151–52, 152–55, 159, 167; technology and craft knowledge in, 136, 146, 148–49, 150, 152–55, 166–67

Cybulski, Jerome, 169

Deagan, Kathleen, 138

DeBoer, Warren R., 7, 87, 97–98, 116, 145, 155

DeCorse, Christopher, 154

"diffusion": cultural transmission and, 135–36, 145, 160

Donald, Leland, 9–10, 33–34, 35, 65, 78, 93–94

drudge wives, 9, 50, 61, 165, 172

Duncan, William, 37

ethnic boundaries. See social boundaries

ethnoarchaeology, 136–37, 141, 142, 143–44, 160, 175n1

ethnogenesis, 111, 123–24, 125–28, 131, 137, 175–76n1

Ethridge, Robbie, 27

Europe: captive taking and slavery in, 9, 39–40, 47, 49, 56–57, 112–13

European contact: impact of, 4–5, 6, 8, 12, 13–14, 19, 20, 22–24, 26–27, 31–32, 35

evolutionary archaeology, 136–37, 138, 141, 175–76n1

Ferguson, R. Brian, 4, 6

foodways: cultural transmission and, 3, 134, 140, 155–59, 167

Fox wars, 22–23

Frank, Barbara, 136, 154

French and Indian Wars, 67

French colonists in North America, 5, 21, 22–23, 31, 66, 67, 129, 154

French Guiana, 125

Fulani group, 114

Gallay, Alan, 27, 69

gender/sexuality: in African captor societies,

37–38, 48, 52, 46, 59–60, 62, 63, 64, 65, 67–68, 82, 86; and captive labor, 50, 63, 64–66; in captive selection and social location, 6, 50–51, 52, 56–57, 59–61, 62–66, 75, 82, 83, 101, 107, 165; among captors, 46, 65–66; in cultural transmission, 138–39; in Northwest Coast slave labor, 65–66; and reproductive abilities of female captives, 62, 63–64, 82, 83, 101, 165; and sex ratios in burial populations, 24, 31–32, 35, 168–69; in South American captor societies, 36, 61–62, 63, 65–66, 170; in Southwest captor societies, 30, 31, 32, 56–57, 63, 122; in state-level societies, 63–64. *See also* women as captives
Genovese, Eugene, 154
German, Catherine, 149
Germanic societies, 8, 39–40, 153
Global Slavery Index (2014), 17
Gosselain, Oliver, 141, 142
Greek societies, 66–67, 90, 152
Gutiérrez, Ramón, 30

Habicht-Mauche, Judith, 88, 154
Haidas, 32, 159–60
Hajda, Yvonne, 33
Hämäläinen, Pekka, 30–31
harems: in state-level societies, 63–64
Harrod, Ryan, 168
Hayden, Brian, 87
Helms, Mary, 146
Hill, Jonathan D., 123
historical archaeology, 136, 137–38, 160, 171
Hochschild, Adam, 17
Holsoe, Svend, 67
"honor": in captive-captor relationships, 56, 111–12, 165–66
honor and shame: dual concepts of, 30, 56–57
Hopis, 106, 160
human remains: prehistoric warfare evidenced by, 24, 27, 35, 167–70
human trafficking, contemporary, 16–17, 164, 171–72
Hurons, 22, 52, 66, 80–81, 160

intercultural transmission. *See* cultural transmission and change
Iroquois, 22, 23, 24, 51–52, 69, 118–20, 129, 139, 160, 170
Islamic slave trade, 37, 39, 89
Island Southeast Asia, 8, 20, 21, 40–41, 98–101, 155, 170

Jesuit missionaries, 22, 118–19, 129

Jewitt, John, 67, 148–49
Junker, Laura, 40–41, 99, 100–101

Kabre society, 58
Kahnawake settlement, 124, 129–30
Kalinago group, 45–46, 61, 89–90, 114, 170
Karras, Ruth, 40, 112–13
Keeley, Lawrence, 4, 167–68
Kelly, Fanny, 148
"kidnapping": captive-taking as, 4, 7, 164
kinship systems: in Africa, 48–49, 58, 70, 107, 126–27; in Asia, 48; captives as "without kin" in, 85, 112, 114; captive social identity in, 44; captive social locations in, 36, 46–47, 48–49, 51–52, 56, 57, 58, 74–75, 120–21; gender and, 52, 56; and maroon communities, 125; marriage in, 50, 52, 81, 107, 121; in Northeast, 49–50, 51–52; in Northwest Coast, 32–33, 47, 49, 90–91, 92, 93; and power, 3, 16, 46, 81, 82, 85, 90, 92, 93, 102–3; slave status and, 47–49, 51, 52, 56, 70, 92, 93, 114–15; and social boundaries, 15, 52, 66, 107, 111, 112, 121; in social organization, 46–47, 121–22; in South America, 36, 52, 121–22; in Southeast, 49–50, 55–56, 114–15; in Southwest, 51, 56–57, 68
Klein, Martin, 38, 46, 64, 65
Kohler, Timothy, 168–69
Kopytoff, Igor, 18, 38, 48–49, 59, 126–27
Kowalewski, Stephen, 123–24
Kristiansen, Kristian, 136, 138
Kristof, Nicholas, 171

labor of captives: and agricultural production, 6, 64, 65, 86–87, 97, 100, 101–2, 150, 156, 157–58; and craft production, 43, 66–67, 87–88, 100, 102, 148–49, 150, 152–55; European contact and, 6, 8, 20; gender and, 38, 40, 41, 50, 63, 64–66, 86, 87, 89–90, 96, 101–2; as source of social and economic power, 16, 33, 46, 50, 78, 81–83, 85–90, 92–93, 97–98, 100–102, 103, 166, 172. *See also* slaves: captives as
Larsson, Thomas, 136, 138
Laudonniére, Rene, 5
Lave, Jean, 141
Legros, Dominique, 33, 81, 89
LeMoyne, Jacques, 5
Lenski, Noel, 39–40, 159

Makú group, 65–66, 113–14, 147–48
maritime chiefdoms, Southeast Asian, 9, 40–41, 98
maroon communities, 124, 125, 126, 129
Martin, Debra, 168

Maschner, Herbert, 33, 80–81, 90
McCormack, Edward, 59–60
McDougall, E. Ann, 117
McIlwraith, Thomas, 116
Meillassoux, Claude, 47, 64
Mendras, H., 139, 140
Miers, Suzanne, 38, 48–49, 59
Miller, Joseph, 38, 117
Mills, Barbara, 138
Mitchell, Donald, 33
Mohaves, 150, *151*
Mohawks, 124, 129–30
Mowachahts, 67, 148–49
Murdock, George, 7–8

Nafana group, 127
Natchez group, 129
Navajos, 29–30, 31, 56, 67, 69, 122, 124, 126, 144–45
network analysis, 137
New France: captive taking in, 22–23, 66, 67
Nieboer, H. J., 3, 7–8
North America, captive taking in. *See* North
    America, Northeast; North America, North-
    west Coast; North America, Southeast; North
    America, Southwest
North America, Northeast: Algonquians in,
    21, 23, 149; captive assimilation into captive
    societies of, 118–20; captive taking in *pays d'en
    haut* of, 21, 22–23, 24; cultural and geographic
    characteristics of, 21–23; cultural transmission
    in, 139, 149, 160; European impact on, 22, 23,
    24; precontact captive taking and warfare in,
    23–24, 170; Fox Wars in, 22–23; Hurons in, 22,
    52, 66, 80–81, 160; Iroquois in, 22, 23, 24, 51–52,
    69, 118–20, 129, 139, 160; Jesuit missionaries
    in, 18–19, 22, 129; kinships systems in, 49–50,
    51–52; slavery in, 24, 51–52; sources used in
    examining, 22–23; women as captives in, 24,
    52, 118, 149, 170
North America, Northwest Coast: captive agency
    in social boundaries of, 116; captive selection
    and social location in, 47, 49, 67–68, 69–70, 90,
    91; captives as source of power and wealth in,
    33, 46, 86, 90–94, *91*; cultural and geographic
    characteristics of, 32–33; cultural transmission
    in, 148–49, 159–60; European impact on, 34;
    gender in slave labor in, 64–65; and kinship
    systems, 32–33, 47, 49, 90–91, 92, 93; precontact
    warfare and captive taking in, 34, 35, 169, 170;
    scholarship on, 33–34; slavery in, 33–34, 35, 46,
    47, 49, 65, 86, 90–94; social stratification in,

33, 46, 49, 90, 92, 93; women and children as
    captives in, 64–65, 86, 90, 91, 92, 169
North America, Southeast: Cahokia chiefdom
    in, 25, 27, 28; Calusas society in, 26; captive
    taking in oral traditions of, 27; captor world-
    view and social construct of captives in, 55–56;
    Cherokee in, 26, 56, 114–15, 123; chiefdoms
    of, 25–26, 27, 128; children as captives in, 51,
    60–61; coalescent societies in, 123–24, 128–29;
    cultural and geographic characteristics of,
    25–26; cultural transmission in, 138–39, 148;
    depopulation in, 25; European impact on,
    26–27, 128–29; evidence of precontact warfare
    and captive taking in, 26–27, *28*; kinship
    systems in, 49–50, 55, 114–15; power and status
    in captive taking in, 46; scholarship on, 26–27;
    social boundaries in, 114–15, 121, 128–29; social
    locations in, 51, 60–61, 67; women as captives
    in, 51, 60–61, 88, 149
North America, Southwest: Apaches in, 29,
    30, 31; captives as cultural intermediaries in,
    30, 68–69, 122; captives and social location
    in, 30, 49–50, 56, 60–61, 63, 68–69, 122; captor
    worldview in social construct of captives in,
    56–57; children as captives in, 30–31, 56, 57, 122;
    Comanches in, 7, 30–31, 51, 60–61, 63, 68; cul-
    tural and geographic characteristics of, 28–30;
    cultural transmission in, 137, 138, 144–45, 148,
    154, 160; evidence of precontact captive taking
    and warfare in, 31–32, 168–69, 170; gender
    in captive taking in, 30, 31, 32, 56–57, 63, 122;
    kinship in, 51, 56–57, 68; Navajos in, 29–30,
    31, 56, 67, 69, 122, 124, 126, 144–45; Pueblos
    in, 29, 30–32, 56, 122, 126, 144, 154, 170, 175n2;
    "sacred violence and exchange" system in, 56,
    57; scholarship on, 29–30; slavery in, 29–30,
    31, 51, 56–57, 60–61; Spanish impact on, 29–31;
    women as captives in, 51, 56, 57, 63, 144–45, 154,
    160, 170; Zuni in, 138, 144
North Pacific Rim, 33, 80–81
Nuer, African, 106, 107

Oatman, Olive, 150, *151*
Oberg, Kalervo, 92
oral traditions: captive taking in, 27, 35, 40, 126,
    127, 170
the "other": conceptions of, 71, 108, 112, 115
Otomaco group, 46

Patterson, Orlando, 7, 10, 66–67, 82, 89, 111–12,
    163, 165

Pawnees, 27, 56

Perdue, Theda, 26, 114

personhood. *See* social personhood

Philippines. *See* Southeast Asian chiefdoms

Piot, Charles, 58

pottery making: cultural transmission through, *135*, 136, 137, 138–39, 143–44

power: captives as social and economic power, 3, 45–46, 78, 81–85, 85–90, 92–93, 97–98, 100–102, 103, 165–66, 172; captives as symbol of, 83, 101; and captives in development of complex societies, 77–78, 101, 102, 103; "competitive feasts" and, 86–87, 97–98, 102; Conibo group and, 94–98, *95;* and control of resources, 77; increase in captive population as source of, 3, 78, 83, 85, 101, 166; kinship systems and, 3, 16, 46, 81, 82, 85, 90, 92, 93, 102–3; in Northwest Coast societies, 90–94, *91;* and prestige and status as motivation for warfare, 6, 20, 24, 26, 46, 48, 78–79, 80–81, 85, 99; and reproduction of women captives, 82, 83, 101; social stratification and, 79–81, 82, 101; in Southeast Asia chiefdoms, 98–101; women and children as source of, 81, 82, 83, 85, 86, 88, 101–2

precontact period: raiding and warfare in, 4–5, 19, 23–24, 27, 31–32, 35–36, 167–70

Pueblos, 29, 30–32, 56, 122, 126, 144, 154, 170, 175n2

raiding and warfare: captive taking as by-product of, 5–6; European contact impact on, 4–5, 6, 12, 13–14, 19, 20, 22–24, 26–27, 31–32, 35; evidence of, 4–7, 19, 23–24, 27, 31–32, 35–36, 167–70; scholarly debate on, 4–5. *See also* children as captives; power; slaves, captives as; women as captives; *specific culture groups and regions by name*

Reedy-Maschner, Katherine, 33, 80–81

Reid, Anthony, 41, 98–99

religious practices: cultural transmission and, 3, 134, 140, 150, 159–60, 161, 167

reproduction: among captive women, 62, 63–64, 82, 83, 101, 165

revenge: as motivator for warfare and captive taking, 6, 23, 26, 81, 91, 120

Richter, Daniel, 22, 119–20

Riesman, Paul, 114

Rígspula legend, 113

Rivaya-Martínez, Joaquín, 31

Robertshaw, Peter, 37, 86

Robertson, Claire, 38, 46, 65

Roman Empire, 8, 39–40, 66–67, 152–53, 159

Roosevelt Redware pottery, 137

Rosomoff, R. N., 156, 158

Roux, Valentine, 139–40

Rowlandson, Mary, 149

Rushforth, Brett, 22–23

Santos-Granero, Fernando, 8–9, 19, 26, 35–36, 47, 54, 55, 61, 77, 113, 116

Scandinavian societies, 8, 9, 20, 40, 49, 89, 112–13, 169

Schmidt, Robert, 62

Seaver, Kristen, 40, 49

"segmentary societies," 3

Service, E. R., 3

sex ratios in burial populations, 24, 31–32, 35, 168–69

Sherbro group, 48–49, 59–60

Shuck-Hall, Sheri, 27

Sidbury, James, 124

Silliman, Stephen, 108, 139

Sioux, 21, 148

situated learning: cultural transmission and, 137, 140–45, 160–61, 166–67

situational opposition: captive taking and, 45, 47, 108–9, 110, 111–15, 130

slavery: global perspective on, 6–11, 17–18, 39–40

slaves, captives as: in Africa, 8, 9, 17, 37–39, 46, 47, 48, 58, 59–60, 62, 63–64, 65, 67–68, 70, 82, 86, 89; and captive agency in assimilation, 116–17; among Comanches, 51; among Cherokee, 26, 56, 114–15; and cultural transmission, 39–40, 150–51, 152–55; in Europe, 9, 39–40, 47, 49, 56–57, 89, 112–13; and gender among slaveholders, 46, 65–66; in kinship systems, 47–49, 51, 52, 56, 70, 92, 93, 114–15; and maroon communities, 124, 125; in Northeast, 24, 51–52; in Northwest Coast, 8, 9–10, 33–34, 35, 46, 47, 49, 86, 64–65, 90–94, 116; and social boundaries, 47–49, 51, 111–15, 116–17; and social identity, 111–15, 117–18; and social location, 59–60, 62, 63–64, 65, 66–68; and social personhood, 54–55; as source of power, 89–90, 98–100; in South America, 8–9, 35–36, 52, 54–55, 89–90, 112, 113–14; among Southeast Asian chiefdoms, 9, 99–100; among Spanish in Southwest, 29–30, 31; in state-level societies, 8, 39–40, 150, 152–54; and value of women, 64, 86, 89–90

Snyder, Christina, 26, 65

social boundaries: in Africa, 107, 126–28; "archaeological cultures" and, 166, 175n2; and captives in ethnogenesis, 106, 111, 122–28, 131;

social boundaries (*continued*)
  and captives as social opposites, 45, 47, 108–9, 110, 111–15, 130; captives in construction and maintenance of, 3, 11, 15, 16, 52, 66, 105–6, 108, 110–11, 115–20, 121–22, 130, 166; among Cherokees, 114–15; coalescence and, 123–24, 127–29; gender, class, and ethnicity in, 106–7, 108; Kahnawake settlement and, 129–30; and kinship systems, 15, 52, 66, 107, 111, 112, 121; and nature of ethnic boundaries, 105, 106–10; in Scandinavian captor societies, 112–13; in South America, 36, 112, 113–14, 116. *See also* social location, captive selection and
social location and captive selection: in Africa, 48–49, 59–60, 62, 63, 64, 65, 67–68, 70; age in, 50, 51, 59–62; captive knowledge, skills, and agency in, 43, 53, 59, 66–69, 75, 165; and captivity as "social death" and "rebirth," 43; captor worldview in, 53–59, 69, 75; circumstances of captive taking in, 44, 69–70; gender in, 50, 51, 56–57, 59, 61, 62–66, 165; inclusion and exclusion in, 44, 46–47; kinship systems and, 36, 46–47, 48–49, 51–52, 56, 57, 58, 74–75, 120–21; in Northeast, 49, 67; in Northwest Coast, 49, 67, 68, 69–70; and social status as changeable, 9, 15–16, 43, 51, 53, 58, 59, 74–75; in South America, 36, 52, 61, 63, 70–74; in Southeast, 49–50, 51; in Southwest, 49–50, 51, 56–57, 60–61. *See also* slaves, captives as; social boundaries
social personhood: concepts of, 50, 53–55, 58, 59, 61
social stratification, 3, 33, 45–46, 78–81, 82, 90, 92, 93, 101, 103, 172
Socolow, Susan, 36, 70
South America: captive selection and location in, 36, 61–62; captives as source of wealth and power in, 94–98; captive worldview in social construct of captives in, 54–55; chiefdoms of, 89, 95; children as captives in, 8, 52, 55, 96–97, 98, 114; Conibo in, 61, 65, 87, 94–98, 95, 135, 142–43, 145, 147–48, 160; cultural transmission in, 142–43, 145, 147–48, 155, 160; evidence of slavery in, 35–36; gender and sexuality in, 36, 62–66, 170; and Helena Valero account, 1, 2, 36, 50, 70–74, 72, 150; kinship systems in, 36, 52, 121–22; scholarship on, 35–36; slaves as social opposites in, 112, 113–14; social boundaries in, 112, 113–14, 121–22; social personhood in, 54–55; Tukanoans in, 65–66, 113–14, 160; women as captives in, 8, 36, 52, 61, 63, 65–66, 96–97, 98,

142–43, 145, 150, 155, 160, 170; Yanomamö group in, 1, 2, 8–9, 36, 52, 70–74, 82, 150
Southeast Asian chiefdoms, 9, 40–41, 98, 99–101, 155, 170
Spiro Mounds, 27, 28, 169–70
Stahl, Ann, 127, 167
Starna, William, 22, 24, 51–52, 118–19
St. Augustine, La Florida, 138

technology and craft production: by captives, 136, 146, 148–49, 150, 152–55, 166–67
Thornton, John, 83
Timucua Indians, 5
Tlingits, 32, 67, 86, 89, 92
torture: captives and, 24, 51, 118
Trafficking in Person Protocol (2003), 16–17
"tribal zones," European contact and, 4
Trigger, Bruce, 22, 23, 24, 80
"tropical America." *See* Santos-Granero, Fernando; South America
Tukanoans, 65–66, 113–14, 160
Turkanoans, 147–48
Turner, Kathryn Kramer, 168–69
Tutchones, 7, 33, 81, 86, 88, 89

Ucayali River Basin, 94–96, 95, 98, 155
United Nations 2012 human trafficking report, 16, 17

Vai group, 48, 67–68
Valero, Helena, 1, 2, 36, 50, 70–74, 72, 150
Viking slave trade, 8, 40, 89, 112–13, 169
Voss, Barbara, 62, 109–10, 123, 138

Wallaert-Pêtre, Helene, 143–44
warfare. *See* raiding and warfare; *specific culture groups and regions by name*
Warren, James, 41
Watkins, Ralph, 22, 24, 51–52, 118–19
Watson, James, 47, 48
"wealth in people": concept of, 54, 57, 63. *See also* power
Wenger, Etienne, 141, 142
Whitehead, Neil, 4
Wilshusen, Richard, 126
Windward Maroons, 125
Witthoft, John, 24
women as captives: in Africa, 37–38, 48, 62, 63, 64, 67–68, 82, 86, 153–54, 159; and age, 59, 60, 61, 62; and captor power, 81, 82, 83, 85, 86, 88, 101–2; as concubines, 9, 48, 50, 57, 61, 63–64, 85, 96, 97, 98, 103, 117, 138–39, 165, 170; in contempo-

rary human trafficking, 16–17; and cultural transmission, *135*, 138–39, 143, 144–45, 148, 149, 153–54, 155, 156, 160; as drudge wives, 9, 50, 61, 165, 172; in Europe, 40, 49; global scope of raiding for, 6–8; in labor systems, 63, 86–87, 96, 101–2; and maroon societies, 125, 126; in Northeast, 24, 52, 118, 149, 170; in North Pacific Rim, 81; in Northwest Coast, 86, 90, 91, 169; reproductive value of, 62, 63–64, 82, 83, 101, 165; and sex ratios in burial populations, 24, 31–32, 35, 168–69; and social location, 40, 45, 49, 50, 51, 52, 61, 62, 63–64, 65; as social intermediaries, 120–22; in South America, 8, 36, 52, 63, 96–97, 98, 142–43, 145, 150, 155, 160, 170; in Southeast, 51, 60–61, 149; in Southeast Asian chiefdoms, 41, 100, 155; in Southwest, 51, 56, 57, 63, 144–45, 148, 154, 160, 168–69, 170. *See also* gender/sexuality; Valero, Helena

WuDunn, Sheryl, 171

Yamasees, 128
Yanomamö group, 1, 2, 8–9, 36, 52, 70–74, 82, 150
Yavapai Indians, *151*
Yoffee, Norman, 103

Zunis, 138, 144

In the Borderlands and Transcultural Studies series

*The Storied Landscape of Iroquoia: History, Conquest,
and Memory in the Native Northeast*
by Chad Anderson

*How the West Was Drawn: Mapping, Indians, and the
Construction of the Tran-Mississippi West*
by David Bernstein

*Chiricahua and Janos: Communities of Violence in the
Southwestern Borderlands, 1680–1880*
by Lance R. Blyth

*The Borderland of Fear: Vincennes, Prophetstown, and the
Invasion of the Miami Homeland*
by Patrick Bottiger

Captives: How Stolen People Changed the World
by Catherine M. Cameron

The Allure of Blackness among Mixed Race Americans, 1862–1916
by Ingrid Dineen-Wimberly

*Intermarriage from Central Europe to Central Asia:
Mixed Families in the Age of Extremes*
edited and introduced by Adrienne Edgar and Benjamin Frommer

Words Like Birds: Sakha Language Discourses and Practices in the City
by Jenanne Ferguson

Transnational Crossroads: Remapping the Americas and the Pacific
edited by Camilla Fojas and Rudy P. Guevarra Jr.

Conquering Sickness: Race, Health, and Colonization in the Texas Borderlands
by Mark Allan Goldberg

Globalizing Borderlands Studies in Europe and North America
edited and with an introduction by John W. I. Lee and Michael North

Illicit Love: Interracial Sex and Marriage in the United States and Australia
by Ann McGrath

Shades of Gray: Writing the New American Multiracialism
by Molly Littlewood McKibbin

The Limits of Liberty: Mobility and the Making of the Eastern U.S.-Mexico Border
by James David Nichols

Native Diasporas: Indigenous Identities and Settler Colonialism in the Americas
edited by Gregory D. Smithers and Brooke N. Newman

Shape Shifters: Journeys across Terrains of Race and Identity
edited by Lily Anne Y. Welty Tamai, Ingrid Dineen-Wimberly,
and Paul Spickard

*The Southern Exodus to Mexico: Migration across
the Borderlands after the American Civil War*
by Todd W. Wahlstrom

To order or obtain more information on these or other University of Nebraska Press
titles, visit nebraskapress.unl.edu.

www.ingramcontent.com/pod-product-compliance
Lightning Source LLC
Chambersburg PA
CBHW020858270326
41928CB00006B/767